Communication: Principles for a Lifetime

Portable Edition

Volume 4: Presentational Speaking

STEVEN A. BEEBE
Texas State University–San Marcos

SUSAN J. BEEBE
Texas State University–San Marcos

DIANA K. IVY
Texas A&M University–Corpus Christi

PEARSON

Boston   New York   San Francisco
Mexico City   Montreal   Toronto   London   Madrid   Munich   Paris
Hong Kong   Singapore   Tokyo   Cape Town   Sydney

Editor in Chief: *Karon Bowers*
Series Editorial Assistant: *Jessica Cabana*
Marketing Manager: *Suzan Czajkowski*
Production Supervisor: *Beth Houston*
Editorial Production Service: *Lifland et al., Bookmakers*
Composition Buyer: *Linda Cox*
Manufacturing Buyer: *JoAnne Sweeney*
Electronic Composition: *Publishers' Design and Production Services, Inc.*
Photo Researcher: *Helane Prottas*
Cover Administrator: *Joel Gendron*

For related titles and support materials, visit our online catalog at
www.ablongman.com.

Between the time website information is gathered and then published, it is not
unusual for some sites to have closed. Also, the transcription of URLs can result in
typographical errors. The publisher would appreciate notification where these errors
occur so that they may be corrected in subsequent editions.

Library of Congress Cataloging-in-Publication Data

Beebe, Steven A., 1950–
    Communication: principles for a lifetime/Steven A. Beebe, Susan J. Beebe,
Diana K. Ivy—Portable ed.
        v. cm.
    Includes bibliographical references and index.
    ISBN-13: 978-0-205-59357-6
    1. Communication. I. Beebe, Susan J. II. Ivy, Diana K. III. Beebe, Susan J.
IV. Ivy, Diana K. V. Title.
    HM1206.B44 2009
    302.2—dc22   2007051355

ISBN-13: 978-0-205-59357-6   ISBN-10: 0-205-59357-7

Printed in the United States of America

10 9 8 7 6 5 4 3 2 1   RRD-IN   11 10 09 08

Contents

4.2 Organizing and Outlining Your Presentation   45

4.3 Delivering Your Presentation   75

Preface

This portable edition of *Communication: Principles for a Lifetime* is for students on the move—those who, on a daily basis, commute, travel, or work and therefore must study in nontraditional settings. The portable edition contains four separate volumes, enabling students to take with them wherever they go, for both reading and self-assessment purposes, only the volume they need.

Students may take only one course in communication during their entire college career. Yet they need to remember essential communication principles and skills for the rest of their lives. In this portable edition of *Communication: Principles for a Lifetime*, our goal is to provide a cogent presentation of what is fundamental to human communication by applying to the study of communication five principles that are inherent in the process of communicating with others.

Communication is essential for life. We want students to view this course not simply as another course in a string of curricular requirements or options, but as a vital, life-enriching course that will help them enhance their communication with others.

The Challenge of a Fundamentals of Communication Course

Most introductory communication courses cover a vast terrain of communication concepts, principles, and skills. Besides several theories of communication, students are presented with what may appear to them to be abbreviated courses in interpersonal communication, group communication, and public speaking. In addition to developing a conceptual understanding of communication, students are expected to master communication skills, including group discussion and problem-solving skills, listening and paraphrasing skills, conflict management skills, and informative and persuasive public speaking competencies. When a typical introductory communication fundamentals course is over, both students and instructors have covered an astounding amount of information and skills; they may not, however, have a coherent vision of what is fundamental about human communication. They may finish the course viewing communication as a fragmented area of study and having little understanding of what is truly fundamental about how we make sense out of the world and share that sense with others.

The Solution

To help students remember and integrate essential information, we've organized the study of human communication around five fundamental communication principles. By synthesizing essential research and wisdom about communication, these principles provide a framework for understanding the importance of communication. They are designed to help introductory communication students see the "big picture"—the role and importance of communication—both as they sit in the classroom and as they live their lives.

Although the communication principles we highlight are included in some way in most introductory communication texts, they are not often used as a scaffolding to lend coherence to the entire course. In most texts, principles are introduced in the first third of the book and then abandoned, as material about interpersonal, group, and public communication is presented. We carefully discuss each principle in the Introduction following this Preface. Then, throughout the four volumes, we gently remind students how these principles relate to interpersonal relationships, group and team discussions, and public presentations. In other words, we cover classic communication content but organize it around five principles.

What are the five fundamental principles?

Principle One: Be aware of your communication with yourself and others.
Principle Two: Effectively use and interpret verbal messages.
Principle Three: Effectively use and interpret nonverbal messages.
Principle Four: Listen and respond thoughtfully to others.
Principle Five: Appropriately adapt messages to others.

A subtext of these five principles is the importance of communicating ethically with others. Throughout the volumes, in a feature entitled *Ethics and Communication*, we invite students to consider the ethical implications of how they communicate with others. We believe that, to be effective, a communication message must achieve three goals: It must be understood, achieve its intended effect, and be ethical. Our five communication principles for a lifetime are designed to help students realize these three goals.

The relationship among the five communication principles is illustrated with a pentagonal model. When a principle is introduced or discussed, the corresponding segment of the model is highlighted.

In addition to knowing the five communication principles, we want students to see how these principles relate to the classic communication contexts of interpersonal communication, group and team communication, and presentational speaking. We link the five communication principles with specific content by using a margin icon to identify a discussion of a skill, a concept, or an idea related to one or more of the principles. The icon, illustrated in the margin here, is explained in detail in the Introduction and appears in each volume to indicate applications of the five principles.

Overview of the Book

The text is organized into four volumes. In Volume 1, Chapter 1.1 covers the fundamentals, and then each principle is discussed and illustrated in a separate chapter. These chapters help students see the value of each principle and its centrality in their lives. Chapter 1.2 discusses the principle of being self-aware. Chapter 1.3 focuses on using and interpreting verbal messages. The emphasis of Chapter 1.4 is on using and interpreting nonverbal messages. Chapter 1.5 discusses the interrelated processes of listening and responding, giving special attention to the importance of being other-oriented and empathic. The last principle, appropriately adapting to others, is presented in Chapter 1.6; we use this principle to illustrate the importance of adapting one's behavior to accommodate to culture and gender differences among people.

Volume 2 links concepts and strategies for understanding interpersonal communication with our five communication principles. Chapter 2.1 helps students better understand the nature and function of communication in relationships. Chapter 2.2 identifies strategies that can enhance the quality of interpersonal relationships with others. Appendix A includes practical strategies for being interviewed and for interviewing others, relating interviewing skills to the five communication principles. Appendix B helps students balance the use of technology with interpersonal communication.

Volume 3 discusses how the five communication principles can enhance communication in small groups and teams. Chapter 3.1 explains how groups and teams work. Chapter 3.2 offers practical strategies for collaboratively solving problems, leading groups and teams, and running and participating in meetings. Volume 3 concludes with Appendix C, relating technology to group communication.

The final volume, Volume 4, presents classic content to help students design and deliver speeches, with references to contemporary research and the latest technological tools. Our popular audience-centered approach to developing a presentation emphasizes the importance of adapting to listeners while also being an ethical communicator. Chapters 4.1 through 4.5 offer information and tips on coming up with ideas for presentations, organizing and outlining messages, delivering presentations (using various kinds of presentational aids), crafting effective informative presentations, and developing ethically sound persuasive messages. Appendix D describes the use of technology in giving presentations. Appendix E includes two examples of recent presentations to illustrate what effective, well-planned presentations look like.

Special Features

A textbook is essentially a "distance learning" tool. When we write the book, we are separated by both time and space from the learner. To help shorten the distance between author and reader and engage students in the learning process, we've incorporated a variety of learning resources and pedagogical features. As noted in the text, information alone is not communication. Communication occurs when the receiver responds to information. Our special features help turn information into a communication message that can affect students' lives.

Principles Model and Icon   Our pentagonal model and margin icons help students see connections among the various communication concepts and skills we present. Throughout the volumes, we provide an integrated framework to reinforce what's fundamental about human communication. We want students to remember the five fundamental principles long after the course is over and they have forgotten the facts they memorized for exams. The principles can also help them remember strategies and concepts for enhancing their interpersonal relationships, improving group and team meetings, and designing and delivering effective presentations.

Principles for a Lifetime: Enhancing Your Skills   In addition to providing a margin icon to highlight text material related to one or more communication principles, we conclude each chapter with *Principles for a Lifetime: Enhancing Your Skills*, a summary of the chapter content organized around the communication principles. In Volume 1, these summaries distill essential information about the individual principle presented in a given chapter. In Volumes 2–4, we summarize the chapter content using all five communication principles for a lifetime as a framework. Miniature versions of the principles icon highlight the five fundamental principles. The purpose of this chapter-end feature is to help students integrate the descriptive and prescriptive information presented in the chapter with the five principles that provide the foundation for it.

Ethics and Communication   To help students apply ethics to what they learn about human communication, each chapter includes a feature called *Ethics and Communication*. In this revised and expanded ethics feature, we present a case study and then pose ethical questions for students to consider, asking them to ponder how they would respond to a specific ethical dilemma. The thought-provoking questions are designed to spark insightful class discussion or to be used in combination with a journal assignment or other learning method to help students see connections between ethics and communication.

Technology and Communication   Because of the importance of technology in our lives today, each chapter includes a feature entitled *Technology and*

Communication. This feature is intended to help students become sensitive to the sometimes mind-boggling impact of new technology on communication with others. The importance and role of technology are also discussed in several chapters throughout the volumes, as well as in appendixes to Volumes 2, 3, and 4. The prevalence of technology in students' lives gives rise to powerful teachable moments, which can be used to help students learn and apply communication principles.

On the Web   We do more than just talk about technology. By including Web resources that link to the topic of each chapter, we encourage students to reach out to the vast array of learning resources on the Internet. These annotated Web links provide background, context, and activities to help students apply course content.

Diversity and Communication   Each chapter includes a *Diversity and Communication* feature to help students see the importance of diversity in their lives. Yet we don't relegate diversity only to a boxed feature. Because diversity is such an important issue in contemporary society, we discuss it not only in a comprehensive chapter on the fifth principle of communication (appropriately adapting messages to others), but throughout the text as well.

Developing Your Presentation Step by Step   The chapters in Volume 4, Presentational Speaking, contain a series of boxes that follow one student's progress through the steps in preparing and giving a presentation. Students receive tips that they can readily apply as they prepare their own presentations.

Comprehensive Pedagogical Learning Tools   To help students master the material, we've built in a wealth of study aids:

- Learning objectives
- Chapter outlines
- Concise Recap boxes that distill key content
- Boldfaced key terms with definitions
- Chapter-end narrative summaries of the chapters
- Chapter-end summaries of the five communication principles
- Chapter-end questions for discussion and review
- Skill-building activities and collaborative learning exercises
- Practice tests

MyCommunicationLab   In this Portable Edition, you will find icons throughout each chapter that refer students to interactive materials available on this book's MyCommunicationLab (www.mycommunicationlab.com; access code required).

- **Watch** icons link to relevant and interesting video clips that supplement a topic being covered in the textbook.

- **Explore** icons link to activities that allow users to gain more knowledge of major topics in the book, reinforcing key concepts taught in the text.

- **Homework** icons link to assignments for students that reinforce material covered in the text.

- **Quick Review** icons link to practice tests that provide reinforcement of key concepts in the context of the book. These Quick Review assessments are not graded and give students an opportunity for self-study.

- **Visual Literacy** icons link to images that help illustrate important concepts.

- **Profile** icons link to relevant self-assessments, which enable students to test and evaluate their communication skills in different contexts.

In addition, the following tools appear in MyCommunicationLab (but not in the printed text).

- A **pre-test icon** appears at each chapter-level page. This icon prompts students to complete a pre-test before reading the chapter in order to gauge their prior knowledge of chapter contents. Results from the pre-test will be stored in the students' individualized study plans.
- A **post-test icon** appears at each chapter-level page. This icon prompts students to complete a chapter post-test after reading and reviewing the chapter content that will indicate a level of understanding of the chapter's material. Results from the post-test will be stored in the students' individualized study plans (see below).
- The results from the chapter pre-test and post-test generate a customized **study plan** for each student, identifying specific areas of weakness and strength. The study plan is organized by chapter and major topic area. Each time a pre-test and/or post-test is taken, the study plan is instantly updated to indicate which topic areas need to be reviewed. The study plan, as well as the pre-test and post-test, are for the students' use only and will not be shared with the instructor. This personalized study and review strategy allows students to track their progress in a topic and to prepare for their tests. This tool allows students to efficiently master the text and course material, save time studying, and perform better on exams.
- **MyOutline** provides students with the opportunity to create customized and specific outlines for their speeches.

In-Text Practice Tests In each chapter of the printed text, we've provided a practice test to help students simulate the test-taking experience. Written by Richard J. Sabatino, Texas State University–San Marcos, these practice tests are derived from the Study Guide that accompanies the main version of this text. Each test gives students the opportunity to gauge their comprehension of the chapter concepts. Answers to the practice tests can be found at the end of each volume.

Our Partnership with Instructors

A textbook is only one tool for helping teachers teach and learners learn. We view our job as providing resources that teachers can use to augment, illustrate, and amplify communication principles and skills. We also offer an array of materials designed for students, to enrich their learning experience.

Instructor Supplements

As part of our partnership with instructors to facilitate learning, we offer an array of print, electronic, and video resources to help teachers do what they do best: teach. Combined with the vast array of learning resources built into the text, this dazzling package of additional resources will help instructors forge both intellectual and emotional connections with their students.

- *MyCommunicationLab.* A place where students learn to communicate with confidence, MyCommunicationLab (www.mycommunicationlab .com) is an interactive and instructive online solution designed to be used as a supplement to a traditional lecture course or as a complete online course. MyCommunicationLab combines multimedia, video, communication activities, research support, tests, and quizzes to make teaching and learning more relevant and enjoyable. Students benefit from a wealth of video clips that include student and professional speeches, small group scenarios, and interpersonal interactions—some with running commentary and critical questions—all geared to help students learn to commu nicate with confidence. Access code required.
- *Instructor's Resource Manual* by Travis Russ, Rutgers University. For each chapter, the Instructor's Resource Manual provides at-a-glance grids that link text objectives to the manual's content as well as to other supplements. Additionally, each chapter includes an outline, discussion and journal questions, classroom activities and assignments, and Internet suggestions. Available electronically through the Instructor's Resource Center (www.ablongman.com/irc). Access code required.
- *Test Bank* by Sue Stewart, Texas State University–San Marcos. The Test Bank contains over 1,500 questions in multiple-choice, true/false, matching, fill-in-the-blank, short answer, and essay formats. Available electronically through the Instructor's Resource Center.
- *Computerized Test Bank*. The Test Bank is also available through Pearson's computerized testing system, TestGen EQ. This fully networkable test-generating software is available for Windows and Macintosh. The user-

friendly interface allows instructors to view, edit, and add questions, transfer questions to tests, and print tests in a variety of fonts. Search and sort features allow instructors to locate questions quickly and to arrange them in a preferred order. Available electronically through the Instructor's Resource Center.

- *A Guide for New Teachers of the Basic Communication Course: Interactive Strategies for Teaching Communication*, Third Edition, by Susanna G. Porter, Kennesaw State University. This guide helps new instructors teach an introductory course effectively. It covers such topics as preparing for the term, planning and structuring your course, evaluating speeches, utilizing the textbook, integrating technology into the classroom, dealing with challenges, and much more.

- *Blockbuster Approach: Teaching Interpersonal Communication with Video*, Third Edition, by Thomas Jewell, Bergen Community College. This guide provides lists and descriptions of popular videos that can be used in the classroom to illustrate complex concepts of interpersonal relationships. Sample activities are also included.

- *Great Ideas for Teaching Speech (GIFTS)*, Third Edition, by Raymond Zeuschner, California Polytechnic State University. This book provides descriptions and guidelines for assignments successfully used by experienced public speaking instructors in their classrooms.

- *Video Workshop for Introduction to Communication*, Version 2.0, by Kathryn Dindia, University of Wisconsin. Video Workshop is a way to bring video into your introductory communication classroom to maximize learning. This total teaching and learning system includes quality video footage on an easy-to-use CD-ROM, plus a Student Learning Guide and an Instructor's Teaching Guide. The result? A program that brings textbook concepts to life with ease and that helps students understand, analyze, and apply the objectives of the course.

- *Allyn and Bacon Digital Media Archive for Communication*, Version 3.0. This CD-ROM contains electronic images of charts, graphs, maps, tables, and figures, along with media elements such as video, audio clips, and related Web links. These media assets are fully customizable and can be used with the pre-formatted PowerPoint™ outlines or imported into the instructor's own lectures. The images are available for both Windows and Mac platforms.

- *Allyn and Bacon PowerPoint Presentation for Introduction to Communication*. This PowerPoint presentation includes approximately 50 slides that cover a range of communication topics: public speaking, interpersonal communication, group communication, mass media, and interviewing. Available electronically through the Instructor's Resource Center.

- *PowerPoint Presentation for Communication: Principles for a Lifetime*, Portable Edition, by James R. Smith, State University of New York, New Paltz. This text-specific package consists of a collection of lecture outlines and graphic images keyed to each chapter in the text. Available electronically through the Instructor's Resource Center.

- *Lecture Questions for Clickers: Introduction to Communication,* by Keri Moe, El Paso Community College. An assortment of questions and activities covering culture, listening, interviewing, public speaking, interpersonal conflict, and more are presented in PowerPoint. These slides will help liven up your lectures and can be used along with the Personal Response System to get students more involved in the material. Available through the Instructor's Resource Center.
- *Communication Video Libraries.* Adopters can choose appropriate video material from Allyn and Bacon's video libraries for Public Speaking, Interpersonal Communication, and Small Group Communication. Please contact your Pearson representative for a list of available videos. Some restrictions apply.

Student Supplements

We also offer an array of materials designed for students to enrich their learning experience.

- *MyCommunicationLab.* A place where students learn to communicate with confidence, MyCommunicationLab (www.mycommunicationlab.com) is an interactive and instructive online solution designed to be used as a supplement to a traditional lecture course or as a complete online course. MyCommunicationLab combines multimedia, video, communication activities, research support, tests, and quizzes to make teaching and learning more relevant and enjoyable. Students benefit from a wealth of video clips that include student and professional speeches, small group scenarios, and interpersonal interactions—some with running commentary and critical questions—all geared to help students learn to communicate with confidence. Access code required.
- *ResearchNavigator.com Guide: Speech Communication.* This updated booklet by Steven L. Epstein of Suffolk County Community College includes tips, resources, and URLs to aid students conducting research on Pearson Education's research Web site, www.researchnavigator.com. The guide contains a student access code for the Research Navigator™ database, offering students unlimited access to a collection of more than 25,000 discipline-specific articles from top-tier academic publications and peer-reviewed journals, as well as the *New York Times* and popular news publications. The guide introduces students to the basics of the Internet and the World Wide Web and includes tips for searching for articles on the site and a list of journals useful for research in their discipline. Also included are hundreds of Web resources for the discipline, as well as information on how to correctly cite research.
- *Speech Preparation Workbook*, by Jennifer Dreyer and Gregory H. Patton, San Diego State University. This workbook takes students through the various stages of speech creation—from audience analysis to writing the speech—and provides supplementary assignments and tear-out forms.

- ***Preparing Visual Aids for Presentations***, Fourth Edition, by Dan Cavanaugh. This 32-page booklet provides a host of ideas for using today's multimedia tools to improve presentations and includes suggestions for planning a presentation, guidelines for designing visual aids and story-boarding, and a PowerPoint presentation walkthrough.

- ***Public Speaking in the Multicultural Environment***, Second Edition, by Devorah A. Lieberman, Portland State University. This booklet helps students learn to analyze cultural diversity within their audiences and adapt their presentations accordingly.

- ***Outlining Workbook***, by Reeze L. Hanson and Sharon Condon, Haskell Indian Nations University. This workbook includes activities, exercises, and answers to help students develop and master the critical skill of outlining.

- ***Study Card for Introduction to Communication.*** Colorful, affordable, and packed with useful information, Pearson's Study Cards make studying easier, more efficient, and more enjoyable. Course information is distilled down to the basics, helping you quickly master the fundamentals, review a subject for understanding, or prepare for an exam. Because it's laminated for durability, you can keep this Study Card for years to come and pull it out whenever you need a quick review.

- ***Introduction to Communication Study Site.*** Accessed at www.abintro-comm.com, this Web site includes Web links to sites with speeches in text, audio, and video formats, as well as links to other valuable Web sites. The site also contains flashcards and a fully expanded set of practice tests for all major topics.

- ***Speech Writer's Workshop CD-ROM***, Version 2.0. This interactive software will assist students with speech preparation and will enable them to write better speeches. The software includes four separate features: (1) a Speech Handbook with tips for researching and preparing speeches plus information about grammar, usage, and syntax; (2) a Speech Workshop that guides students through the speechwriting process and includes a series of questions at each stage; (3) a Topics Dictionary containing hundreds of speech ideas, divided into subcategories to help students with outlining and organization; and (4) a citation database that formats bibliographic entries in MLA or APA style.

- ***Video Workshop for Introduction to Communication***, Version 2.0, by Kathryn Dindia, University of Wisconsin. Video Workshop includes quality video footage on an easy-to-use CD-ROM plus a Student Learning Guide. The result is a program that brings textbook concepts to life with ease and that helps students understand, analyze, and apply the objectives of the course.

Acknowledgments

Although our three names appear on the cover as authors of the book you are holding in your hands, in reality hundreds of people have been instrumental in making this book possible. Communication scholars who have dedicated their lives to researching the importance of communication principles, theories, and skills provide the fuel for the book. We thank each author we reference in our endnotes for the research conclusions that have led to our contemporary understanding of communication principles. We thank our students who have trusted us to be their guides in a study of human communication. They continue to enrich our lives with their enthusiasm and curiosity. They have inspired us to be more creative by their honest, quizzical looks and have challenged us to go beyond textbook answers with their thought-provoking questions.

We are most appreciative of the outstanding editorial support we continue to receive from our colleagues and friends at Allyn and Bacon. We thank Joe Opiela for helping us keep this project moving forward when we wondered if the world needed another communication book. Vice President Paul Smith has been exceptionally supportive of our work since we've been members of the Allyn and Bacon publishing family. Karon Bowers, Editor in Chief, has continued to provide valued support and encouragement. Our thoughtful and talented development editor, Carol Alper, helped us polish our ideas and words. Karen Black, Diana Ivy's sister, who conducted permissions research, was a true blessing, providing skilled assistance with important details and administrative support. We acknowledge and appreciate the ideas and suggestions of Mark Redmond, a valued friend, gifted teacher, and skilled writer at Iowa State University. His co-authorship with us of *Interpersonal Communication: Relating to Others* significantly influenced our ideas about communication, especially interpersonal communication.

We are grateful to the many educators who read the manuscript and both encouraged and challenged us. We thank the following people for drawing on their teaching skill, expertise, and vast experience to make this a much better book:

Lawrence Albert, Morehead State University
Leonard Assante, Volunteer State Community College
Dom Bongiorni, Kingwood College
Michael Bruner, University of North Texas
Jo Anne Bryant, Troy University
Cherie Cannon, Miami–Dade College
Diana O. Cassagrande, West Chester University
Dan B. Curtis, Central Missouri State University
Terrence A. Doyle, Northern Virginia Community College
Dennis Dufer, St. Louis Community College
Julia F. Fennell, Community College of Allegheny County, South Campus

Annette Folwell, University of Idaho

Thomas Green, Cape Fear Community College

Gretchen Harries, Austin Community College

Mike Hemphill, University of Arkansas at Little Rock

Teri Higginbotham, University of Central Arkansas

Phil Hoke, The University of Texas at San Antonio

Lawrence Hugenberg, Youngstown State University

Stephen Hunt, Illinois State University

Carol L. Hunter, Brookdale Community College

Dorothy W. Ige, Indiana University Northwest

A. Elizabeth Lindsey, The New Mexico State University

Xin-An Lu, Shippensburg University of Pennsylvania

Robert E. Mild, Jr., Fairmont State College

Timothy P. Mottet, Texas State University–San Marcos

Alfred G. Mueller II, Pennsylvania State University, Mont Alto Campus

Sara L. Nalley, Columbia College

Kay Neal, University of Wisconsin–Oshkosh

Penny O'Connor, University of Northern Iowa

Kathleen Perri, Valencia Community College

Evelyn Plummer, Seton Hall University

Kristi Schaller, University of Hawaii

David Shuhy, Salisbury University

John Tapia, Missouri Western State College

Charlotte C. Toguchi, Kapi'olani Community College

Beth M. Waggenspack, Virginia Tech University

Gretchen Aggert Weber, Horry-Georgetown Technical College

Kathy Werking, Eastern Kentucky University

Andrew F. Wood, San Jose State University

Debra Sue Wyatt, South Texas Community College

We have each been influenced by colleagues, friends, and teachers who have offered support and inspiration for this project. Happily, colleagues, friends, and teachers are virtually indistinguishable for us. We are each blessed to know people who offer us strong support.

Steve and Sue thank their colleagues at Texas State University–San Marcos for their insights and ideas that helped shape key concepts in this book. Cathy Fleuriet and Tom Burkholder, who served as basic course directors at Texas State, influenced our work. Tim Mottet, currently a basic course director at Texas State, is a valued, inspirational friend and colleague who is always there to listen and freely share his ideas and experience. Richard Cheatham, Dean of the College of Fine Arts and Communication, continues to provide enthusiastic encouragement for this project. Kosta Tovstiadi, from the University of Oklahoma, provided skilled research assistance to help us draw on the most contemporary communication research. Michael Hennessy and Patricia Margerison are Texas State English faculty who have been especially supportive of Sue's work. Finally, Steve thanks his skilled and dedicated support team at Texas State. Administrative Assistant Sue Hall, who continues to be Steve's right hand, is a cherished friend and colleague. Manuscript typist Sondra Howe and technical support expert Bob Hanna are two other staff members who provide exceptional support and assistance for this project and many others.

Ivy is grateful to her students, colleagues, and friends at Texas A&M University–Corpus Christi for their patience and unwavering support for her involvement in this book project. In particular, Michelle Maresh, Jason Pruett, Kelly Quintanilla, Flicka Rahn, Nada Frazier, Chair Don Luna, Deans Paul Hain and Richard Gigliotti, and Provost Sandra Harper constantly reaffirmed the value of a well-written, carefully crafted book—one that speaks to students' lives. Their support of Ivy's research efforts, along with constant "fueling" from her wonderful students, has made this project a real joy. Ivy's deepest thanks also go to Steve and Sue Beebe for their generosity in bringing her into this project, and for their willing mentorship.

Finally we express our appreciation to our families. Ivy thanks her ever-supportive family, parents Herschel and Carol Ivy, sister Karen Black (who supplied the permissions research and constant encouragement), and nephew Brian Black (whose humorous e-mails provided great comic relief). They have been constant and generous with their praise for her writing accomplishments. Ivy is especially grateful to her father, Herschel Ivy, for lovingly offering many lessons about living the highly ethical life.

Sue and Steve especially thank their parents, Herb and Jane Dye and Russell and Muriel Beebe, who taught them much about communication and ethics that truly are principles for a lifetime. They also thank their sons, Mark and Matthew Beebe, for teaching life lessons about giving and receiving love that will remain with them forever.

Steven A. Beebe
Susan J. Beebe
San Marcos, Texas

Diana K. Ivy
Corpus Christi, Texas

Communication Principles for a Lifetime

Underlying human communication are five principles that provide the foundation for all effective communication, whether we are communicating with others one on one, in groups or teams, or by presenting a public speech to an audience. We will emphasize how these principles are woven into the fabric of each communication context. The five communication principles for a lifetime are

Principle One: Be aware of your communication with yourself and others.

Principle Two: Effectively use and interpret verbal messages.

Principle Three: Effectively use and interpret nonverbal messages.

Principle Four: Listen and respond thoughtfully to others.

Principle Five: Appropriately adapt messages to others.

These five principles operate together rather than independently to form the basis of the fundamental processes that enhance communication effectiveness. The model on the next page illustrates how the principles interrelate. The first principle, being aware of your communication with yourself and others, is followed by the two principles that focus on communication messages: Principle Two on verbal messages and Principle Three on nonverbal messages. The fourth principle, on listening and responding, is followed by appropriately adapting messages to others (Principle Five). Together, these five principles help explain why communication can be either effective or ineffective. A violation of any one principle can result in inappropriate or poor communication.

Principle One: Be Aware of Your Communication with Yourself and Others

The first foundation principle is to be aware of your communication with yourself and others. Effective communicators are conscious, or "present," when communicating. Ineffective communicators mindlessly or thoughtlessly say and do things that they may later regret. Being aware of your communication includes

Communication Principles for a Lifetime

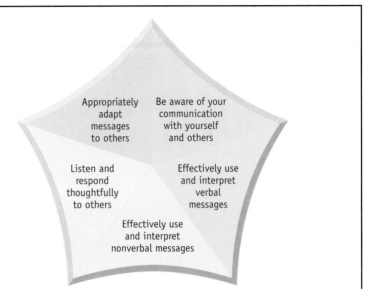

being conscious not only of the present moment, but also of who you are, your self-concept, your self-worth, and your perceptions of yourself and others. Being aware of your typical communication style is also part of this foundation principle. For example, some people realize that their communication style when interacting with others is emotional. Others may be shy.

Self-awareness includes being conscious of your intrapersonal communication messages. **Intrapersonal communication is communication that occurs within yourself, including your thoughts, your emotions, and your perceptions of yourself and others.** Talking to yourself is an example of intrapersonal communication. Although our intrapersonal communication is often the focus of psychologists, our intrapersonal messages also form the basis of our communication with others.[1]

Competent communicators are aware of the choices they make when they communicate both intrapersonally and with others; incompetent communicators react to others' messages with thoughtless, quick, knee-jerk responses. Because they do not mindfully censor themselves, they may blurt out obscene, offensive, or profane words. Ineffective communicators operate in an unthinking "default" mode. Being aware of our communication is a foundation principle because all of the choices we make when communicating rest on our ability to make conscious choices when we respond to others.

Human communication is the process of making sense out of the world and sharing that sense with others. Being aware of who we are and how we perceive, or "make sense" of, what we observe is a fundamental principle that helps explain both effective and ineffective communication.

Principle Two: Effectively Use and Interpret Verbal Messages

The second principle we introduce here is using and interpreting verbal messages effectively. Verbal messages are created with language. A **language is a system of symbols (words or vocabulary) structured by rules (grammar) that make it possible for people to understand one another.**

A symbol is a word, sound, gesture, or other visual signal that represents a thought, concept, object, or experience. When you read the words on this page, you are looking at symbols that trigger meaning. The word is not the thing it represents; it simply symbolizes the thing or idea.

Your reading skill permits you to make sense out of symbols. The word *tree*, for example, may trigger a thought of the tree you may be reading under now, a tree in your own yard or a nearby park, or a giant sequoia you saw on your family vacation in Yosemite National Park. Effective communicators use appropriate symbols to create accurate meaning. Author Daniel Quinn once commented, "No story is devoid of meaning, if you know how to look for it. This is as true of nursery rhymes and daydreams as it is of epic poems."[2] Meaning is created when people have a common or shared understanding.

The effective communicator both encodes and decodes messages accurately; he or she selects appropriate symbols to form a message and interprets carefully the messages of others. The process of using and interpreting symbols is the essence of how we make sense out of the world and share that sense with others.

Words have power. The words we use to describe ourselves and our world have considerable influence on how we perceive what we experience. Any good advertising copywriter knows how to use words to create a need or desire for a product. Political consultants tell politicians how to craft sound bites that will create just the right audience response. And words can hurt us. Words have the ability to offend and create stress. For example, derogatory words about someone's gender or race can do considerable harm. We will present strategies and suggestions for selecting the best word or symbol to enhance your listeners' understanding.

Principle Three: Effectively Use and Interpret Nonverbal Messages

Messages are also nonverbal. Nonverbal communication is communication by means other than written or spoken language that creates meaning for someone. Nonverbal messages can communicate powerful ideas or express emotions with greater impact than mere words alone. An optimistic hitchhiker's extended thumb and an irate driver's extended finger are nonverbal symbols with clear and intentional meaning. But not all nonverbal symbols are clearly interpreted or even consciously expressed. You may not be aware of your frown when someone asks if he or she may sit next to you in a vacant seat in a restaurant. Or your son may excitedly be telling you about his field trip to the fire station while you stare into the pages of your newspaper. You have no intention of telling your son he is not important, but your lack of nonverbal responsiveness speaks volumes.

One of the most important reasons our unspoken messages are significant is that they are the primary way we communicate feelings and attitudes toward others. With someone whom you like or love very much, you may spend a very small percentage of your time verbalizing your affection and friendship. The other person can discern your interest and admiration based on your nonverbal expressions and the amount of time you spend together. Your eye contact, facial expression, and tone of voice communicate your pleasure in his or her company. You may also know someone who doesn't like you. This less-than-friendly person may never have to come right out and say, "I don't like you." But you know you're not on friendly terms based on nonverbal cues: A scowl, an uninterested tone of voice, and a lack of eye contact signal that you're not held in high esteem. Our nonverbal messages communicate how we feel toward others.

When there is a contradiction between what you say and what you do, your nonverbal message is more believable than your verbal message. When asked how your meal is, you may tell your server that the meal is "great," but your nonverbal message—facial expression and tone of voice—clearly communicates your unhappiness with the cuisine. Our nonverbal cues often tell people how to interpret what we are saying.

Effective communicators develop skill in interpreting nonverbal messages of others. They also monitor their own messages to avoid unintentionally sending contradictory verbal and nonverbal messages. It's sometimes hard to interpret nonverbal messages because they don't have a neat beginning and ending point—the flow of information is continuous. It may not be clear where one gesture stops and another begins. Cultural differences, and the fact that so many different nonverbal channels (such as eye contact, facial expression, gestures, posture) can be used at the same time, make it tricky to "read" someone's nonverbal message accurately.

Principle Four: Listen and Respond Thoughtfully to Others

So far, our list of principles may appear to place much of the burden of achieving communication success on the person sending the message. But effective communication with others also places considerable responsibility on the listener. Because communication is a transactional process—both senders and receivers are mutually and usually simultaneously expressing and responding to symbols—listening to words with sensitivity and "listening between the lines" to nonverbal messages join our list of fundamental principles.

Listening can be hard because it looks easy. You spend more time listening than performing any other communication activity—probably more than any other thing you do except sleep.[3] Despite spending the greatest portion of our communication time listening, there is evidence that many, if not most, of us do not always listen effectively. What's tricky about listening? Both psychological, or internal, noise (our own thoughts, needs, and emotions) and external distractions (noise in the surroundings in which we listen) can create barriers to effective listening. The fact that it is perceived to be a passive rather than an active task makes listening and accurately interpreting information a challenge. Effective listening is *not* a passive task at all; the effective and sensitive listener works hard to stay on task and focus mindfully on a sender's message.

At the heart of this principle is developing sensitivity to others. By sensitivity we are not talking about the touchy-feely, emotional, what-I-hear-you-saying approach to interpersonal relationships. We are, however, suggesting that you develop an orientation or sensitivity to others when you listen and respond. **When you are other-oriented, you consider the needs, motives, desires, and goals of your communication partners while still maintaining your own integrity.** The choices you make in both forming the message and selecting when to share it should consider your partner's thoughts and feelings.

Most of us are egocentric—self-focused. We are born with an innate desire to meet our own needs. As we grow and mature, we develop a consciousness of more than our own needs. Scholars of evolution might argue that it is good that we are self-focused; looking out for number one is what perpetuates the human race.

Yet an *exclusive* focus on ourselves inhibits effective communication. Do you know anyone who is self-absorbed? Most of us find such a person tedious and uncomfortable to be around. People who are skilled communicators both listen and respond with sensitivity; they are other-oriented.

Principle Five: Appropriately Adapt Messages to Others

It is not enough to be sensitive and to accurately understand others; you must use the information you gather to modify the messages you construct. It is important to adapt your response appropriately to your listener. **When you adapt a message, you adjust both what is communicated and how the message is communicated and make choices about how best to for-**

mulate a message and respond to others to achieve your communication goals. Adapting to a listener does not mean that you tell a listener only what he or she wants to hear. That would be unethical. Adapting involves appropriately editing and shaping your responses so that others accurately understand your messages and so that you achieve your goal without coercing or using false information or other unethical means. To adapt a message is to make choices about all aspects of message content and delivery.

Regardless of whether you are giving a presentation, talking with a friend, or participating in a small-group meeting, as an effective communicator you consider who the listeners are when deciding what to say and how best to say it. One of the elements of a message that you adapt when communicating with others is the structure or organization of what you say. Informal, interpersonal conversations typically do not follow a rigid, outlined structure. Our conversation freely bounces from one topic to another. Formal presentations delivered in North America, however, are usually expected to have a more explicit structure—an introduction, a body, and a conclusion. The major ideas of a formal presentation are expected to be clearly identified. North American audiences also seem to prefer a presentation that could be easily outlined. Other cultures, such as those in the Middle East, expect a greater use of stories, examples, and illustrations, rather than a clearly structured, outlined presentation. Knowing your audience's expectations can help you adapt your message so that it will be listened to and understood.

You also adapt the general style or formality of your message to the receiver. If you are speaking to your lifelong best friend, your style is less formal than if you are speaking to the president of your university. The language you use and jokes you tell when around your best chums will undoubtedly be different than your language and humor when you are attending a meeting with your boss or with faculty members from your school. Our point is that effective communicators not only listen and respond with sensitivity; they use the information they gather to shape the message and delivery of their responses to others. Adapting to differences in culture and gender, for example, may mean the difference between a message that is well received and one that creates hostility.

Throughout the volumes of this book, we remind you of how these principles can be used to organize the theory, concepts, and skills we offer as fundamental to human communication. Chapters 4.1 through 4.5 will apply these principles to one of the most prevalent communication situations we experience each day—giving a talk or presentation.

Developing Your Presentation

CHAPTER OUTLINE

CHAPTER OBJECTIVES

After studying this chapter, you should be able to

1. Explain the practical value of presentational speaking skills.

2. List the nine components of the audience-centered public speaking model.

3. Define speaker anxiety, explain what causes it, and offer at least three suggestions for managing it.

4. Suggest three questions and three strategies that can help a speaker discover a topic.

5. List the three general purposes for presentations.

6. Explain how to write an audience-centered specific-purpose statement.

7. List and explain four criteria for a central idea.

8. Explain how to generate main ideas from a central idea.

9. Describe three sources and five types of supporting material for a presentation, and offer guidelines for using each type effectively.

10. List six types of library resources.

Freedom of speech is of no use to a man who has nothing to say.

Franklin D. Roosevelt

Jacob Lawrence, The Library, 1960. Tempera on fiberboard, 24 × 29 7/8 in. (60.9 × 75.8 cm). Smithsonian American Art Museum, Washington, DC. Photo credit: Smithsonian American Art Museum, Washington, DC/Art Resource, NY. © 2007 The Jacob and Gwendolyn Lawrence Foundation, Seattle/Artists Rights Society (ARS), New York.

A good friend of ours who has lived in Hong Kong for several years recently remarked that she found traveling back to the United States exhausting. Her reason? Not so much the long plane trip or the 13-hour time difference, but, as she explained, "When I begin to hear airport public announcements in English instead of Cantonese, I suddenly feel compelled to pay attention to every word. All that listening wears me out!"

Few of us can take for granted that others will listen to us merely because we are speaking their native language. However, when we study the presentational speaking process and learn its component skills and principles, we certainly increase the likelihood that others will listen to us out of genuine, compelling interest.

Far from being a rare talent possessed only by an inspired few, **public speaking, or presentational speaking, is a teachable, learnable process—a process of developing, supporting, organizing, and presenting ideas orally.** It is a process that has much in common with expository writing. Yet preparing an oral presentation and writing a paper are not exactly the same. For one thing, the language you use when you speak is less formal and more conversational than the language you use when you write. You are more likely to use shorter words, more first- and second-person pronouns (*I* and *you*), and shorter sentences when you speak than when you write. Second, while a writer can rely on parenthetical citations and Works Cited pages to document his or her sources, a speaker must document sources orally, within the text of the speech itself. And third, perhaps the most important way in which presentational speaking and writing differ is that speaking is more redundant than writing. What might seem unnecessary repetition in a paper is essential in a presentation. A person listening to a presentation does not have the luxury of rereading something he or she missed or did not understand the first time. Neither can the listener rely on paragraphing to indicate when a speaker is moving on to another point or idea. Instead, the listener must depend on the speaker to repeat important ideas and to provide oral organizational cues, such as transitions, previews, and summaries. Certainly you can apply to presentational speaking some of the skills and strategies you have learned as a writer. But you will also learn new and sometimes slightly different ones. As with the writing process, the more you practice, the easier and more "natural" the presentational speaking process will become.

Still not convinced that you want or need to learn presentational speaking? Perhaps you will feel more motivated if you consider that the skills you will develop as you study presentational speaking will be of practical use in the future. They will give you an edge in other college courses that require oral presentations. They may help you convince some current or future boss that you deserve a raise. And they may even land you a job. Ethernet inventor Bob Metcalf recently told a group of MIT students (who expected, no doubt, to hear technology-related advice) that "Communication is key" to their success.[1] Young entrepreneurs in technical fields need presentation skills, Metcalf pointed out, to "secure funding, win customers, recruit talented employees, and talk with the media."

The communication skills that Metcalf was talking about are grounded in the five communication principles for a lifetime and can be learned and practiced in the various stages of the presentational speaking process. Let's begin our discussion of presentational speaking with an overview of that process. Then—because even if you are fully convinced of the value of learning to speak in public, you may still feel nervous about delivering a presentation—we will explore why you feel that way and offer suggestions for managing your anxiety and developing confidence. In the final pages of this chapter, we will focus more closely on the first five stages of the public speaking process, which involve generating, exploring, and developing ideas for presentations.

An Overview of the Presentational Speaking Process

Chances are that you didn't complete a driver-education course before you got behind the wheel of a car for the first time. Similarly, you don't have to read an entire book on public speaking before you give your first presentation. An overview of the presentational speaking process can help you with your early assignments, even if you have to speak before you have a chance to read Chapters 4.2 through 4.5.

Figure 4.1.1 illustrates the presentational speaking process. Viewing the model as a clock, you find "Select and narrow topic" at 12 o'clock. From this stage, the process proceeds clockwise, in the direction of the arrows, to "Deliver presentation." Each stage is one of the tasks of the public speaker:

1. Select and narrow topic.
2. Identify purpose.
3. Develop central idea.
4. Generate main ideas.
5. Gather supporting material.

FIGURE 4.1.1
An Audience-Centered Model of the Presentational Speaking Process

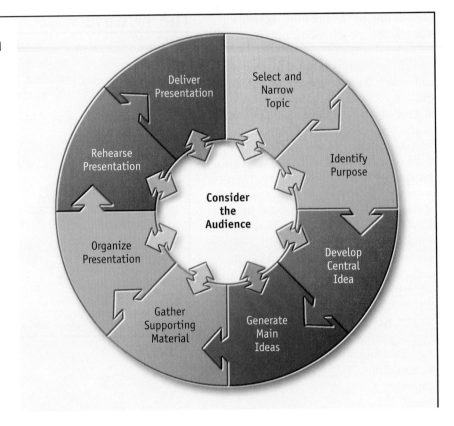

6. Organize presentation.
7. Rehearse presentation.
8. Deliver presentation.

Note that a ninth component, "Consider the audience," appears at the center of the model. Double-headed arrows connect this center with every other stage, illustrating that at any point you may revise your ideas or strategies as you learn more about your audience. Your audience influences every decision you make.

Audience-centered presentational speakers consider and adapt to the audience at every stage of the speaking process. They are inherently sensitive to the diversity of their audiences. While guarding against generalizations that might be offensive, they acknowledge that cultural, ethnic, and other traditions affect the way people process messages. They apply the fundamental principle of appropriately adapting their messages to others. How? They might choose to use pictures to help them communicate. They might select topics and use illustrations with universal themes such as family and friendship. They might adjust the formality of their delivery and even their dress to whatever is expected by the majority of the audience members. The fundamen-

Adapt

Developing Your Presentation
STEP BY STEP

Consider Your Audience

A well-known Chinese proverb says that a journey of a thousand miles begins with a single step. Developing and delivering a presentation may seem like a daunting journey. But we believe that if you take it one step at a time and keep your focus on your audience, you'll be rewarded with a well-crafted and well-delivered message.

To help you see how the audience-centered presentation process unfolds step by step, we will explore each step of that process by showing how one student prepared and delivered a presentation. Ben Johnson, a student at the University of Nevada, Reno, participated in the 132nd annual contest of the Interstate Oratori-

cal Association. His presentation, "Coricidin: No Prescription Needed," is outlined in Chapter 4.2.[2] In the pages ahead, we will walk you through the process Ben used to develop his award-winning presentation.

Ben thought about his audience even before selecting his topic. Realizing that his listeners would include both students and faculty, he decided to look for a topic that was relevant to both groups. And he knew that he could discuss complex issues, using a fairly advanced vocabulary. The Developing Your Presentation Step by Step feature will provide a window through which you can watch Ben at work on each step of the presentational speaking process.

tal communication principle of adapting to the audience is the key to the success of any presentation.

Understanding Speaker Anxiety

The above overview of the stages of the public speaking process should help to increase your understanding of how to prepare for your first speaking assignment. However, if you still feel nervous at the prospect, you are definitely not alone. One study found that more than 80 percent of the population feel anxious when they speak to an audience.[3] Another survey discovered that people are more afraid of public speaking than of death![4]

Also known as stage fright or communication apprehension, **speaker anxiety is anxiety about speaking in public that is manifested in physiological symptoms such as rapid heartbeat, butterflies in the stomach, shaking knees and hands, quivering voice, and increased perspiration.** You might be surprised at the names of some of the people who have admitted to experiencing speaker anxiety. John F. Kennedy and Winston Churchill, among the greatest orators of the twentieth century, were anxious about speaking in public. Contemporary public figures who have talked about their speaker anxiety include Katie Couric, Conan O'Brien, Jay Leno, and Oprah Winfrey.[5] In fact, almost everyone feels at least some anxiety about speaking or performing in public. Why?

To answer this question and to manage your own anxiety, you need both accurate information and practical advice. Even if the prospect of giving a presentation makes you feel a sense of heightened excitement rather than fear, you can use these suggestions to make your excitement help you, rather than distract you.

It is important to understand that speaker anxiety results from your brain signaling your body to help with a challenging task. The body responds by increasing its breathing rate and blood flow and by pumping more adrenaline, which in turn results in the all-too-familiar symptoms of a rapid heartbeat, butterflies in the stomach, shaking knees and hands, quivering voice, and increased perspiration.

Although these physical symptoms may annoy and worry you, remember that they indicate that your body is trying to help you with the task at hand. The same increased oxygen, blood flow, and adrenaline that cause the uncomfortable symptoms can actually be helpful. You may find that you speak with heightened enthusiasm. Your brain thinks faster and more clearly than you would have believed possible. Your state of increased physical readiness can help you speak better.

Keep in mind, too, that most speakers feel more nervous than they look. Although the antiperspirant advertising slogan "Never let 'em see you sweat" suggests that our increased perspiration, along with our shaking hands and knocking knees, is likely to be visible to our audience, rarely is this true. Communication researchers call **the mistaken belief that the physical manifestations of a speaker's nervousness are apparent to an audience the illusion of transparency** and have found that simply informing speakers that their nervousness is not as apparent as they think can improve the quality of their speeches.[6]

Speaker anxiety is a normal physiological reaction. It can actually help us in our speaking tasks. Its physical symptoms are seldom apparent to anyone else; rarely does it become so severe that it is actually debilitating. Still, it can be uncomfortable. Some practical tips can help you manage that discomfort and further build your confidence in your speaking ability.

Managing Speaker Anxiety

Perhaps you've read books or magazine articles that address the topic of speaker anxiety with such advice as "Look over the audience's heads, rather than at them" and "Imagine that your audience members are naked." Interesting though they may be, these techniques are not particularly helpful in reducing speaker anxiety. (After all, wouldn't you be pretty anxious if you had to talk to a group of naked people?) In addition, these strategies create new problems. Gazing at the back wall robs you of eye contact with your audience, an important source of information about how they are responding to your speech. And your audience can tell if you are looking over their heads instead of at them. Rather than pay attention to your speech, they may begin to glance surreptitiously over their shoulders to find out what in the world you're staring at.

If these techniques won't help, what will? Fortunately, several proven strategies exist for managing anxiety.

Know How to Develop a Presentation

Communication researchers have found that public speaking instruction decreases students' perception of their own speaker anxiety.[7] If you have read the first part of this chapter, then you have already taken this first step toward managing anxiety—learning about the public speaking process. Just knowing what you need to do to develop a presentation can boost your confidence in being able to do it.

Be Prepared

Being well prepared will also mean less anxiety. Being prepared includes selecting an appropriate topic, researching that topic thoroughly, and organizing your ideas logically. But perhaps most important, it also includes rehearsing your presentation. Research

Even performers like Barbra Streisand suffer from communication anxiety; we all need to take positive steps to control anxiety before a performance.

suggests that people who experience high speaker anxiety typically spend less time rehearsing than do those who report lower speaker anxiety.[8]

When you rehearse your presentation, imagine that you are giving it to the audience you will actually address. Stand up. If you cannot rehearse in the room where you will deliver the presentation, at least imagine that room. Practice rising from your seat, walking to the front of the room, and beginning your presentation. Speak aloud, rather than rehearsing silently. Thorough preparation that includes realistic rehearsal will increase your confidence when the time comes to deliver your presentation.

HOMEWORK

Focus on Your Audience

The fundamental communication principle of being audience-centered is key to reducing speaker anxiety. As you are preparing your presentation, consider the needs, goals, and interests of your audience members. As you rehearse your presentation, visualize your audience and imagine how they may respond; practice adapting your presentation to the responses you imagine. The more you know about your audience and how they are likely to respond to your message, the more comfortable you will feel about delivering that message. And as you finally deliver your presentation, focus on connecting to your

Adapt

listeners. The more you concentrate on your audience, the less you can attend to your own nervousness.

Focus on Your Message

Verbal

Focusing on your message can also be a constructive anxiety-reducing strategy. Like focusing on your audience, it keeps you from thinking too much about how nervous you are. In the few minutes before you begin your presentation, think about what you are going to say. Mentally review your main ideas. Silently practice your opening lines and your conclusion. Once you are speaking, maintain your focus on your message and your audience, rather than on your fears. Communication researchers have found that **most public speakers become progressively more comfortable as they speak,** a phenomenon they term **habituation.**[9]

Give Yourself a Mental Pep Talk

Aware

Even if you focus primarily on your audience and your message, you are bound to have some lingering thoughts about your performance. Rather than allowing yourself to dwell on how worried or afraid you are, make a conscious effort to think positively. Remind yourself that you have chosen a topic you know something about. Give yourself a mental pep talk before getting up to speak: "I know I can give this presentation. I have prepared and practiced, and I'm going to do a great job." This kind of positive thinking can help you manage your anxiety.

Use Deep-Breathing Techniques

Two of the physical symptoms of nervousness are shallow breathing and rapid heart rate. To counter these symptoms, take a few slow, deep breaths before you get up to speak. As you slowly inhale and exhale, try to relax your entire body. These simple strategics will increase your oxygen intake and slow your heart rate, making you feel calmer and more in control.

Take Advantage of Opportunities to Speak

As you gain public speaking experience, you will feel more in control of your nervousness. Past successes build confidence. This course will provide opportunities for frequent practice, which will increase your skill and confidence.

Seek Professional Help

For a few people, the above strategies may not be enough help. These people may still experience a level of speaker anxiety that they consider debilitating. If you feel that you may be such a person, ask your communication instructor where you might turn for additional help. Some college or university departments of communication maintain communication labs that teach students various additional strategies to help manage counter-productive anxiety.

One such strategy is **systematic desensitization, which helps you learn to manage anxiety through a combination of general relaxation techniques and visualization of successful and calm preparation and delivery of a presentation.**

Another proven strategy is **performance visualization: viewing a videotape of a successful effective speaker, becoming familiar enough with the videotaped presentation that you can imagine it, and eventually visualizing yourself as the speaker.**[10] This process may offer one of the best long-term strategies for managing speaker anxiety. Studies suggest that student speakers who practice performance visualization view themselves as more positive, vivid, and in-control speakers both immediately after performance visualization and up to several months later.[11]

Additional services may be available through university counseling or other student support services. If you think that you might benefit from professional help, find out what is available and use it.

RECAP

Managing Speaker Anxiety

- Know how to develop a presentation.
- Be prepared.
- Focus on your audience.
- Focus on your message.
- Give yourself a mental pep talk.
- Use deep-breathing techniques.
- Take advantage of opportunities to speak.
- Seek professional help.

QUICK REVIEW

Your task of selecting a topic is made easier if you think about the needs of the audience who will be listening to your presentation.

Selecting and Narrowing Your Topic

Sometimes a speaker is invited or assigned to speak on a certain topic and doesn't have to think about selecting one. At other times, however, a speaker is given some guidelines—such as time limits and perhaps the general purpose for the presentation—but otherwise allowed freedom to choose a topic. When this happens to you—as it almost certainly will in your communication class—you may find your task made easier by exploring three questions: Who is the audience? What is the occasion? What are my interests and experiences?

Who Is the Audience?

As we have noted several times throughout this book, the principle of appropriately adapting messages to others is central to the communication process. In presentational speaking, that adaptation begins with topic selection. Who are the members of your audience? What interests and needs do they have in common? Why did they ask you to speak?

One professional speaker calls the answers to such questions "actionable intelligence"—information that you can use as you select your topic.[12] Your college classmates are likely to be interested in such topics as college loans and the job market. Older adults might be more interested in hearing a speaker address such topics as the cost of prescription drugs and investment tax credits. Thinking about your audience can often yield an appropriate topic.

Adapt

What Is the Occasion?

You might also consider the occasion for which you are being asked to speak. A Veteran's Day address calls for such topics as patriotism and service to one's country. A university centennial address will focus on the successes of the institution's past and a vision for its future.

What Are My Interests and Experiences?

Self-awareness, another communication principle you already know, can also help you discover a topic. Exploring your own interests, attitudes, and experiences may suggest topics about which you know a great deal and feel passionately, and result in a presentation that you can deliver with energy and genuine enthusiasm. One speaker thinking about her own interests and experiences quickly produced the following list of possible topics:

> San Diego, California: city of cultural diversity
> Are world climates really changing?
> The reconstructed Globe Theatre
> Working at Six Flags
> What a sociologist does

Even after considering audience, occasion, and personal interests and experiences, you may still find yourself facing a speaking assignment for which you just cannot come up with a satisfactory topic. When that happens, you might try silent brainstorming, scanning Web directories and Web pages, or listening and reading for topic ideas.

Silent Brainstorming

Silent brainstorming, discussed in Chapter 3.2 as **a technique used by small groups to generate creative ideas,** is a useful strategy for generating topics for presentations. A silent brainstorming session of about 3 minutes yielded the following list of 11 potential topics:

> Gargoyles
> Gothic architecture
> Notre Dame
> French food
> Disney's *The Hunchback of Notre Dame*
> Collecting Disney movie celluloids
> Grammy Award winning movie themes
> Academy Award winning movies of the 1940s
> The Motion Picture Academy's Lifetime Achievement Award
> John Wayne
> The California Gold Rush

On the Web

The Internet can be a useful source to help you search for an interesting speech topic. Remember, the best topic is one that relates to your audience, the occasion, and your own interests and background. Consider using a Web directory such as Yahoo! to help you find a topic that meets the three criteria we've noted. Here's the address:

www.yahoo.com

Another interesting source of speech ideas is current headlines. Here's a source that has links to many media outlets, including most major news networks:

www.totalnews.com

Having generated a list of topics, you can now go back to it and eliminate topics that don't have much promise or that you know you would never use. For example, you may not have any real interest in or reason for discussing the California Gold Rush. However, perhaps your film course has given you good background for discussing Academy Award winning movies of the 1940s or some other decade. Keep the topics you like in your class notebook. You can reconsider them for future assignments.

Scanning Web Directories and Web Pages

You know how addicting it can be to surf the Web—to follow various categories and links out of interest and curiosity. What may seem an idle pastime can actually be a good way to discover potential speech topics. For example, a recent random search on Yahoo! starting with the general category of Health yielded the following subcategories and possible topics, arranged from broad to narrow:

Diseases and conditions
Depression
Prevention of depression
Benefits of fish

An additional advantage of this strategy is that you now have both a broad topic and one or more potential sources for your presentation. An article found in the final subcategory discusses the role of omega-3 fats, found in fish, as a critical component of nerve cells.

Listening and Reading for Topic Ideas

Listen and Respond

It is not unusual to see on television or read in a newspaper something that triggers an idea for a presentation. For example, the following list of quite varied topics was suggested by the headlines in a recent daily newspaper:

Corporate accounting scandals
Forest fires in the southwestern United States
Diagnosing breast cancer
U.S. government aid to foreign nationals
Political turmoil in South America

The nightly news is not the only media source of potential topics. You might also get topic ideas from television talk shows or from general interest or news magazines. Or you might get an idea from a book. Perhaps you have just read Daniel Goleman's *Working with Emotional Intelligence*. You might decide to give a speech on what emotional intelligence is and why it is important in the workplace.

Developing Your Presentation
STEP BY STEP

Select and Narrow Your Topic

*W*hile lazily scanning the newspaper headlines one Sunday afternoon, Ben happens on one that catches his eye. He settles down to read the article, which discusses a relatively new form of drug abuse—the abuse of common over-the-counter cold medications. Ben is surprised. He had no idea that such medications could produce the kind of side effects that would lead to their abuse. As he finishes the article, another thought goes through his mind: Maybe the abuse of over-the-counter cold medicines would make a good topic for his upcoming persuasive presentation.

You might also find a topic in material you have studied for a class. Perhaps you recently had an interesting discussion of minimum mandatory sentencing in your criminology class. It might make a good topic for a presentation. And your instructor would probably be happy to suggest additional resources.

Even a topic that comes up in casual conversation with friends may make a good speech topic. Perhaps everyone in your dorm seems to be sniffling and coughing all at once. "It's sick-building syndrome," gasps one. Sick-building syndrome might be an interesting topic for a presentation.

The point is to keep your eyes and ears open. You never know when you might see or hear a potential topic. If you do, write it down. Nothing is so frustrating as to know you had a good idea for a topic but not to be able to remember what it was!

If you discover potential topics through brainstorming, surfing the Web, or listening or reading, you should still consider the communication principles of adapting to your audience and being aware of your own interests and experiences before you make your final topic selection. And you will also need to consider the time limits of the speaking assignment. Many good topics need to be narrowed before they are appropriate for a given assignment. Be realistic. Although many beginning speakers worry about how they will ever fill 3 minutes, in reality more speakers run over their time limits than under.

One strategy for narrowing topics is to construct the kinds of categories and subcategories created by Web directories. Write your general topic at the top of a list, making each succeeding word or phrase more specific and narrow. For example, in order to narrow the topic "animals," write it down and then write an increasingly specific list of topics under it:

Aware
Adapt

Animals
Pets
Reptiles
Bearded dragons
Caring for a bearded dragon

If you have 10 minutes for your presentation, you might decide that the last topic is too narrow. If so, just go back one step. In 10 minutes, you may be able to discuss characteristics and habits of bearded dragons, as well as how to care for them.

Select and Narrow Your Topic

- Consider the audience, the occasion, and your interests and experiences.
- Practice silent brainstorming.
- Scan Web directories and Web pages.
- Listen and read for topic ideas.
- Narrow your topic by generating increasingly specific categories and subcategories.

Identifying Your Purpose

Now that you have a topic in mind, you need to clarify your purpose for your presentation. If you are unclear about exactly what you hope to accomplish, you probably won't accomplish anything, except to ramble about your topic in some sort of vague way. A clear purpose, on the other hand, can help you select main ideas, an organizational strategy, and supporting material, and can even influence the way in which you deliver the presentation. You should determine both your general purpose and your specific purpose for every presentation that you give.

General Purpose

Your general purpose is the broad reason for giving your presentation: to inform, to persuade, or to entertain. When you inform, you teach. You define, describe, or explain a thing, person, place, concept, or process. You may use some humor in your presentation; you may encourage your audience to seek out further information about your topic. But your primary purpose for speaking is to give information.

If you are using information to try to change or reinforce your audience's ideas or convictions or to urge your audience to do something, your general purpose is persuasive. The insurance representative who tries to get you to buy life insurance, the candidate for state representative who asks for your vote, and the coordinator of Habitat for Humanity who urges your fraternity to get involved in building homes all have persuasive general purposes. They may offer information about life expectancy, the voting record of an incumbent opponent, or the number of people in your community who cannot afford decent housing, but they use this information to convince you or to get you to do something. Their primary purpose is persuasive.

The speaker whose purpose is to entertain tries to get the members of his or her audience to smile, laugh, and generally enjoy themselves. For the audience members, learning something or being persuaded about something is secondary to having a good time. Most after-dinner speakers speak to entertain. So do most stand-up comedians and storytellers.

In your speech class, the general purpose for each assignment will probably be set by your instructor. Because the general purpose influences the way you develop and organize your presentation, as well as the way you deliver it, it is important that you be aware of your general purpose throughout the process of developing and delivering your presentation.

Aware

Specific Purpose

Knowing whether you want to inform, persuade, or entertain clarifies your general purpose for speaking. You also need to determine your specific purpose. **A specific purpose is a concise statement of what your listeners should be able to do by the time you finish your presentation.** In other words, a specific purpose is an audience-centered behavioral goal for your presentation. You can begin a specific-purpose statement for any presentation with these words:

Verbal

> At the end of my presentation, the audience will . . .

And then specify a behavior. For example, if you are giving an informative presentation on eating disorders, you might state,

> At the end of my presentation, the audience will be able to explain the causes and most successful treatments for anorexia and bulimia.

If your topic is Zen meditation and your general purpose is to persuade, you might say,

> At the end of my presentation, the audience will try Zen meditation.

Wording your specific purpose like the examples above will help you keep your audience foremost in your mind during the entire presentation preparation process.

Every subsequent decision you make while preparing and delivering your presentation should be guided by your specific purpose. As soon as you have formulated it, write it on a note card and keep it with you while you are working on your presentation. Think of it as a compass pointing true north—toward your audience. Refer to it often.

Identify Your Purpose

General Purpose

- To inform—to define, describe, or explain a thing, person, place, concept, or process
- To persuade—to change or reinforce audience members' ideas or convictions, or to urge them to do something
- To entertain—to amuse an audience

Specific Purpose

- Specifies what you want audience members to be able to do by the end of your presentation
- Uses the words "At the end of my presentation, the audience will . . ."

Examples of General Purposes	Examples of Specific Purposes
To inform	At the end of my presentation, the audience will be able to list two benefits for adults of learning to play a musical instrument.
To persuade	At the end of my presentation, the audience will enroll in a music appreciation course.
To entertain	At the end of my presentation, the audience will be laughing at my misadventures as an adult cello student.

QUICK
REVIEW

Developing Your Central Idea

While your specific purpose indicates what you want your audience to know or do by the end of your presentation, **your central idea makes a definitive point about your topic.** It focuses on the content of the speech.

Professional speech coach Judith Humphrey explains the importance of a central idea:

> Ask yourself before writing a speech . . . "What's my point?" Be able to state that message in a single clear sentence. Everything else you say will support that single argument.[13]

Sometimes, as in the following example, wording the central idea can be as simple as copying the part of the specific purpose statement that specifies what the audience should be able to do.

Developing Your Presentation
STEP BY STEP

Determine Your Purpose

*B*en's assignment is to prepare and deliver a persuasive presentation, so he knows that his general purpose is to persuade. He will have to try to change or reinforce his audience's attitudes and beliefs about the abuse of common over-the-counter cold medications and perhaps also get his listeners to take some sort of action.

Ben also knows that his specific purpose should begin with the phrase "At the end of my presentation, the audience will . . . ." So he jots down,

> At the end of my presentation, the audience will know about the cold medication Coricidin.

As Ben thinks further about this draft specific purpose, he sees some problems with it. How can he determine what his audience "knows" at the end of his presentation? And just what is it the audience should know about Coricidin? He edits his purpose statement to read,

> At the end of my presentation, the audience will be able to discuss the current epidemic of abuse of the common cold medication Coricidin.

This version is more specific, but perhaps more appropriate for an informative speech than a persuasive one. What does he want his audience to *do* about the problem? Maybe a better statement would be

> At the end of my presentation, the audience will take steps to end the abuse of the cold medication Coricidin.

Ben is pleased with this third version. It is a concise statement of what he wants his audience to do at the end of his speech. He is ready to move to the next step of the process.

TOPIC:	Foreign-language education
SPECIFIC PURPOSE:	At the end of my presentation, the audience will be able to explain two reasons foreign-language education should begin in the elementary grades.
CENTRAL IDEA:	Foreign-language education should begin in the elementary grades.

Even though they may seem similar, the specific purpose and central idea are used quite differently. The specific purpose guides you as you prepare your presentation; the central idea will guide the audience as they listen to the presentation. Although the specific purpose is never actually stated in the presentation itself, the central idea is, usually at or near the end of the speaker's introduction. It provides the focus for the body of the presentation.

The most successful central ideas meet the following criteria: They are audience-centered; they reflect a single topic; they are complete declarative sentences; and they use direct, specific language. Let's consider each of these criteria in turn.

Adapt

Effective speakers state their central idea during their introductory remarks to help their audience focus on the main points covered in the body of the speech.

Audience-Centered

If your specific purpose is audience-centered, your central idea probably will be, too. It should reflect a topic in which the audience has a reason to be interested and should provide some knowledge they do not already have or make some claim about the topic that they may not have previously considered. The second of the following central ideas is more appropriate to an audience of college students than the first.

> INAPPROPRIATE: Taking Advanced Placement classes in high school can help fulfill your general education requirements. *(Inappropriate because taking Advanced Placement classes is something college students either did or did not do in the past. They cannot make any decisions about them at this point.)*

> APPROPRIATE: Taking Web-based classes can help fulfill your general studies requirements. *(Appropriate because students are probably looking for various options for completing required courses. They can choose to take courses on the Web.)*

A Single Topic

A central idea should reflect a single topic. Trying to cover more than one topic, even if multiple topics are related, only muddles your presentation and confuses the audience.

> MULTIPLE TOPICS: Clubbing and running in marathons are two activities that appeal to many college students.

> SINGLE TOPIC: Clubbing appeals to many college students.

A Complete Declarative Sentence

Your central idea should be more than just the word or phrase that is your topic—it should make a claim about your topic. Questions may help you come up with a central idea, but questions themselves are not good central ideas, because they don't make any kind of claim. A central idea should be a **declarative sentence—a complete sentence that makes a statement, as opposed to asking a question.**

> TOPIC: Study abroad

> QUESTION: Should students consider opportunities to study abroad?

> CENTRAL IDEA: Study abroad provides significant advantages for students in most fields of study.

Verbal

Developing Your Presentation
STEP BY STEP

Develop Your Central Idea

*B*en knows from reading Chapter 4.1 of *Communication: Principles for a Lifetime* that his central idea should be a complete declarative sentence that states a single audience-centered idea. He knows too that sometimes you can develop your central idea by copying the part of your specific purpose statement that specifies what the audience should do. So he writes,

> We should take steps to end the abuse of the cold medication Coricidin.

Direct, Specific Language

A good central idea should use direct, specific language, rather than qualifiers and vague generalities.

Verbal

VAGUE: Crop circles are not what they seem to be.
SPECIFIC: Although they have been variously attributed to alien forces and unknown fungi, crop circles are really just a clever hoax.

RECAP

The Central Idea Should . . .

Be audience-centered.

Reflect a single topic.

Be a complete declarative sentence.

Use direct, specific language.

QUICK REVIEW

Generating Main Ideas

If the central idea of a presentation is like the thesis statement of a paper, **the main ideas of a presentation correspond to the paragraph topics of a paper. They support or subdivide the central idea and provide more detailed points of focus for developing the presentation.**

Getting from the central idea to related but more specific main ideas can seem a challenging task, but actually you can use the central idea to generate main ideas. Here's how.

Write the central idea at the top of a sheet of paper or a word-processing document. Then ask yourself three questions:

1. Does the central idea have *logical divisions?*
2. Can I think of several *reasons* the central idea is true?
3. Can I support the central idea with a series of *steps* or a *chronological sequence?*

You should be able to answer yes to one of these questions and to write down the corresponding divisions, reasons, or steps. Let's apply this strategy to several examples.

Does the Central Idea Have *Logical Divisions*?

Suppose that your central idea is "Most accomplished guitarists play three types of guitars." The phrase "three types" is a flag that indicates that this central idea does indeed have logical divisions—those being, in this case, the three types of guitars. You list the three that come to mind:

1. Acoustic
2. Classical
3. Electric

You don't need to use Roman numerals or to worry particularly about the order in which you have listed the types of guitars. Right now you are simply trying to generate main ideas. They aren't set in concrete, either. You may revise them—and your central idea—several times before you actually deliver the presentation. For example, you may decide that you need to include steel guitars in your list. So you revise your central idea to read "four types of guitars" and add "steel" to your list.

Can You Think of Several *Reasons* the Central Idea Is True?

If your central idea is "Everyone should study a martial art," you may not be able to find readily apparent logical divisions. Simply discussing judo, karate, and taekwando would not necessarily support the argument that everyone should study one of them. However, the second question is more productive: You can think of a number of *reasons* everyone should study a martial art. You quickly generate this list:

1. Martial arts teach responsibility.
2. Martial arts teach self-control.
3. Martial arts teach a means of self-defense.

Unlike the list of types of guitars, this list is written in brief complete sentences. Whether words, phrases, or sentences, the purpose of your first list of main ideas is just to get the ideas in written form. You can and will revise them later.

Developing Your Presentation
STEP BY STEP

Determine Your Main Ideas

*W*ith his central idea in hand, Ben knows that he next needs to generate main ideas for his presentation. He asks three questions:

- Does the central idea have logical divisions?
- Can I think of several reasons the central idea is true?
- Can I support my central idea with a series of steps or a chronological sequence?

Ben's central idea does not seem to have logical divisions, but he can certainly provide reasons it is true. He jots down his central idea and writes *because* at the end of it:

We should take steps to end the abuse of the cold medication Coricidin <u>because</u>

And then he adds,

1. Coricidin abuse is rapidly becoming a significant problem.
2. Coricidin is widely available to teenagers.
3. Parents and teachers have only compounded the problem.

Ben thinks at first that these might make three good main ideas for his speech. Then he realizes that ideas 2 and 3 are really subdivisions of the same point—why Coricidin abuse is a growing trend. Additionally, glancing back at his purpose statement reminds him that he wants his audience to take steps to end Coricidin abuse. So he revises his original list of main ideas to read,

1. Coricidin abuse is rapidly becoming a significant problem.
2. Coricidin poses a problem because it is widely available to teenagers and because parents and teachers remain largely unaware of its abuse potential.
3. In addition to government and retailer regulation, personal action is needed to solve the problem of Coricidin abuse.

Now Ben has main ideas that both support his central idea and fulfill his specific purpose.

Can You Support the Central Idea with a Series of *Steps* or a *Chronological Sequence*?

"The events of September 11, 2001, were the climax of a decade of deadly terrorist attacks against the United States." It seemed like a pretty good central idea when you came up with it. But now what do you do? It doesn't have any logical divisions. You couldn't really develop reasons that it is true. However, you could probably support this central idea with a chronological sequence or a history of the problem. You jot down the following list:

1. 1993—Bomb explodes in the underground parking garage of the World Trade Center, killing six people.
2. 1995—Car bomb in Riyadh, Saudi Arabia, kills seven people, five of them American military and civilian National Guard advisers.
3. 1996—Bomb aboard a fuel truck explodes outside a U.S. Air Force installation in Dhahran, Saudi Arabia, killing 19 U.S. military personnel.
4. 1998—Bombs destroy the U.S. embassies in Nairobi, Kenya, and Dar es

Salaam, Tanzania. Three hundred and one people are killed, including 13 Americans.

5. 2000—Bomb damages the *USS Cole* in the port of Aden, Yemen, killing 17 American sailors.

6. 2001—Hijacked airliners crash into the World Trade Center in New York, the Pentagon in Washington, D.C., and a field in Pennsylvania, killing more than 3000.[14]

These six fatal terrorist attacks, arranged in chronological order, could become the main ideas of your speech.

How many main ideas should you have? Your topic and time limit will help you decide. A short presentation (3 to 5 minutes) might have only two main ideas. A longer one (8 to 10 minutes) might have four or five. If you find that you have more potential main ideas than you can use, decide which main ideas are likely to be most interesting, relevant, and perhaps persuasive to your audience. Or combine two or more closely related ideas.

Gathering Supporting Material

By the time you have decided on your main ideas, you have a skeleton presentation. Your next task is to flesh out that skeleton with **supporting material,** both verbal and visual. **Verbal supporting material includes illustrations, explanations, descriptions, definitions, analogies, statistics, and opinions—material that will clarify, amplify, and provide evidence to support your main ideas and your thesis. Visual supporting material includes objects, charts, graphs, posters, maps, models, and computer-generated graphics. You can also support your speech with audio aids such as music or sounds from a CD-ROM or DVD.** The speaker who seeks out strong verbal and visual supporting material is adhering to the fundamental communication principles of effectively using verbal and nonverbal messages.

Sources of Supporting Material

Like a chef who needs to know where to buy high-quality fresh fruits and vegetables for gourmet recipes, you need to know where to turn for supporting material that will effectively develop your presentation and achieve your specific purpose. We will discuss three potential sources of supporting material: you and people you know, the Internet, and the library.

You and People You Know   You needn't look far for at least some of the supporting material for your presentation. If you were self-aware as you selected your topic, you may be your own source. You may have chosen a topic about your hobby—collecting CDs, raising cockatiels, or cooking. You may have chosen a topic with which you have had some personal experience, such as undergoing plastic surgery or negotiating a favorable apartment lease. Or you may have discovered your topic through listening to others. Your roommate may have confided in you about her mother's treatment for melanoma. Your political science professor may have delivered a fascinating lecture on the changes in Hong Kong after its 1998 return to China.

The point is that you don't necessarily need to consult the Internet or run to the library for every piece of supporting material for every topic on which you speak. For the presentations mentioned above, it would be logical to begin by considering your own personal experience in having plastic surgery or negotiating a favorable apartment lease or by interviewing your roommate or your political science professor. It is true that most well-researched presentations will include some objective material gathered from the Internet or from library resources. But don't overlook your own expertise and experience or that of people you know. As an audience-centered speaker, realize, too, that personal knowledge or experience has the added advantage of heightening your credibility in the minds of your listeners. They will respect your authority if they realize that you have firsthand knowledge of the topic on which you are speaking.

Aware
Listen and Respond

The Internet   Only a few short years ago, the **Internet (a vast collection of hundreds of thousands of computers accessible to millions of people all over the world)** was more of a research curiosity than a serious source of supporting material. Now it is the first place many of us turn when faced with a research task.

The most popular Internet information-delivery system is the World Wide Web. You have probably accessed material on the Web through a **directory (an Internet site that offers the user ever-more-specific categories through which to search the Web)** or through **a search engine**

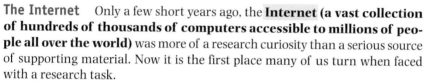

Technology *and* Communication

A New Kind of Search Engine

For the past several years Google and Yahoo! have been the leading Internet search engines. However, vertical search engines, designed to select only certain types of information from the Internet, have been increasing in both number and popularity.

One such engine is Ziggs, which can help you find people with certain specific characteristics. For example, one person who has tested the search engine explains, "it might help you find a lawyer in Washington specializing in international trade, or an alumnus of Brandeis University who lives in Delaware."[15]

Another vertical search engine is Indeed.com, a search engine for job openings, which indexes more than 500 job Web sites (including Monster.com), newspaper-ad sites, and corporate sites. You can use Indeed.com to search for all jobs in a given location or at a given company, all jobs that require certain specific qualifications.

Whether vertical search engines will compete seriously with Google and Yahoo! remains to be seen. One reference librarian suggests that it is "more likely what we're seeing is a maturation of the industry that allows for both general purpose search engines and verticals to co-exist."[16]

TABLE 4.1.1
Popular World Wide Web Directories and Search Engines*

AltaVista	www.altavista.com AltaVista is both a directory and a keyword search engine.
Google	www.google.com In addition to providing both a directory and a keyword search engine, Google enables the user to conduct specific image searches.
Teoma	www.teoma.com A vertical search engine, Teoma both narrows and improves the relevance of a search by ranking sites based on the number of same-subject pages that reference them.
Yahoo!	www.yahoo.com Both a directory and a search engine, Yahoo! is one of the best for browsing a wide-ranging topical list of sites. Each topic branches to additional topical subcategories.

*If some of these or other URLs provided in this chapter change or become unavailable at a later date, you may be automatically forwarded to new sites. If not, you can search for the sites by name. And if you still can't find a site, chances are that several new and better ones have taken its place.

(an Internet site that works much like a traditional card catalog or index, allowing the user to perform a subject or keyword search of the Web) such as Yahoo!, Alta Vista, or another of the sites listed in Table 4.1.1.

You can use directories and search engines in two ways: by clicking on subject categories that are in turn broken down into ever-more-specific subcategories or by entering keywords or phrases into a designated space and clicking on a "Find" command. In either case, you will then have to sort through **the hits—the listed Web sites (locations on the Web that include a number of related Web pages) and Web pages (individual files or screens that may be part of a larger Web site) dealing with the topic you entered.**

The Web sites and Web pages you discover may include personal pages, books, periodicals, newspapers and wire services, reference material, and government documents. In addition, you may discover indexes and catalogs for accessing these various kinds of resources. You can even find sites designed to help you prepare and deliver your presentations. Although the sheer volume of material may be overwhelming for even the most experienced researchers, two strategies can help.

First, explore the advanced or Boolean search capabilities of your directory or search engine. **A Boolean search is a Web search in which words are tied together so that a search engine can hunt for the resulting phrase.** Most offer directions on how to limit your search to those sites that are most relevant to what you are looking for. For a Boolean search, you enclose phrases in quotation marks or parentheses so that the search yields only those sites on which all the words of the phrase appear together, rather than sites that contain any one of the words. You can also insert the word *or* between two parenthetical phrases, directing your search to include documents in which either phrase appears. Or you can insert the word *and* between parenthetical phrases to indicate that you wish to see results that contain both phrases. These relatively simple strategies can help you narrow a list of hits from, in some cases, millions to a more workable number.

A second strategy for sorting through information you discover on the World Wide Web has to do with the principle of appropriately interpreting verbal and nonverbal messages. Specifically, you need to evaluate the sites you discover, according to a consistent standard. The following six criteria can serve as such a standard:[17]

1. *Accountability.* Find out what organization or individual is responsible for the Web site. A good place to start is to examine the domain, indicated by the last three letters of the site's URL. The following domains are used by the types of organizations indicated:[18]

.com or *.net*	commercial sites
.org	nonprofit groups
.edu	educational institutions
.gov	government agencies
.mil	military groups

   You can also try entering the name of the organization, enclosed in quotation marks, in a search engine. If you cannot identify or verify the author or sponsor of a Web site, be extremely wary of the site. If no one is willing to be accountable for the information, you cannot be accountable to your audience for using it. Search elsewhere.

2. *Accuracy.* Sources of facts should be documented on a Web site just as they are in a print source. An additional advantage of the Web is that it can provide a hyperlink to any original source. **Hyperlinks are usually colored and underlined words or images in the text. Clicking with your mouse on a hyperlink will take you directly to the linked site.**

   Web sites should also be relatively free of errors in grammatical usage and mechanics. If a site contains such errors, it might also contain errors in content.

3. *Objectivity.* As noted above, you need to know who has posted the site. Consider the philosophies and possible biases of the organization or individual responsible for the site. Are those beliefs, interests, and biases likely to slant the information? The more objective the author, the more credible the facts and information.

4. *Date.* Many sites include information about when the site was posted and when it was last updated. In most cases, when you are concerned with factual data, the more recent, the better.

5. *Usability.* If you have spent much time exploring the Internet, you have probably at one time or another called up a site that contained such complex graphics that it took a long time to load or even caused your computer

to crash. Frames, graphics, and multimedia resources can enhance a site, or they can simply complicate it. Consider the practical efficiency of the sites you explore.

6. *Sensitivity to diversity.*   A diversity-sensitive Web site will be free of bias against either gender, against any ethnic, racial, or sexual-preference sub-group, and against people with disabilities.[19]

Federal agencies are required by law to make their Web sites accessible to people with disabilities. For example, federal Web sites must be accessible in a mode that allows people with low vision to view them without relying on audio input.[20] Other requirements include making sure hyperlinks can be detected by color-blind users and providing audio and video clips with written captions for people with hearing disabilities.[21]

Using the World Wide Web as a Source of Supporting Material

- Use a directory or search engine to find relevant sites.
- Expect to discover a wide variety of sites: personal pages, books, periodicals, newspapers and wire services, reference material, government documents, and indexes and catalogs.
- Evaluate Web sites according to six criteria: accountability, accuracy, objectivity, date, usability, and sensitivity to diversity.

The Library Despite the explosion of World Wide Web resources in recent years, the library remains a rich source of supporting material. Most libraries, from the largest research university library to the smallest village public library, house the following kinds of resources:

Books
Periodicals
Full-text databases
Newspapers
Reference resources
Government documents
Special services

Books   The word *library* is almost synonymous with the word *book.* In spite of the predictions of some that electronic resources will someday make books obsolete, for now books remain central to the holdings of most libraries.
A library's books are housed in the stacks, often several floors of shelves of books. Books are organized in the stacks according to **call number,**

Title:	Ethics in the workplace : a systems perspective / William F. Roth.
Author:	Roth, William F.
Call Number:	HF5487 .R674 2005
Publisher:	Upper Saddle River, N.J. : Pearson Education, c2005.
Subject Heading(s):	Business ethics.
	0424L

(**Display Related Subjects**)

Description:	xiii, 140 p. ; 23 cm.
Notes:	Includes bibliographic references (p. 129-133) and index.
ISBN:	0131848151 (pbk.)
DBCN:	AFF-9865
Holdings:	**Item Holdings**

**FIGURE 4.1.2
Entry from an
Electronic Card
Catalog**

a reference number assigned to each book, which encodes the subject or topic, as well as the author. **Most libraries use the Library of Congress classification system of call numbers.**

A library's central catalog of all its books is called the card catalog. Today, most card catalogs are electronic ones. Banks of computer monitors in a central location in the library provide directions for looking up the books you need. Many college and university card catalogs these days are also accessible from remote locations, meaning that you can search them online and build preliminary bibliographies of books and call numbers before ever coming to the library building itself. Figure 4.1.2 illustrates a sample entry from a computerized card catalog.

You may be able to print out the card catalog records for the books you want. If you have to copy them from the screen, be sure to include the author's name, title of the book, publisher and date of publication, and the library's call number. Use a consistent format so that later you can easily interpret the information.

Books will be important sources as you prepare your presentations. They can provide in-depth coverage of topics, which is not possible in shorter publications. However, because most books are written 2 or 3 years before they are published, they are inherently outdated. If your presentation addresses a current topic or if you want to use current examples, you will probably not find the information you need in books. You will turn instead to periodicals and newspapers, available both online and in hard copy.

Periodicals   **The term periodicals refers both to magazines,** such as *Time, People,* and *Sports Illustrated,* **and to professional journals,** such as *College English* and the *Quarterly Journal of Economics.* Both types of periodicals can be useful for presentations.

Ethics *and* Communication

The Question of Speechwriting

From at least the time of Franklin Delano Roosevelt, speechwriters have written many of the best speeches made by U.S. presidents, including George W. Bush's speech to Congress and the nation following the September 11 terrorist attacks. More recently, former *Wall Street Journal* editor William McGurn became Bush's chief speechwriter and helped to fashion Bush's 2005 State of the Union address. Is such use of speechwriters ethical? Is it ethical to credit presidents with memorable lines from speeches that were written for them by professionals?

Periodical indexes are the equivalent of card catalogs in helping you locate information you need; **they contain a listing of bibliographical data for articles published in a group of magazines or journals during a given time period.** A number of such indexes cover many topics and most of the thousands of periodicals published. Many periodical indexes are available on CD-ROM, and many can be accessed either from the library or from remote locations. In most periodical indexes, entries are indexed alphabetically according to both subject and author. Most people use them by searching for subjects or keywords, much as they would conduct a World Wide Web search. Some periodical indexes are **full-text databases, meaning that you can access not only bibliographical information but also the texts of the articles themselves.**

Following are some frequently used periodical indexes and full-text databases:

- *The Reader's Guide to Periodical Literature* is the oldest periodical index and the one that many researchers first learn to use. It indexes popular magazines and a few trade and professional journals. Libraries can subscribe to the *Reader's Guide* either in hard copy or as an electronic database.
- *Info Trac* is a collection of indexes available through a single source. *Info Trac* includes the *Expanded Academic Index* and the *Business Index Backfile.*
- *The Public Affairs Information Service (P.A.I.S.) Bulletin,* available in both hard copy and electronic formats, indexes both periodicals and books in such fields as sociology, political science, and economics.
- *LEXIS/NEXIS* is an extensive full-text subscription database of periodicals, newspapers, and government documents. It is an excellent source of very current information.
- *Academic Search Premier* is billed as the world's largest multidisciplinary academic database. Updated daily, it provides full text of more than 4700 scholarly publications in virtually every academic field.

Newspapers   You can find information that is only hours old by reading the latest edition of a daily newspaper. Newspapers also offer the most detailed coverage available of current events.

Developing Your Presentation
STEP BY STEP

Gather Supporting Material

*W*ith a draft of his specific purpose, central idea, and main ideas in hand, Ben begins to research Coricidin abuse. Fortunately, he had kept the newspaper article that gave him the idea for the topic, so he has one source already. Because this first source is a newspaper, Ben decides to check out other newspapers.

He goes online to his university library's Web site. There he accesses the database *Newspaper Source,* where he discovers another article entitled "Latest Trend in Drug Abuse: Youths Risk Death for Cough-Remedy High," in the December 29, 2003, issue of *USA Today. Newspaper Source* provides the full text of that article.

While Ben is online, he uses Google to search for additional information on his topic and discovers a site called *TheAntiDrug.com*. The National Youth Anti-Drug Media Campaign, an initiative of the White House Office of National Drug Control Policy, maintains the site. Ben decides it is another credible source.

Ben records in MLA format on note cards the essential bibliographical information for these and other sources he discovers. Then he begins to read carefully and take notes. As he does so, he copies verbatim material accurately and puts quotation marks around it.

Newspapers today exist in three formats. The first is the traditional newsprint format. However, libraries usually keep only the most recent newspapers (probably less than a week old) in their racks because they take up so much storage space. Back issues are kept on microfilm, the second format. And in recent years, many newspapers, from major national newspapers to local and college newspapers, have also become available online.

As with books and periodicals, you need a subject index to help you find newspaper articles of potential value to your research. **Newspaper indexes, listing bibliographic data for articles published in a newspaper or group of newspapers during a given time period,** are published by a number of medium-to-large newspapers. Your library may subscribe to several of these. In addition, electronic indexes such as the *National Newspaper Index* reference multiple newspapers. *Newspaper Source* also provides full texts of selected articles from some 30 national and international newspapers and more than 200 regional U.S. newspapers. Keep in mind, too, that if you need information about a specific event and you know the day on which it occurred, you can locate a newspaper from that or the following day and probably find a relevant news story about the event.

Reference Resources   **A library's reference resources include encyclopedias, dictionaries, directories, atlases, almanacs, yearbooks, books of quotations, and biographical dictionaries.** As a speaker, you may at one time or another use most of these types of materials. Like periodicals, newspapers, and microfilm, reference resources are usually available only for in-house research and cannot be checked out.

Government Documents   Government agencies at all levels publish information on almost every conceivable subject, as well as keeping records of most official proceedings. **Once a dauntingly complex collection of pamphlets, special reports, and texts of speeches and debates, government documents today are much more readily accessible through the World Wide Web.**

The most important index of government documents has long been the *Monthly Catalog of U.S. Government Publications*, available online in recent years. At present, several government agencies are in the final stages of developing a more comprehensive online *National Bibliography of U.S. Government Publications*.[22]

Special Services   Interlibrary loan and reciprocal borrowing privileges are among the special services that can help you find resources not otherwise available through your own library or online. Say you are reading an article and discover a reference to a book you would like to see. Your library does not own the book. **You might be able to use interlibrary loan to locate the book at another library and have it sent to your library within a few days.** Or, if your library has **reciprocal borrowing privileges** with another library, **you may be able to go to that library yourself and locate the book.**

Types of Supporting Material

If you have explored your own knowledge and insights and those of people you know, discovered material on the Internet, and examined a variety of library resources, you probably have a wealth of potential supporting material. Now you will need to decide what to use in your presentation. Keeping in mind your audience's knowledge, interests, and expectations will help you to determine where an illustration might stir their emotions, where an explanation might help them to understand a point, and where statistics might convince them of the significance of a problem. Let's discuss these and other types of supporting material and consider suggestions for using them effectively.

Verbal

Illustrations   **Illustrations offer an example of or tell a story about an idea, issue, or problem a speaker is discussing.** They can be as short as a word or phrase or as long as a well-developed paragraph. Sometimes speakers will offer a series of brief illustrations, as Illinois State Senator Barack Obama did in his address to the Democratic National Convention in July 2004:

> . . . we have more work to do. More to do for the workers I met in Galesburg, Illinois, who are losing their union jobs at the Maytag plant that's moving to Mexico, and now are having to compete with their own children for jobs that pay seven bucks an hour. More to do for the father I met who was losing his job and choking back tears, wondering how he would pay $4,500 a month for the drugs his son needs without the health benefits he counted on. More to do for the young woman in East St. Louis, and thousands more like her, who has the grades, has the drive, has the will, but doesn't have the money to go to college.[23]

Other speakers may offer longer and more detailed illustrations:

> Toby Lee, six years old, was sitting in the bleachers at the Hutchinson Ice
> Arena, just outside Minneapolis, Minnesota. He got up and walked toward his
> mother to get money for the concession stand. To the horror of his parents,
> Toby slipped and fell through the 13-inch space between the seat and the foot-
> board, dropped 8 feet and landed headfirst on the concrete floor. Still con-
> scious, he was rushed to the hospital, where he later died of severe head
> injuries.[24]

Obama's illustrations and the story of Toby Lee are true examples. However, sometimes a speaker will use instead a **hypothetical illustration—one
that has not actually occurred.** If you decide to use a hypothetical illustration, it is important to make clear to your audience that the scene you describe
never really happened. Note how Matthew uses the word *imagine* to make clear
to his audience that his illustration is hypothetical:

> Imagine an evening outing: You and your two children decide to have a fun
> night out. You look up to your rearview mirror to see a car slam into the back
> of your car—WHAM—killing your children. You survive the crash and so
> does the individual who rear-ended you.[25]

Whether you choose to use brief or extended illustrations, true or hypothetical ones, remember this principle: Everybody likes to hear a story. An illustration almost always ensures audience interest. In addition, communication
researchers have found that listeners are less likely to generate counterargu-
ments to a persuasive message supported by examples and personal
narratives.[26]

The following suggestions should help you use illustrations effectively in
your presentations.

- Be sure that your illustrations are directly relevant to the idea or point they
  are supposed to support.
- Choose illustrations that are typical, not exceptions.
- Make your illustrations vivid and specific.
- Use illustrations with which your listeners can identify.
- Remember that the most effective illustrations are often personal ones.

Verbal

Descriptions and Explanations   Probably the most commonly used forms
of supporting material are descriptions and explanations. To describe is to provide detailed images that allow an audience to see, hear, smell, touch, or taste
whatever you are describing. **Descriptions—word pictures—**can make people and scenes come alive for an audience, as does this description of an all-
too-common encounter:

> You're walking down the main street when a loud thumping bass sound
> approaches you. To your annoyance, it is one of those hot rod drivers with all
> his car windows down, and from his tiny capsule, irritating, distorted sound
> waves of "Did It for the Nookie" hit your ears at 90 decibels.[27]

This speaker effectively uses an electronic presentation aid to complement his use of descriptions and explanations.

Verbal

An explanation of how something works or why a situation exists can help an audience understand conditions, events, or processes. In her presentation on "superbugs," Amanda explains how disease-resistant strains of bacteria develop:

> Bacteria are able to mutate when they are continually exposed to an antibiotic, rendering the antibiotic virtually useless against it. And the frequency with which antibiotics are prescribed today makes our pharmacies virtual classrooms for infections.[28]

Although descriptions and explanations are part of most presentations, they lack the inherent interest factor that illustrations have. The following suggestions may help you to keep audiences from yawning through your descriptions and explanations:

- Avoid too many descriptions and explanations.
- Keep your descriptions and explanations brief.
- Describe and explain in specific and concrete language.

Verbal

Definitions   For each technical or little-known term in their presentations, speakers should offer a **definition, or statement of what the term means.** However, they do not need to define terms with which most or all audience members are likely to be familiar. If you determine that you should define a word or phrase for your audience, consider whether you can best define it by **classification, the format of a standard dictionary definition,** or by an **operational definition, explaining how the word or phrase works or**

what it does. Joni uses both kinds of definition in this excerpt from her speech on the dangers of oral polio vaccination:

> Polio is a virus which attacks the tissue in the spinal cord and brain, causing inflammation. The effects of this inflammation range from fever and vomiting to bodily paralysis and damage to the nerve cells which control breathing and circulation.[29]

The first sentence defines *polio* by placing it in the general category in which it belongs (viruses) and then differentiating it from other viruses. This is a definition by classification. The second sentence describes what polio does. This is an operational definition.

To use definitions effectively, consider the following suggestions:

- Use definitions only when necessary.
- Be certain that your definitions are understandable.
- Be sure that any definition you provide accurately reflects your use of the word or phrase throughout the presentation.

Analogies   **An analogy demonstrates how unfamiliar ideas, things, and situations are similar to something the audience already understands.** Speakers can use two types of analogies in their presentations. The first is **a literal analogy, or comparison of two similar things.** Kyle uses a literal analogy to compare the African slave trade to other historical travesties:

Verbal

> The trans-Atlantic slave trade was one of the greatest tragedies in human history, rivaled by such horrible events as the Jewish Holocaust and the Spanish invasion of the Americas.[30]

The second type of analogy is **a figurative analogy, a comparison of two seemingly dissimilar things that in fact share a significant common feature.** In a recent speech to an environmental group, former Colorado Governor Richard Lamm drew on a figurative analogy that compared humanity's continuing long-term challenges to the flow of a river:

> . . . River issues were the long-term flowing issues, which went on over generations if not centuries. The full sweep of history reveals some issues like the fight for religious freedom, the gradual, if glacial, emancipation of women, the search for freedom for self-government, the fight against authoritarian governance, etc. These issues can be observed in some form over the sweep of history.[31]

Two suggestions can help you use analogies more effectively in your presentations:

- Be certain that the two things you compare in a literal analogy are very similar.
- Make the similarity between the two things compared in a figurative analogy apparent to the audience.

Statistics   **Statistics, or numerical data,** can represent hundreds or thousands of illustrations, helping a speaker express the significance or magnitude

Verbal

HOMEWORK

Verbal

of a situation. Statistics can also help a speaker express the relationship of a part to the whole. In this brief excerpt from a presentation on bogus airline parts, Jon uses both types of statistics:

> . . . 26 million parts are installed on airplanes every year in the U.S., and the FAA estimates that at least 2% of these parts are counterfeits.[32]

Skilled speakers learn how to use statistics to their greatest advantage. For example, they try to make huge numbers more readily understandable and more dramatic to their audiences. Nicole emphasizes the vast amount of computer waste with a memorable image:

> . . . outdated computer waste in America alone could fill the area of a football field piled one mile high.[33]

Or a speaker might present statistics about the world's growing population in these terms:

> In an average minute, 245 people are born and 107 die, for a net gain by the minute of 138 . . . 8300 an hour, 200,000 per day, 6 million per month, and 72 million a year.[34]

In addition to simplifying and dramatizing your statistics, you can use statistics more effectively if you utilize the following three suggestions:

- Round off large numbers.
- Use visual aids to present your statistics.
- Cite the sources of your statistics.

Opinions   The opinions of others can add authority, drama, and style to a presentation. A speaker can use three types of opinions: expert testimony, lay testimony, and literary quotations.

Expert testimony (the opinion of someone who is an acknowledged expert in the field under discussion) is perhaps the type of opinion most frequently employed by speakers. If you lack authority on your topic, cite someone who can offer such expertise. In her speech on the college credit card crisis, Jeni realized that her audience might not believe that the misuse of credit cards by college students is a widespread problem. So Jeni quoted an expert:

> Ruth Suswein, executive director of the Bankcard Holders of America, told the . . . *Pittsburgh Post Gazette*, "I defy you to go on any college campus and find any student who doesn't know some other student who has messed up using credit cards."[35]

In the days and weeks that followed the September 11, 2001, terrorist attacks, countless eyewitnesses and people affected in various ways by the tragedy told their personal stories to reporters and news anchors. Audiences already aware of the magnitude of the tragedy—the number of lives lost and the damage inflicted—were perhaps even more moved by the stories of such individuals as Lisa Jefferson. Jefferson was the GTE customer care representative who stayed on the line for 15 minutes with Todd Beamer, a passenger on United Flight 93 that eventually crashed in Pennsylvania. Of course, few speakers will have eyewitnesses at hand when they speak. But they can use **lay testimony by quoting firsthand witnesses of dramatic or traumatic events.** Such lay testimony can stir an audience's emotions and provide the most memorable moments of a presentation.

Finally, speakers may wish to include **literary quotations (citations from a work of fiction or nonfiction, a poem, or another speech)** in their presentations. Newspaper publisher Mike Curtin quoted science fiction writer H. G. Wells in his speech on the importance of language education:

> H. G. Wells, the English writer who achieved fame with his publication of *The Time Machine* and *The War of the Worlds,* . . . wrote, "Civilization is a race between education and catastrophe."[36]

Whether you use expert testimony, lay testimony, or literary quotations, consider the following suggestions for using opinions effectively in your presentations:

- Be certain that any authority you cite is actually an expert on the subject you are discussing.
- Identify your sources.
- Cite unbiased authorities.
- Cite opinions that are representative of prevailing opinion. If you cite a dissenting viewpoint, identify it as such.
- Quote or paraphrase your sources accurately and note the context in which the remarks were originally made.
- Use literary quotations sparingly.

Acknowledgment of Supporting Material

Once you have supporting material in hand, you must decide whether it must be credited to a source. Some information is so widely known that you may not need to acknowledge a source. For example, you need not credit a source if you say that former FBI official Mark Felt has been identified as the long-anonymous Watergate informant "Deep Throat." This fact is general knowledge and is widely available in a variety of sources. However, if you decide to use any of the following, then you must give credit:

- Direct quotations, even if they are only brief phrases
- Opinions, assertions, or ideas of others, even if you paraphrase them rather than quote them verbatim
- Statistics
- Any nonoriginal visual materials, including graphs, tables, and pictures

Integrating an **oral citation (an oral recounting of information about a source, such as the author, title, and publication date)** into your presentation is not difficult. For example, you might say,

> According to an article entitled "Wider Student Use Is Urged for New Meningitis Vaccine," published in the May 27, 2005, edition of *The New York Times,* the U.S. Centers for Disease Control and Prevention are now recommending

Diversity *and* Communication

Adapting to Diverse Audiences

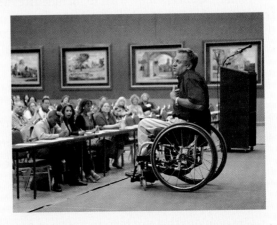

One of the principles we've stressed throughout this book is the importance of adapting your message to others. Many, if not most, of the presentations you give will be to audiences that represent a mix of cultures and backgrounds rather than a single cultural tradition. Although you may not have immediate plans to deliver a presentation in Singapore, Moscow, Tokyo, or Warsaw, it will not be unusual for you to face audience members who come from one of these cities when you speak on campus or in your hometown.

People from the predominant culture in North America usually prefer a structured presentation that follows an outlined pattern; they also prefer an introduction that previews the ideas you'll present and a conclusion that crisply summarizes the essential points you've made. But a Russian or Eastern European audience would expect a less tightly structured presentation. When you're in doubt about listener preferences, we recommend being structured and organized. But realize that not all audience members may expect information to be presented as *you* prefer. One study found that members of some cultures prefer a more formal oratorical style of delivery than the conversational, extemporaneous style that is usually taught in American presentational speaking classes.[37] For example, Japanese speakers addressing a predominantly Japanese audience begin a presentation by making respectful references to their audience.

You may still be wondering, "So, what should I do when I speak to people who have a cultural background different from my own?" Here are some ideas

that may help you.[38] First, consider using a variety of different types of supporting materials. A mix of stories, examples, statistics, and other supporting illustrations can appeal to a wide range of audience backgrounds. Also consider the power of images over words. Use visual aids to illustrate your talk. Pictures and images can communicate universal messages—especially emotional ones. Telling a good story to illustrate your ideas is another effective strategy to appeal to a wide range of audience preferences. Most audiences value a good story with a point or moral that is relevant to the point you want to make. Our overarching suggestion: Be aware of who will be in your audience. If you're unsure of your listeners' speaking-style preferences, ask for tips and strategies from audience members or people you trust before you design or deliver your presentation.

Aware
Verbal
Nonverbal
Listen and Respond
Adapt

"wider use of a new meningitis vaccine for adolescents and college freshmen," including routine vaccination for 11- and 12-year olds.[39]

As you select your illustrations, descriptions, explanations, definitions, analogies, statistics, and opinions, be guided not only by the suggestions provided in this chapter for each type of supporting material but also by the five communication principles for a lifetime. The best supporting material reflects self-awareness, taking advantage of your own knowledge and experience. Effective verbal supporting material is appropriately worded, concrete, and

RECAP

Supporting Your Speech

Type of Supporting Material	Guidelines for Use
Illustrations	• Make illustrations directly relevant to the idea or point they support. • Choose illustrations that are typical. • Make illustrations vivid and specific. • Use illustrations with which your listeners can identify. • Remember that the most effective illustrations are often personal ones.
Descriptions and Explanations	• Avoid too many descriptions and explanations. • Keep descriptions and explanations brief. • Describe and explain in specific and concrete language.
Definitions	• Use definitions only when necessary. • Be certain that definitions are understandable. • Be sure that a definition accurately reflects your use of the word or phrase.
Analogies	• Be certain that the two things you compare in a literal analogy are very similar. • Make apparent to the audience the similarity between the two things compared in a figurative analogy.
Statistics	• Round off large numbers. • Use visual aids. • Cite your sources.
Opinions	• Be certain that any authority you cite is actually an expert on the subject you are discussing. • Identify your sources. • Cite unbiased authorities. • Cite representative opinions, or identify dissenting viewpoints as such. • Quote or paraphrase accurately and in context. • Use literary quotations sparingly.

QUICK REVIEW

vivid enough that your audience can visualize what you are talking about. Effective visual supporting material enhances, rather than detracts from, your verbal message. Sensitivity to your audience will help you choose the verbal and visual supporting material that is most appropriately adapted to them. If a presentation is boring, it is probably because the speaker has not used the fundamental principles of communication as criteria for selecting supporting material.

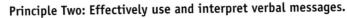

PRINCIPLES FOR A LIFETIME: Enhancing Your Skills

Principle One: Be aware of your communication with yourself and others.
- Give yourself a pep talk before getting up to speak.
- Consider your own interests and experiences when searching for a topic.
- Remember that the most effective illustrations are often personal ones.

Aware

Principle Two: Effectively use and interpret verbal messages.
- Focus on your message to help manage speaker anxiety.
- Search for topics on the Web, in the media, and in books.
- Wording your specific purpose in terms of your audience will help you keep your focus on them.
- A central idea should reflect a single topic, be a complete declarative sentence, and use specific language.
- Consider the accountability, accuracy, objectivity, date, usability, and diversity sensitivity of verbal material you find on Web sites.
- Be sure that your illustrations are directly relevent to the idea or the point they are supposed to support.
- Make your illustrations vivid and specific.
- Avoid too many descriptions and explanations.
- Keep descriptions and explanations brief.
- Describe and explain in specific and concrete language.
- Make your definitions readily understandable, and be certain they accurately reflect how you use the word or phrase in the speech.
- Round off statistics to make them more readily understandable.
- Cite unbiased authorities.
- Cite opinions that are representative of prevailing opinion.
- Quote or paraphrase accurately and in context.
- Use literary quotations sparingly.
- Integrate oral citations of your sources into your presentation.

Verbal

Principle Three: Effectively use and interpret nonverbal messages.
- Remember that the physical symptoms of speaker anxiety are rarely visible to an audience.
- Consider the accountability, accuracy, objectivity, date, usability, and diversity sensitivity of pictures and graphics you find on Web sites.
- Use visual aids to present statistics.

Nonverbal

Listen and Respond

Principle Four: Listen and respond thoughtfully to others.

- Seek out information about your audience and how they are likely to respond to your message to increase your comfort with speaking in public.
- Listen for topic ideas in the course of casual conversation with friends.

Adapt

Principle Five: Appropriately adapt messages to others.

- Revise your ideas or strategies at any point in the presentation-preparation process, as you seek out and learn more about your audience.
- Be audience-centered to reduce speaker anxiety.
- Be sensitive to and adapt to the diversity of your audience.
- Consider your audience's interests and expectations as you select the topic for your presentation.
- Keep in mind your audience's knowledge, interests, and expectations as you select supporting material for your presentation.
- Use illustrations with which your audience can identify. Consider making your audience members part of the scenario in a hypothetical illustration.
- Make the similarity between the two things compared in a figurative analogy apparent to your audience.

SUMMARY

Public speaking is a teachable, learnable process of developing, supporting, organizing, and presenting ideas. Presentational speaking skills can help you in other college courses and in the workplace.

The stages of the public speaking process center around consideration of the audience, who influence every decision a speaker makes. A speaker's tasks include selecting and narrowing a topic, identifying a general and specific purpose for speaking, developing the central idea of the presentation, generating main ideas, gathering supporting material, organizing the presentation, and finally, rehearsing and delivering the presentation.

Nearly everyone feels some anxiety about speaking in public. Speaker anxiety triggers physiological responses that may be worrisome but are actually your body's attempt to help you. Focusing on your audience and message and giving yourself mental pep talks can help you manage speaker anxiety, as can knowing how to develop a presentation, being well prepared, and seeking out opportunities to speak. Professional help is available for those few who continue to suffer debilitating speaker anxiety.

As you begin to prepare your presentation, you will first have to select and narrow your topic, keeping in mind the audience, the occasion, and your own interests and experiences. You may find helpful such strategies as silent brainstorming, scanning Web directories and Web pages, and listening and reading for topic ideas. Once you have a topic, you need to identify both your general and your specific purpose. General purposes include to inform, to persuade, and to entertain. Specific purposes are determined by the general purpose, the topic, and the audience. You will also need to decide on the central idea for the presentation. You can use that central idea to help you generate your main ideas, which are usually logical divisions of the central idea, reasons the central idea is true, or a series of steps or a chronological sequence that develops the central idea.

Next, you will need to discover support for your main ideas. As a presentational speaker, you have at least three potential sources of supporting material: yourself and people you know, the Internet, and the library. Personal knowledge and experience increase the likelihood that the audience will find you a credible speaker. To supplement your own knowledge and experience, you might turn to the vast resources available on the Internet. And most likely, you will still use library resources—books, periodicals, newspapers, reference resources, government documents, and various special services—as sources of supporting material.

The types of supporting material you can use in a presentation include illustrations, descriptions, explanations, definitions, analogies, statistics, and opinions. Simple guidelines can help you use each of these types of supporting material effectively and cite your sources correctly.

DISCUSSION AND REVIEW

1. Explain how presentational speaking skills can be of practical use, both while you are in college and afterward.
2. Sketch and label the stages of the audience-centered public speaking model.
3. Explain what causes the symptoms of speaker anxiety.
4. Offer at least three suggestions for managing speaker anxiety.
5. Suggest both criteria and strategies for discovering a good presentation topic.
6. What are the three general purposes for presentations?
7. With what phrase should an audience-centered, specific-purpose statement begin?
8. In what ways does a central idea differ from a specific purpose?
9. What are the characteristics of a good central idea?
10. List the three questions that you can apply to generate main ideas from a central idea.
11. Where might you find supporting material for a presentation?
12. List and explain the six criteria for evaluating Web sites.
13. What resources are available in most libraries?
14. What types of supporting material might you use in your presentations?

PUTTING PRINCIPLES INTO PRACTICE

1. Interview someone who regularly speaks in public as part of his or her job. Ask that person how he or she deals with speaker anxiety and what stages or steps he or she goes through in developing a speech.

2. Brainstorm a list of at least ten possible topics for an informative classroom presentation.

3. Write a specific-purpose statement for an informative presentation and a persuasive presentation on each of the following topics:

   Rap music

   Graduate school

   Primary elections

   Athletes as role models

   Credit cards

4. Generate at least three main ideas from each of the following central ideas. Apply the questions suggested in this chapter: Does the central idea have logical divisions? Can you think of several reasons the central idea is true? Can you support the central idea with a series of steps or a chronological sequence?

   Students who commute have at least three advantages over students who live on campus.

   Diplomatic relations between the United States and China have been strained over the last decade.

   Sleep deprivation is dangerous.

   Three specific strategies can help you deal with unsolicited telemarketers.

   Women should have annual mammograms.

5. Use a World Wide Web search engine to answer the following questions.[40] They're not as obvious as you think!

   a. How long did the Hundred Years War last?
   b. Which country makes Panama hats?
   c. From what animal do we get catgut?
   d. What is a camel's hair brush made of?
   e. The Canary Islands in the Pacific are named after what animal?
   f. What was King George VI's first name?
   g. What color is a purple finch?
   h. Where are Chinese gooseberries from?

6. Read a story in a newspaper or national news magazine. See how many different types of supporting material you can identify in the story.

7. The following passage comes from a book entitled *Abraham Lincoln, Public Speaker*, by Waldo W. Braden:

   > The Second Inaugural Address, sometimes called Lincoln's Sermon on the Mount, was a concise, tightly constructed composition that did not waste words on ceremonial niceties or superficial sentiment. The shortest Presidential inaugural address up to that time, it was only 700 words long, compared to 3700 words for the First, and required from 5 to 7 minutes to deliver.[41]

   Now determine which of the following statements should be credited to Braden if you were to use them in a presentation:

   - Lincoln's Second Inaugural is "sometimes called Lincoln's Sermon on the Mount."
   - Because he was elected and sworn in for two terms as President, Abraham Lincoln prepared and delivered two inaugural addresses.
   - Lincoln's Second Inaugural was 700 words and 5 to 7 minutes long.

Chapter 4.1   *Practice Test*

MULTIPLE CHOICE.   Choose the *best* answer to each of the following questions.

1. _____is helpful when you are choosing a topic for your presentation.
   a. Speaker anxiety
   b. Identifying your purpose
   c. Brainstorming
   d. Writing an introduction

2. Which of the following would **not** be considered a periodical?
   a. *The Quarterly Journal of Speech*
   b. *Encyclopedia Britannica*
   c. *Newsweek*
   d. *Rolling Stone*

3. Which of the following identifies what your audience should know or be able to do at the conclusion of your presentation?
   a. general purpose
   b. specific purpose
   c. central idea
   d. supporting material

4. In your presentation, you should cite a source for all of the following **except**
   a. historical events if they are well known.
   b. others' opinions that you have paraphrased.
   c. statistics.
   d. direct quotations if they are very brief.

5. Destiny gave an informative presentation in class with the following central idea: "Good study habits and time management skills are key to a successful college experience." Her instructor deducted points from her grade because Destiny's central idea
   a. is not a complete declarative statement.
   b. is not audience-centered.
   c. uses vague and abstract language.
   d. should be a single topic.

6. Research in the area of speaker anxiety has found that about _____ of speakers experience anxiety.
   a. 20%
   b. 40%
   c. 60%
   d. 80%

7. After choosing and narrowing your topic, determining your _____ is the next step in the presentation preparation process.
   a. specific purpose
   b. general purpose
   c. audience
   d. central idea

8. Which of the following strategies will help you manage speaker anxiety?
   a. Thoroughly research your topic.
   b. Imagine your audience members are naked.
   c. Look over your audience members' heads when speaking.
   d. Expect the worst and be happy when it does not happen.

9. Informing, persuading, and entertaining are the three types of
   a. general purposes.
   b. specific purposes.
   c. central ideas.
   d. supporting material.

10. Which of the following questions will **not** help you generate main ideas from your central idea?
    a. Does the idea have logical divisions?
    b. Can you think of several reasons why the central idea is true?
    c. How have other people treated the central idea?
    d. Does the central idea occur in a series of steps or chronological sequence?

11. When using statistics in a presentation, you should usually do all of the following *except*

    a. cite the sources of your statistics.

    b. use visual aids to present your statistics.

    c. cite specific numbers rather than rounding them off.

    d. make statistics readily understandable to the audience.

12. Whenever Linda gets nervous about giving a presentation, she takes a look at a video of Martin Luther King's "I Have a Dream" presentation so she can imagine herself being that effective. Linda is practicing

    a. systematic desensitization.

    b. focusing on her audience.

    c. performance visualization.

    d. deep-breathing techniques.

13. All of the following questions are useful in selecting a presentation topic *except*

    a. "What is the occasion?"

    b. "How much time do I have?"

    c. "Who is the audience?"

    d. "What are my interests and experiences?"

14. Internet searches that allow you to specify various combinations of intact phrases to search for are known as

    a. Einsteinian searches.

    b. Boolean searches.

    c. multi-level searches.

    d. hypersearches.

15. The comparison of two seemingly dissimilar things in order to reveal a common feature is known as a(n)

    a. definition.

    b. literal analogy.

    c. figurative analogy.

    d. illustration.

16. Dallin is planning to use information about population growth in the United States in his speech. From which top-level domain should he gather his information if he uses the Internet?

    a. .com

    b. .org

    c. .gov

    d. .mil

17. When assessing the accuracy of information in her sources, Gabriella should look at

    a. what organization or individual is responsible for the content.

    b. whether or not the sources of the facts are cited.

    c. the philosophies or biases of the organization or individual responsible for the content.

    d. when the information was posted or published.

18. During a speech on global warming, Rosalinda says, "Imagine spending spring break on the Gulf Coast, but instead of going to South Padre Island, you drive to Austin, Texas." What type of support is Rosalinda using?

    a. description

    b. hypothetical illustration

    c. literal analogy

    d. opinion

19. During a speech on alternative energy, Luis explains, "The American Petroleum Institute's Web site explains that the need for alternative energy sources is exaggerated because the current known oil supplies are expected to last for almost 100 more years." Which standard for evaluating Web sites did Luis most likely overlook?

    a. accountability

    b. accuracy

    c. objectivity

    d. date

20. Joseph is preparing a speech on nanotechnology. He wants to describe his topic in a way that the audience can comprehend, so he writes the following: "Nanotechnology refers to new technologies and devices that are smaller than ever previously imagined, allowing us to do things not previously imagined. Look at one of the

hairs on your arm and how small across that hair is. If that hair were as wide as a basketball, a nano-robot for curing cancer would still only be the size of a golf ball in comparison." To help his audience's comprehension, Joseph is using

a. statistics.
b. literal analogy.
c. figurative analogy.
d. hypothetical illustration.

TRUE/FALSE.   Indicate whether the following statements are *true* or *false*.

1. T or F   The use of illustrations increases the likelihood that the audience will be interested in the presentation.

2. T or F   When presenting new terms with which the audience is familiar, it is important to clearly define the terms.

3. T or F   It is important to clearly identify all of the sources of your supporting evidence.

4. T or F   You should use only factual illustrations in your presentations.

5. T or F   "To persuade my audience that the federal government should institute a patient bill of rights" is an example of a well-worded central idea.

6. T or F   Literal analogies compare two similar things.

7. T or F   When using statistics for evidence, it is unethical to round large numbers.

8. T or F   When evaluating a Web site for sensitivity to diversity, it is important to examine how accessible the Web site is.

9. T or F   The World Wide Web has replaced the library as the main source of supporting material for a presentation.

10. T or F   When referring to facts that are common knowledge, it is not necessary to cite your source.

FILL IN THE BLANK.   Complete the following statements.

1. If you share a fictional story with your audience to help them understand your ideas, you are using a(n) _____ _____.

2. The rapid heartbeat and butterflies that some speakers experience are a result of speaker _____.

3. Progressing through a series of relaxation techniques before you give a presentation is an example of _____ _____.

4. The process of developing, supporting, organizing, and presenting ideas is _____ speaking.

5. The _____ _____ of a presentation is either to inform, to persuade, or to entertain.

6. In the statement "4 out of 5 dentists recommend chewing gum after eating a meal," the phrase "4 out of 5 dentists" is an example of a(n) _____.

7. Your central idea should be subdivided into _____ _____.

8. Another term for the thesis statement of your presentation is the _____ _____.

9. The _____ _____ of a presentation identifies what the audience should know or be able to do after hearing the presentation.

10. Any statement that creates a word picture of something for your audience is a(n) _____.

Organizing and Outlining Your Presentation

CHAPTER OUTLINE

CHAPTER OBJECTIVES

After studying this chapter, you should be able to

1. List and explain five strategies for organizing main ideas in a presentation.

2. Define the principles of primacy, recency, and complexity and explain how each can be applied to organizing main ideas.

3. List and explain five strategies for organizing supporting material in a presentation.

4. Explain three ways to organize a presentation for the ears of others.

5. List and explain the five functions of a presentation introduction.

6. Suggest at least five strategies for getting an audience's attention in a presentation introduction.

7. List and explain the four functions of a presentation conclusion.

8. Define a preparation outline and explain how a speaker would use one.

9. Outline a presentation according to standard outline format.

10. Define a delivery outline and explain how a speaker would use one.

Don't agonize. Organize.

Florynce R. Kennedy

Jim Macbeth, Mostly Round & Flat, © Jim Macbeth/SuperStock, Inc.

D eveloping a presentation is like building a house. Just as a building contractor frames out a house early in the building process, a speaker frames
out a presentation by completing the first four stages of the speech preparation process—selecting and narrowing a topic, identifying a general and a specific purpose, determining a central idea, and generating main ideas. Framing
completed, the contractor assembles all the materials needed for the house:
windows, doors, cabinets, hardware, and flooring; the speaker finds and adds
supporting material to the presentation "frame," the fifth stage of the process.
Once the house is framed out and the building materials are ready, the contractor must organize the work of the electricians, plumbers, carpenters, and car-
pet layers. Similarly, the speaker must organize ideas and supporting material.

In this chapter, we will discuss strategies for organizing and outlining your
presentation, and we will explore ways to introduce and conclude your presentation effectively. Grounded in the five communication principles for a lifetime with which you are now familiar, these suggestions and strategies will
result in an essentially complete "house"—a presentation that is ready to be
rehearsed and delivered.

Organizing Your Main Ideas

You have already completed the first five stages of audience-centered presentation preparation:

- Select and narrow a topic.
- Determine your purpose.
- Develop your central idea.
- Generate main ideas.
- Gather supporting material.

Now it is time to put your presentation together, organizing the ideas and information you have generated and discovered.

Verbal

Logical organization is one way you can communicate your verbal message
effectively. A logically organized presentation has three major divisions—an
introduction, a body, and a conclusion. The introduction catches the audience's attention and previews the body. The body presents the main content
of the presentation. The conclusion summarizes the main ideas and provides
memorable closure to the presentation.

Professional speaker Larry Tracy suggests a strategy he calls "3–1–2" for
drafting the organization of a presentation.[1] It works like this:

1. Take a stack of 3 × 5 cards. Label one card "3" and write on it your "bottom line" message. This is the core of your conclusion.
2. Label another card "1" and write on it where the presentation will go—
   your preview.

3. Next, place the supporting points that flow from "1" to "3" on a series of cards marked "2a," "2b," "2c," etc. These will become the main ideas of the body of your presentation.

The advantage of the "3–1–2" strategy, says Tracy, is that it clarifies from the start of the drafting process where the presentation is going, ensuring more logical structure. He adds, "Just remember: You draft 3–1–2, but . . . you deliver 1–2–3."

Regardless of whether you use Tracy's drafting process, one recommended by your public speaking instructor, or one of your own devising, you will need to consider early on how best to organize your main ideas. Then you will organize your supporting material for maximum impact, and devise signposts to lead your audience through your presentation. Finally, you will need to develop an effective introduction and conclusion. Once you have made the necessary decisions about these component parts, you will be ready to outline the entire presentation.

Organizing Ideas Chronologically

If you determine that you can best develop your central idea through a series of steps, you will probably organize those steps—your main ideas—chronologically. **Chronological organization is based on sequential order, according to when each step or event occurred or should occur.** If you are explaining a process, you will want to organize the steps of that process from first to last. If you are providing a historical overview of an event, movement, or policy, you might begin with the end result and trace its history backward in time. Examples of topics that might lend themselves to chronological organization include the process for stripping and refinishing a piece of furni-

If you intend to describe a series of different types of procedures in your presentation, you may find that it works well to organize your main ideas topically.

ture, the four hurricanes that hit Florida in 2004, and the history of higher education for women.

Organizing Ideas Topically

If your main ideas are natural divisions of your central idea, you will probably arrange them according to topical organization. Topical organization may be simply an arbitrary arrangement of main ideas that are fairly equal in importance. For example, if you are giving an informative presentation on the various instrument families of the modern symphony orchestra, your main ideas will probably be strings, woodwinds, brass, and percussion. The order in which you discuss these instrument groups may not really matter.

At other times, topical organization is less arbitrary. **The principle of recency suggests that audiences remember best what they hear last.** If you want to emphasize the string section of an orchestra, you will purposefully place that family last in your presentation.

Another principle that can help guide your topical organization is **the principle of primacy, which suggests that you discuss your most convincing or least controversial idea first**. To adapt to an audience who may be skeptical of some of your ideas, discuss first those points on which you all agree. If you are speaking to an anti–gun-control audience about ways to protect children from violence in schools, don't begin by advocating gun control. Instead, begin by affirming family values and education in the home, perhaps move on to the importance of small classes and adequate counseling in schools, and only then discuss gun control as a possible preventive measure.

One other type of topical organization is **organization according to complexity, moving from simple ideas and processes to more complex ones.** Many skills you have learned in life have been taught by order of complexity. In first grade, you learned to read easy words first, then moved on to more difficult ones. In third grade, you learned single-digit multiplication tables before moving on to more complex double- and triple-digit multiplication problems. In junior high school, you learned to use the library's catalog before you began a research project. And in high school, you learned to drive by practicing simple maneuvers in the parking lot before going out on the highway. Similarly, if you are giving a presentation on how to trace your family's genealogy, you might discuss readily available, user-friendly Internet sources before explaining how to access old courthouse records or parish registries of births, deaths, and baptisms.

Organizing Ideas Spatially

"Go down the hill two blocks and turn left by the florist. Then go three blocks to the next stoplight and turn right. The place you're looking for is about a block farther, on your right." When you offer someone directions, you organize your ideas spatially. **Spatial organization means arranging items according to their location, position, or direction.**

Presentations that rely on description are good candidates for spatial organization. For example, discussions of the route taken by Sir Edmund Hillary and Tenzing Norgay when climbing Mt. Everest in 1953 and the molecular structure of DNA would lend themselves to spatial organization. Or, rather than organizing your presentation on Florida's 2004 hurricanes chronologically, you might choose to organize it spatially, according to where each hurricane made landfall.

Organizing Ideas to Show Cause and Effect

Cause-and-effect organization actually refers to two related patterns: identifying a situation and then discussing the resulting effects (cause–effect) and presenting a situation and then exploring its causes (effect–cause).

A speaker discussing the consequences of teenage pregnancy might use a cause–effect pattern, establishing first that teenage pregnancy is a significant social issue and then discussing various consequences or effects. On the other hand, a speaker who speaks on the same topic but who chooses to explore the reasons for the high rate of teen pregnancy will probably use an effect–cause pattern, discussing teenage pregnancy first as an effect and then exploring its various causes. As the recency principle would suggest, a cause–effect pattern emphasizes effects; an effect–cause pattern emphasizes causes.

Organizing Ideas by Problem and Solution

If, instead of exploring causes or consequences of a problem or issue, **you want either to explore how best to solve the problem or to advocate a particular solution, you will probably choose problem-and-solution organization.** For example, if you were speaking on how listeners can protect themselves from mountain lion attacks in the American West, you might first establish that a significant problem exists, then talk about solutions to that problem. Or if you were talking about ending discrimination against overweight people, you could first establish that such discrimination exists and is harmful, then talk about the solutions. Although you can use problem-and-solution organization for either informative or persuasive presentations, you are more likely to use it when your general purpose is to persuade—to urge your audience to support or adopt one or more of the solutions you discuss.

Note that the topics in both of the above examples also lend themselves to organization by cause and effect. You could, for example, discuss mountain lion attacks as an effect and explore why the frequency of such attacks has increased in recent years (causes). Or you could talk about discrimination against the overweight as a cause and discuss the harmful effects of such discrimination. How do you decide which organizational pattern to use? Return to your specific purpose. If it is for your audience to be able to explain how best to guard against mountain lion attacks, select the problem-and-solution organizational strategy. If it is for your audience to be able to explain the harmful effects of discrimination against those who are overweight, use the cause-and-effect strategy of organization. Let both your general and your specific purpose continue to guide your presentation as you organize your main ideas.

RECAP

Organizing Your Main Ideas

Strategy	Description
Chronological	Organization by time or sequence
Topical	Arbitrary arrangement of topics or organization according to recency, primacy, or complexity
Spatial	Organization according to location or position
Cause-and-effect	Organization by discussing a situation and its causes or a situation and its effects
Problem-and-solution	Organization by discussing a problem and then various solutions

Organizing Your Supporting Material

Once you have organized your main ideas, you are ready to organize the supporting material for each idea. Suppose that you find that you have two brief illustrations, a statistic, and an opinion in support of your first main idea. How should you organize these materials to communicate your verbal message most effectively?

The same organizational patterns you considered as you organized your main ideas can also help you organize your supporting material. For example, you might arrange a group of brief illustrations chronologically. At other times, you might find it more useful to organize supporting material according to the principle of recency, primacy, or complexity. You would employ the principle of recency if you saved your most convincing statistic for last. You would use primacy if you decided to present first the opinion with which you were certain your audience would agree. And you might arrange two explanations according to the principle of complexity, presenting the simplest one first and working up to the more complex one. Two additional principles that may help you organize supporting material are specificity and arrangement from "soft" to "hard" evidence.

Sometimes your supporting material includes both very specific illustrations and a more general explanation. **The principle of specificity suggests**

that you offer your specific information and follow it by your general explanation or make your general explanation first and then support it with your specific illustrations. In his speech on wearing ribbons to show support for a cause, Tony offers a series of brief illustrations first, followed by a more general explanation:

> Battling AIDS, surviving breast cancer, putting your life back together after 9/11, just being brave while your country is at war; all of these are situations that cause people to seek out support and comfort in others. We start looking for ways to connect with people around us, even total strangers. A simple way proven effective in the past and possible for the future is simply cutting off a ribbon and pinning it to your clothes.[2]

Another principle that can help you organize your supporting material is moving from "soft" evidence to "hard" evidence. **Hypothetical illustrations, descriptions, explanations, definitions, analogies, and opinions are**

Diversity and Communication

Acknowledging Cultural Differences in Organizing Messages

*W*hat's the shortest distance between two points? Why, going in a straight line, of course. In organizing a message, it may seem that the most logical strategy is to develop a structure that moves from one idea to the next in a logical, "straight" way. But not every culture organizes ideas using that logic. In fact, each culture teaches its members unique patterns of thought and organization that are considered appropriate for various occasions and audiences. In general, U.S. speakers tend to be more linear and direct than do Semitic, Asian, Romance, or Russian speakers.[3] Semitic speakers support their main points by pursuing tangents that might seem "off topic" to many U.S. listeners. Asians may allude to a main point only through a circuitous route of illustra-

tions and parables. And speakers from Romance and Russian cultures tend to begin with a basic principle and then move to facts and illustrations that only gradually are related to a main point. The models in Figure 4.2.1 illustrate these culturally diverse patterns of organization.[4] Of course, these are very broad generalizations. As an effective speaker who seeks to adapt to your audience, you should investigate and perhaps acknowledge or even consider adopting the customary organizational strategy of your particular audience. In addition, when you are listening to a presentation, recognizing the existence of cultural differences can help you appreciate and understand the organization of a speaker from a culture other than your own.

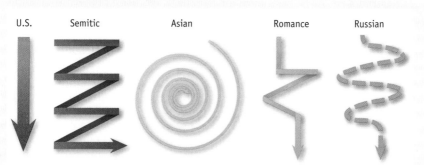

FIGURE 4.2.1
Organizational Patterns by Culture

Developing Your Presentation
STEP BY STEP

Organize Your Speech

*A*s he begins to integrate his supporting material in his speech on Coricidin abuse, Ben finds that he has four items to help him explain the ingredient in Coricidin that is the catalyst for abuse. He decides to arrange these four items in order of complexity—from stating where DXM can be found, to explaining its physical side effects:

1. DXM is found in over 100 cold medications, including those with "DM" or "Tuss" in their names.
2. Coricidin is the drug of choice because it's

easier than swallowing several bottles of Robitussin.
3. As the National Institute on Drug Abuse indicates on TheAntiDrug.com Web site, last updated April 11, 2004, DXM closely resembles PCP and, when taken in excess, causes hallucinations.
4. According to *USA Today* of December 29, 2003, when abused, Coricidin can cause depressed breathing, an irregular heartbeat, seizures, coma, and even death.

usually considered soft evidence. Hard evidence includes factual examples and statistics. Allie moves from soft evidence to a hard statistic as she discusses the widespread prescribing of selective serotonin reuptake inhibitors, or SSRIs:

> The *PR Newswire* of April 14, 2003, explains that when people suffer from depression or an anxiety disorder, there could be a problem with their serotonin balance. Thus, it is unsurprising that SSRIs are frequently prescribed for a variety of mood disorders. *ABC News* of June 21, 2003, reports that one out of every eight Americans has been prescribed at least one SSRI.[5]

RECAP

Organizing Your Supporting Material

Strategy	Description
Chronology	Organization by time or sequence
Recency	Most important material last
Primacy	Most convincing or least controversial material first
Complexity	From simple to more complex material
Specificity	From specific information to general overview or from general overview to specific information
"Soft" to "hard" evidence	From hypothetical illustrations and opinions to facts and statistics

Organizing Your Presentation for the Ears of Others

You now have a fairly complete, logically organized plan for your presentation. But if you tried to deliver it at this point, your audience would probably become confused. What are your main ideas? How is one main idea related to the next? What supporting material develops which main idea? To adapt your logically organized message to your audience, you need to provide **signposts, or organizational cues for their ears.** You do this by adding previews, transitions, and summaries that allow you to move smoothly from one idea to the next throughout the presentation.

Adapt

Previews

A preview "tells them what you're going to tell them"—it is a statement of what is to come. Previews help your audience members anticipate and remember the main ideas of your presentation. They also help you move smoothly from the introduction to the body of your presentation and from one main idea to the next. **The initial preview is usually presented in conjunction with, and sometimes as part of, the central idea.** Note how Yarmela states her central idea and then previews her three main ideas near the end of the introduction to her presentation on genetic testing:

> Genetic testing is seen as the wave of the future, but too many Americans are putting their faith in these tests that simply are not adequate. In order to understand this problem, we will first examine the problems that are occurring with genetic testing, then look at the causes, and finally discuss the solutions that must occur in order to stop more tragedies from taking place.[6]

In addition to offering an initial preview, a speaker may also offer **internal previews at various points throughout a presentation. These previews introduce and outline ideas that will be developed as the presentation progresses.** Meleena provides an internal preview just before the final main idea of her presentation on sexual harassment in schools:

Ethics and *Communication*

The Ethics of Primacy and Recency

Jessica knows that, according to the principle of recency, she should discuss last what she wants her audience to remember best. However, in her presentation on the risk of counterfeit prescription drugs, Jessica thinks that it may be more ethical to reveal immediately to her audience how costly the problem is in terms of both dollars and human lives. Is it ethical for Jessica to save that important statistic for last?

Now . . . we can look at some things that we can all do, as parents, teachers, and students, to stop sexual harassment in our schools. There are two ways to prevent these causes from recurring. The first is education and the second is immediate action.[7]

When Meleena delivers this preview, her listeners know that she is going to talk about two possible solutions to the problem she has been discussing. Their anticipation increases the likelihood that they will hear and later remember these solutions.

Verbal and Nonverbal Transitions

Verbal
Nonverbal

A transition signals to an audience that a speaker is moving from one idea to the next. Effective **verbal transitions** **are words or phrases that show relationships between ideas in your presentation.** They include simple enumeration *(first, second, third)*; synonyms or pronouns that refer to earlier key words or ideas (the word *they* at the beginning of this sentence refers to the phrase "verbal transitions" in the previous sentence); and words and phrases that show relationships between ideas *(in addition, not only . . . but also, in other words, in summary, therefore, however)*. As you begin to rehearse your presentation, you might need to experiment with various verbal transitions to achieve a coherence that seems natural and logical to you. If none of the verbal alternatives seems quite right, consider a nonverbal transition.

Nonverbal transitions are sometimes used alone and sometimes in combination with verbal transitions. An effective **nonverbal transition might take the form of a facial expression, a pause, a change in vocal pitch or speaking rate, or movement.** Most good speakers will use a combination of verbal and nonverbal transitions to help them move from one idea to the next throughout their presentations.

Canadian Prime Minister Jean Charest uses a nonverbal signpost to help listeners follow his transitions.

Summaries

Like previews, **a summary—a recap of what has been said**—provides an additional opportunity for the audience to grasp a speaker's most important ideas. Most speakers use two types of summaries: internal summaries and a final summary.

Internal summaries, like internal previews, **occur within and throughout a presentation and recap what has been said so far in the presentation.** You might want to use an internal summary after you have discussed two or three main ideas, to ensure that the audience keeps them firmly in mind as you move into another main idea. You can combine an internal summary with an internal preview. Rebecca clarifies what she has just discussed, as well as what she will discuss next, in this combined internal summary/preview from her presentation on Rohypnol, the so-called date-rape drug:

> Having examined the problem of Rohypnol and why it has become such a danger in today's society [summary], we can now explore solutions at the commercial and personal levels to purge this drug from our system [preview].[8]

You may also want to provide your audience with **a final opportunity to hear and remember your main ideas, in the form of a final summary in your conclusion.** While your initial preview gave your audience their first exposure to your main ideas, your final summary will give them their last exposure to those ideas. Near the end of Stephanie's presentation on cruise ship violence, she provides this final summary of her three main ideas:

> Today we outlined violence on cruise ships and the need for recourse; we then discussed the nature of these criminal environments and lack of laws; and finally, we explored solutions for handling or avoiding these crimes even if the authorities are not supportive.[9]

Adding previews, transitions, and summaries to your well-organized presentation applies the fundamental principles of using both verbal and nonverbal messages effectively and of adapting your message to others, increasing the likelihood that your audience will grasp your main ideas and the logic of your organizational strategy.

QUICK REVIEW

Verbal
Nonverbal
Adapt

Introducing and Concluding Your Presentation

At this point, you have pretty well developed the ideas and content of the body of your presentation, and you have strategies for organizing that material. But you have not yet given much thought to how you are going to begin and end the presentation. That's okay. Even though you will deliver it first, you usually plan your introduction last. You need to know first what you're introducing—especially your central idea and main ideas. Once you do, it is time to plan how you are going to introduce and conclude your presentation. While they make up a relatively small percentage of the total presentation, your introduction

Adapt

and conclusion provide your audience with first and final impressions of you and your presentation. They are important considerations in adapting your message to others.

Introductions

Your introduction should convince your audience to listen to you. More specifically, it must perform five functions: get the audience's attention, introduce the topic, give the audience a reason to listen, establish your credibility, and preview your main ideas. Let's briefly consider each of these five functions.

Get the Audience's Attention   If an introduction does not capture the audience's attention, the rest of the presentation may be wasted on them. You have to use verbal messages effectively to wake up your listeners and make them want to hear more.

There are several good ways to gain an audience's attention. One commonly used and quite effective one is to open with an illustration. Tony opens his speech on forgiveness with a moving personal illustration:

> For my fifteenth birthday, my mother promised that we would spend the whole day together, and she would take me anywhere I wanted to go and buy me anything I wanted. You see, my mother was a single mom, and the true gift to me was just spending time with her; she was always at work. Well, I was so excited that the night before my birthday I couldn't sleep, and I woke up at dawn on my birthday, and I waited. And I waited, and I waited, and I waited. Well, 1:00 PM came around, and my mother was still sleeping. You see, I knew that she'd been up drinking all night the night before, and that she'd probably wake up angry at me if I was to wake her up. So I waited. And then 5:00 PM came around, and I gathered up the courage to wake her up. And when I did, she slapped me; she threw $60 at me and said, "Get out of my face."[10]

Other strategies are to ask a rhetorical question, relate a startling fact or statistic, quote an expert or a literary text, tell a humorous story, or refer to historical or recent events. Federal Reserve Chairman Alan Greenspan used humor to capture the attention of the 2005 graduating class of the Wharton School of the University of Pennsylvania:

> I have more in common with you graduates than people might think. After all, before long, after my term at the Federal Reserve comes to an end, I too will be looking for a job.[11]

Eileen uses a historical reference to open her presentation on mental health privacy:

> A bright political future loomed ahead of Thomas Eagleton in 1972. George McGovern had chosen him as his vice presidential running mate for the '72 elections, and his popularity was high among Americans. But then the press

found out that Eagleton had received shock treatment for depression when he was younger. Eagleton was immediately dropped from the ticket and shunned from the political world.[12]

Still other speakers might get their audience's attention by referring to a personal experience, referring to the occasion, or referring to something said by a preceding speaker. While not all of these strategies will work for all presentations, at least one of them should be an option for any presentation you make. And with a little practice, you may find yourself being able to choose from several good possibilities for a single presentation.

The 5th Wave   By Rich Tennant

Introduce the Topic

Within the first few seconds of listening to you, your audience should have a pretty good idea of what your topic is. The best way to achieve this objective is to include a statement of your central idea in your introduction.

Give the Audience a Reason to Listen

Not only do you have to get your audience's attention and introduce your topic—you have to motivate your listeners to continue to listen. Show the audience how your topic affects them and those they care about. Catherine uses rhetorical questions to drive home to her audience the relevance and importance of her speech on a healthy diet:

Verbal

> What if I told you that, by decreasing one food item in your and your loved ones' diet, you could significantly lessen the chance for metabolic syndrome (or obesity); heart disease; coronary artery disease; osteoporosis due to calcium depletion; high blood pressure; colon, kidney, breast, prostate, and liver cancer? Would you change the menu at your and your loved ones' next meal?[13]

By the end of your introduction, your audience should be thinking, "This concerns *me*!"

WATCH

Establish Your Credibility

A credible speaker is one whom the audience judges to be believable, competent, and trustworthy. Be aware of the skills, talents, and experiences you have had that are related to your topic. You can increase your credibility by telling your audience about your expertise. For example, in your introduction to a persuasive presentation on studying abroad, you might say:

> I know first-hand how studying abroad can broaden your worldview, increase your understanding of another culture, and enrich your academic studies. Last fall, I studied at the Sorbonne in Paris.

On the Web

We've emphasized the importance of catching your listeners' attention when you begin your presentation. The Internet can be a good place to find an attention-gaining quote, story, statistic, or illustration. Here are some Web addresses that may help you find what you need to begin your presentation in a memorable way:

Famous quotations: dir.yahoo.com/Reference/quotations

Humorous quotations: directory.google.com/Top/Recreation/Humor/Quotations

Stories from literature: www.literature.org/Works

Statistics from the U.S. Census Bureau: www.census.gov

Preview Your Main Ideas   As we discussed above, you should provide an initial preview of your main ideas at or near the end of your introduction, to allow your listeners to anticipate the main ideas of your presentation.

Conclusions

While your introduction creates a critically important first impression, **your conclusion leaves an equally important final impression.** Long after you finish speaking, your audience will hear the echo of effective final words. An effective conclusion serves four functions: to summarize the presentation, to reemphasize the main idea in a memorable way, to motivate the audience to respond, and to provide closure. Let's consider each of these functions.

Summarize the Presentation   The conclusion offers a speaker a last chance to repeat his or her main ideas. Most speakers summarize their main ideas between the body of the presentation and its conclusion or in the first part of the conclusion.

Verbal

Reemphasize the Central Idea in a Memorable Way   The conclusions of many famous speeches contain many of the lines we remember best:

> . . . that government of the people, by the people, for the people, shall not perish from the earth. *(Abraham Lincoln)*[14]

> Old soldiers never die; they just fade away. *(General Douglas MacArthur)*[15]

> Free at last! Free at last! Thank God almighty, we are free at last! *(Martin Luther King Jr.)*[16]

Use your final verbal message effectively. Word your thoughts so that your audience cannot help but remember them.

Motivate the Audience to Respond   Think back to your specific purpose. What do you want your audience to be able to do by the end of your presentation? If your purpose is to inform, you may want your audience to think about your topic or to seek more information about it. If your purpose is to persuade, you may want your audience to take some sort of action—to write a letter, make a phone call, or volunteer for a cause. Your conclusion is where you can motivate your audience to respond. Travis closes his presentation on sleep deprivation with this admonition:

> Before we are all, literally, dead on our feet, let's take the easiest solution step of all. Tonight, turn off your alarm, turn down your covers, and turn in for a good night's sleep.[17]

Provide Closure   You may have experienced listening to a presentation and not being certain when it was over. That speaker did not achieve the last purpose of an effective conclusion: providing **closure, or a sense that the presentation is finished.**

One good way to provide closure is to refer to your introduction by finishing a story, answering a rhetorical question, or reminding your audience of your introduction. Kyle had opened his presentation by quoting President Theodore Roosevelt, who declared in 1907 that depletion of America's natural resources would diminish the future prosperity of the country. Kyle provides closure to his presentation by referring again to Roosevelt's warning:

> If President Theodore Roosevelt were alive today, he'd certainly be concerned at the state and the future of our national forests. Therefore, it's so important that we heed his advice and we do everything that we can to protect our national forests—for our physical well-being, our financial well-being, and for the prosperity of future generations.[18]

You can also achieve closure by using verbal and nonverbal signposts. For example, you might use such transitions as "finally" and "in conclusion" as you move into your conclusion. You might pause before you begin the conclusion, slow your speaking rate as you deliver your final sentence, or signal by falling vocal inflection that you are making your final statement. Experiment with these strategies until you are certain that your presentation "sounds finished."

Sarah Ferguson, Duchess of York, knows that a good conclusion is key to reinforcing the motivational purpose of her speech.

RECAP

The Purposes of Introductions and Conclusions

Your introduction should . . .
- Get your audience's attention.
- Introduce your topic.
- Give your audience a reason to listen.
- Establish your credibility.
- Preview your main ideas.

Your conclusion should . . .
- Summarize your presentation.
- Reemphasize your central idea in a memorable way.
- Motivate your audience to respond.
- Provide closure.

Verbal
Nonverbal

WATCH

QUICK
REVIEW

Outlining Your Presentation

WATCH

With your introduction and conclusion planned, you are almost ready to begin rehearsing your presentation. By this point, you should have your preparation outline nearly complete. **A preparation outline is a fairly detailed outline of central idea, main ideas, and supporting material and may also include the specific purpose, introduction, and conclusion.** A second outline, which you will prepare shortly, is a delivery outline, the notes from which you will eventually deliver your presentation.

Preparation Outline

Aware

Although few presentations are written in manuscript form, most speakers develop a fairly detailed preparation outline that helps them to ensure that their main ideas are clearly related to their central idea and are logically and adequately supported. A speaker who creates a preparation outline is applying the first fundamental principle of communication: becoming increasingly aware of his or her communication. In addition to helping the speaker judge the unity and coherence of the presentation, the preparation outline also serves as an early rehearsal outline and is usually the outline handed in as part of a class requirement.

Instructors who require students to turn in a preparation outline will probably have their own specific requirements. For example, some instructors ask you to include your introduction and conclusion as part of your outline, while others ask you to outline only the body of the presentation. Some ask that you incorporate signposts into the outline or write your specific purpose at the top of the outline. Be certain that you listen to and follow your instructor's specific requirements regarding which elements to include.

EXPLORE

Technology *and* **Communication**

Using Outlining Software

*W*ord processing programs such as Microsoft Word have features that allow you to set the style of, and various levels within, an outline. The feature will then apply the appropriate number, letter, and indentation to each heading you provide.

If you are using MyCommunicationLab in your communication course, you have access on that site to Outline icons that will allow you to create customized, specific outlines of your presentations.

Try using one or both of these outlining resources to prepare either your preparation outline or your delivery outline for your next presentation. Then evaluate the resource you used. Explain whether it made outlining easier or harder for you than outlining by hand.

Almost certainly, your instructor will require that you use standard outline format. **Standard outline format, which uses numbered and lettered headings and subheadings, lets you become more aware of the exact relationships among various main ideas, subpoints, and supporting material in your presentation.** Even if you haven't had much experience with formal outlines, the following guidelines can help you produce a correct outline.

Aware

Use Standard Numbering   Outlines are numbered by using Roman and Arabic numerals and uppercase and lowercase letters followed by periods, as follows:

I. First main idea
    A. First subdivision of I
    B. Second subdivision of I
       1. First subdivision of B
       2. Second subdivision of B
          a. First subdivision of 2
          b. Second subdivision of 2
II. Second main idea

You will probably not need to subdivide beyond the level of lowercase letters in most presentation outlines.

Use at Least Two Subdivisions, If Any, for Each Point   You cannot divide anything into fewer than two parts. On an outline, every I should have a II, every A should have a B, and so on. If you have only one subdivision, fold it into the level above it.

Line Up Your Outline Correctly   Main ideas, indicated by Roman numerals, are written closest to the left margin. The *periods* following these Roman numerals line up, so that the first letters of the first words also line up:

I. First main idea
II. Second main idea
III. Third main idea

Letters or numbers of subdivisions begin directly underneath the first letter of the first *word* of the point above:

I. First main idea
    A. First subdivision of I
    B. Second subdivision of I

If a main idea or subdivision takes up more than one line, the second line begins under the first letter of the first word of the preceding line:

I. First main idea
    A. A rather lengthy subdivision that
        runs more than one line
    B. Second subdivision

Within Each Level, Make the Headings Grammatically Parallel   Regardless of whether you write your preparation outline in complete sentences or in phrases, be consistent within each level. In other words, if I is a complete sentence, II should also be a complete sentence. If A is an infinitive phrase (one that begins with *to* plus a verb, such as "to guarantee greater security"), B should also be an infinitive phrase.

Following is a sample preparation outline for the presentation we've been watching Ben Johnson prepare in the Developing Your Presentation Step by Step feature.[19] Your instructor may give additional or alternative requirements for what your preparation outline should include or how it should be formatted.

SAMPLE PREPARATION OUTLINE

Writing the purpose statement at the top of the outline helps the speaker keep it in mind. But always follow your instructor's specific requirements for how to format your preparation outline.

Purpose

At the end of my presentation, the audience will take steps to end the abuse of the cold medication Coricidin.

Introduction

Ben catches his reader's attention by opening his presentation with an illustration. Other strategies for effectively getting audience attention were discussed earlier in the chapter.

Three days before Christmas, Jill and Jim Darling went to check on their daughter to make sure she was getting ready for school. When they opened the door to the bathroom, they found their daughter Jennifer unconscious on the floor. Jill frantically called 911, and then they waited helplessly for the paramedics. Only moments after the ambulance arrived, the high school senior was pronounced dead. The cause of Jennifer's death remained a mystery until investigators discovered a small plastic bag in her room containing 32 red pills. According to the January 27, 2003, issue of *University Wire*, the pills were an over-the-counter cold medication known as Coricidin. When used by adults, these pills are an effective method for decreasing the symptoms of the common cold, but in the hands of a child they become a dangerous hallucinogenic drug. These seemingly harmless pills are part of a new national epidemic of substance abuse by teenagers and children as young as 6.

Central Idea

Ben writes out and labels his central idea and preview. Again, follow your instructor's requirements.

We should take steps to end the abuse of the cold medication Coricidin.

Preview

For this reason we must first educate ourselves about the danger of Coricidin and the threat it poses for teens, and next uncover the cause for this growing trend, so that finally we may pose some viable solutions to safeguard our children's health.

Body Outline

The first main idea of the presentation is indicated by the Roman numeral I. This main idea has two subpoints, indicated by A and B.

I. Coricidin abuse is rapidly becoming a significant problem.
   A.   Coricidin contains the cough suppressant Dextromethorphan, or DXM.

1. DXM is found in over 100 cold medications, including those with "DM" or "Tuss" in their names.
2. Coricidin is the drug of choice because it's easier than swallowing several bottles of Robitussin.
3. As the National Institute on Drug Abuse indicates on *TheAntiDrug.com* Web site, last updated April 11, 2004, the drug closely resembles PCP, and when taken in excess, causes hallucinations.
4. According to *USA Today* of December 29, 2003, when abused, Coricidin can cause depressed breathing, an irregular heartbeat, seizures, coma, and even death.

B. Coricidin abuse is widespread.
   1. The American Association of Poison Control Centers told the *Boston Globe* of January 11, 2004, that there were over 14,000 calls to poison control centers last year to report the intentional overdose of cold medication.
   2. According to the January 29, 2004, Scripps Howard News Service, there were more than 3000 cases of Coricidin abuse in 2003 alone.
   3. A report by *CNN* on December 30, 2003, explains that overdoses tend to occur in clusters. A 13-year-old girl brought 80 Coricidin tablets to her middle school in Naples, Florida, and gave some to six of her friends. Each friend took at least five pills. The recommended dose for an adult is no more than one pill every six hours. The school was in chaos as three students lost consciousness and had to be rushed to the hospital. The girl who distributed the pills thought it would be "fun to feel messed up and act. . . drunk."

Signpost: So if the drug poses such a threat, why has nothing been done to stop it? There are two main reasons that Coricidin has become such a problem. First, the pills and information on how to use them are widely available to teenagers. Second, there is a lack of awareness from parents and teachers.

II. Coricidin abuse has become a problem for two reasons.
   A. Coricidin is widely available to teenagers.
      1. *CBS News* reports on December 29, 2003, that some stores have begun keeping Coricidin behind the counter, but for the most part the pills are easily obtainable by teens.
      2. A box of 16 pills only costs about $5, and because the drug is safe when taken correctly, the Food and Drug Administration has made no move to regulate it. Jeff Hegelson, a 19-year-old abuser, told ABC's *20/20* on January 9, 2004, "As far as drugs go, you don't need to know a dealer. If you can find a Walgreen's or a grocery store, you're set."
      3. The Internet has contributed to the problem.
         a. The *Milwaukee Journal Sentinel* of October 24, 2003, explains that full-strength DXM can be purchased online. Two Wisconsin teens were arrested after purchasing a 50-gram bottle of DXM over the Internet and then reselling the pills.
         b. A simple Web search returns hundreds of sites giving detailed instructions on how many pills to take to get high.

Subpoints 1, 2, 3, and 4 provide supporting material for A.

Ben's oral citation for this Web site is sufficient; he should also have the Web address available for his instructor or any other audience member who might want it.

This signpost summarizes Ben's first main idea—that Coricidin abuse is significant—and previews his second main idea—why the problem has occurred.

        c.   There are even recipes explaining how to extract DXM from Coricidin in order to achieve a more potent drug.

    4. In an interview with the previously cited *Boston Globe*, Dr. Michael Shannon, Chief of Emergency Medicine at Children's Hospital in Boston, says, "It's rampant. Look at who's taking it. These are kids who are unable to buy alcohol, unable to buy cigarettes. . . and now you've got something that you know is in many households. It's cheap, it's legal, and it's easy to obtain and nobody questions you if you have it in your backpack."

  B. The attitudes of parents and teachers also complicate the problem.

    1. Donna Oldham suspected that her son was abusing drugs, but she was shocked when she learned that he was getting his fix legally at the local pharmacy. Donna told the *Chicago Daily Herald* of September 8, 2003, "Most parents would have no idea their kids were doing this. It's not like pot or cocaine. It's this legal drug that a lot of people probably have in their own medicine cabinets. Unless you know what to look for, you're going to miss it."

    2. The February 19, 2004, *Modesto Bee* explains that approximately 2/3 of teen drug abuse is from drugs found in the home or ones that you can get at the drugstore. Traditionally, parents and school officials watch out for illegal substances and alcohol. If a student were caught with a bottle of alcohol or marijuana, he or she would be suspended. But when a box of Coricidin is found in that student's backpack, school officials don't give it a second thought.

Having established the problem and discussed its causes, Ben turns to solutions.

Signpost: After exploring the problem and cause of this drug abuse, it's clear that Coricidin poses a threat, and something must be done to stop it.

  III. Solutions at both the national and personal levels can ensure that no more harm is done.

    A. On a national level, the use of Coricidin by minors needs to be regulated more carefully.

      1. According to the *San Antonio Express News* of January 11, 2003, a bill was introduced in New Mexico making it illegal to sell products with DXM to minors and requiring stores to keep the pills behind the counter or in areas that require assistance. Other state governments need to follow suit.

      2. Retailers can also help solve the problem. The previously cited *Chicago Daily Herald* reports that last year Wal-Mart started requiring customers to be at least 18 if they wanted to buy Coricidin, and they weren't allowed to purchase more than three boxes at a time.

A final signpost makes clear that Ben will talk about what individual audience members can do about Coricidin abuse.

Signpost: However, restrictions alone are not enough to stop this problem; action must be taken at the personal level as well.

    B. We must begin to create awareness about the danger of Coricidin.

      1. Parents should watch for boxes of the drug in their child's room or backpack and ask questions if they notice cold pills being used frequently.

2. Those people without children can log on to *Drugfreeamerica.org* or *TheAntiDrug.com* to learn more about drug prevention as well as additional ways to join the fight against this abuse.
   a. Donate time or money.
   b. Inform your friends and family about the dangers of Coricidin.

Aware that many of his listeners are not parents, Ben suggests appropriate actions for both groups.

Conclusion

It's been a year since Jim and Jill Darling watched helplessly as their daughter died on the bathroom floor, but the drugs that took her life still pose a tremendous danger to children and teens across the country. Today we gained an understanding of the dangers of Coricidin, next uncovered the cause for this trend, and finally posed some viable solutions to safeguard our youth. Jim Darling said he "hopes his daughter's death has served as a wake-up call for law enforcement, teachers and parents." No parents should ever have to watch their child die, but as long as Coricidin remains easily available, the lives of our children will be at risk.

In his conclusion, Ben returns to the illustration with which he began the presentation.

Delivery Outline

As you rehearse your presentation, you will find yourself needing to look at your preparation outline less and less. You have both the structure and the content of your presentation pretty well in mind. At this point, you are ready to develop a shorter delivery outline.

Your delivery outline should provide all the notes you will need to make your presentation as you have planned, without being so detailed that you will be tempted to read it rather than speak to your audience. Here are a few suggestions for developing a delivery outline:

- *Use single words or short phrases whenever possible.*
- *Include your introduction and conclusion in abbreviated form.* Even if your instructor does not require you to include your introduction and conclusion on your preparation outline, include an abbreviated version of them on your delivery outline. You might even feel more comfortable delivering the presentation if you have your first and last sentences written out in front of you.
- *Include supporting material and signposts.* Write out in full any statistics and direct quotations and their sources. Write your key signposts—your initial preview, for example—to ensure that you will not have to grope awkwardly as you move from one idea to another.

It might have been easier for this student to deliver an effective message if she had prepared a concise delivery outline on note cards.

- *Do not include your purpose statement.*   Because you will not actually say your purpose statement during your presentation, do not put it on your delivery outline.
- *Use standard outline form.*   Standard outline form will help you find your exact place when you glance down at your speaking notes. You will know, for example, that your second main idea is indicated by II.

Here is a delivery outline for Ben Johnson's presentation on the abuse of Coricidin.

SAMPLE DELIVERY OUTLINE

For the delivery outline, Ben does not need to write his purpose statement, as he will not actually state it in the presentation.

Ben writes his introduction as a bullet list so that he will be able to see each part at a glance.

Introduction
- 3 days before Christmas, Jill and Jim Darling check on daughter—find Jennifer unconscious on floor.
- 911—paramedics—dead.
- ? until small plastic bag of 32 red pills found.
- January 27, 2003, *University Wire*: over-the-counter cold medication Coricidin
- Adults—C. effective for decreasing cold symptoms.
- Child—C. dangerous hallucinogenic drug, part of ntl. epidemic of substance abuse by teens & children as young as 6.

Central Idea
We should take steps to end the abuse of the cold medication C.

Ben includes and labels his initial preview and signposts throughout the outline so that he can find them quickly.

Although both main ideas and subpoints are shorter than in the preparation outline, source citations are still provided in full.

Part of the "shorthand" of the delivery outline may include such symbols as > or < for "greater than" or "less than"; @ for "at"; and w/ for "with." Ben also uses abbreviations in his delivery outline.

Preview
1. Educate ourselves about the danger & threat of C.
2. Uncover cause for trend.
3. Pose viable solutions.

Body Outline
I. Significant problem.
   A. C. contains cough suppressant Dextromethorphan (DXM).
      1. DXM found in > 100 cold meds., incl. those w/ "DM" or "Tuss" in name.
      2. C. the drug of choice because easier than swallowing several bottles of Robitussin.
      3. National Institute on Drug Abuse, *TheAntiDrug.com* Web site, last updated April 11, 2004—resembles PCP & when taken in excess causes hallucinations.
      4. *USA Today*, December 29, 2003—when abused, C. can cause depressed breathing, irregular heartbeat, seizures, coma, & death.
   B. Abuse widespread.
      1. American Ass. of Poison Control Centers told *Boston Globe*, January 11, 2004 → 14,000 calls to poison control centers last year.

2. CNN, December 30, 2003—overdoses occur in clusters.
    a. 13-year-old girl brought 80 C. to middle school, Naples, Florida.
    b. Gave to 6 friends.
    c. Each took > 5.
    d. (Rec. adult dose = 1 pill/6 hrs.)
    e. Chaos: 3 lost consciousness & rushed to hospital.
    f. Girl thought it would be "fun to feel messed up and act . . . drunk."

Ben lists the elements of the CNN illustration separately so he can quickly see any detail he needs.

Signpost: So if the drug poses such a threat, why has nothing been done to stop it? There are two main reasons that C. has become such a problem. First, the pills and information on how to use them is widely available to teenagers. Second, there is a lack of awareness from parents and teachers.

II. 2 reasons.
   A. Widely available to teenagers.
      1. *CBS News*, December 29, 2003—some stores keep C. behind counter, but usually easily obtainable by teens.
      2. Box of 16 pills = $5; Food & Drug Admin. has made no move to regulate. Jeff Hegelson, 19-year-old abuser, told ABC's *20/20*, January 9, 2004, "As far as drugs go, you don't need to know a dealer. If you can find a Walgreen's or a grocery store, you're set."
      3. Internet has contributed to problem.
         a. The *Milwaukee Journal Sentinel*, October 24, 2003—full-strength DXM can be purchased online; 2 Wis. teens arrested after purchasing 50-gram bottle of DXM over Internet and reselling pills.
         b. Web search = hundreds of sites w/detailed instructions on how many pills to take to get high.
         c. Recipes explaining how to extract DXM from C. in order to achieve a more potent drug.
      4. Interview w/*Boston Globe*, Dr. Michael Shannon, Chief of Emergency Medicine at Children's Hospital in Boston—"It's rampant. Look at who's taking it. These are kids who are unable to buy alcohol, unable to buy cigarettes . . . and now you've got something that you know is in many households. It's cheap, it's legal, and it's easy to obtain and nobody questions you if you have it in your backpack."
   B. Attitudes of parents & teachers complicate.
      1. Donna Oldham suspected son, but shocked to learn was getting fix legally @ local pharmacy. Donna told *Chicago Daily Herald*, Sept. 8, 2003, "Most parents would have no idea their kids were doing this. It's not like pot or cocaine. It's this legal drug that a lot of people probably have in their own medicine cabinets. Unless you know what to look for, you're going to miss it."
      2. Feb. 19, 2004, *Modesto Bee*—approx 2/3 teen drug abuse from drugs found in home or drugstore. Parents & school officials watch for illegal substances & alcohol. Student w/bottle of alcohol or marijuana wd. be suspended. Box of C.: not a 2nd thought.

To ensure that he quotes Jeff Hegelson and others accurately, Ben writes out their statements in full.

Signpost: After exploring the problem and cause of this drug abuse, it's clear that C. poses a threat, and something must be done to stop it.

III. Ntl. & personal.
    A. Ntl.: C. regulated more carefully.
        1. *San Antonio Express News*, January 11, 2003—bill in N.M. makes it illegal to sell products with DXM to minors & requires stores to keep pills behind counter. Others need to follow suit.
        2. Retailers: *Chicago Daily Herald*—
           a. Wal-Mart started requiring customers to be > 18 to buy C.
           b. Not allowed to purchase > 3 boxes @ a time.

Signpost: However, restrictions alone are not enough to stop this problem; action must be taken at the personal level as well.

    B. Personal awareness
        1. Parents: Watch & ask ?.
        2. No children—*Drugfreeamerica.org* or *TheAntiDrug.com* to learn about drug prevention & how to fight.
           a. Donate time or money.
           b. Inform friends & family.

Conclusion
- A yr. since Jim and Jill Darling watched daughter die.
- Drugs that took her life still pose tremendous danger to children & teens.
- Today,
    1. Understanding of dangers of C.
    2. Uncovered cause for trend.
    3. Posed viable solutions.
- Jim Darling said he "hopes his daughter's death has served as a wake-up call for law enforcement, teachers and parents."
- No parents should ever have to watch their child die, but as long as C. remains easily available, the lives of our children will be at risk.

Ben writes out his final sentence, to ensure that he can end his presentation fluently.

    Although you may write the first version of your delivery outline on paper, eventually you will probably want to transfer it to note cards. They don't rustle as paper does, and they are small enough to hold in one hand. Two or three note cards will probably give you enough space for your delivery outline. Type or print neatly on one side only, making sure that the letters and words are large enough to read easily. Plan your note cards according to logical blocks of material, using one note card for your introduction, one or two for the body of your presentation, and one for your conclusion. Number your note cards to prevent getting them out of order while you are speaking.

    A final addition to your note cards as you rehearse your presentation will be **delivery cues such as "Louder," "Pause," or "Walk two steps left." These will remind you to communicate the nonverbal messages you have planned.** Write your delivery cues in a different color ink so that you don't confuse them with your verbal content.

RECAP

Two Types of Presentation Outlines

Type	Purpose
Preparation Outline	Allows speaker to examine presentation for completeness, unity, coherence, and overall effectiveness. May serve as first rehearsal outline.
Delivery Outline	Serves as speaking notes; includes delivery cues.

PRINCIPLES FOR A LIFETIME: Enhancing Your Skills

Aware

Principle One: Be aware of your communication with yourself and others.

- Use the introduction of your presentation to help establish your own credibility; be aware of the skills, talents, and experiences you have that can enhance your credibility with your listeners.
- Use a preparation outline to demonstrate to yourself that your main ideas are clearly related to your central idea and are logically and adequately supported.

Verbal

Principle Two: Effectively use and interpret verbal messages.

- Organize your presentation logically to communicate your verbal message effectively.
- Use verbal transitions to show relationships between ideas in your presentation.
- Introduce your topic and preview your main ideas in your introduction.
- Use stories, examples, illustrations, statistics, a quotation, or other techniques to capture your listeners' attention when you begin your talk.
- In your conclusion, summarize your presentation and reemphasize your main idea in a memorable way.

Nonverbal

Principle Three: Effectively use and interpret nonverbal messages.

- Use nonverbal transitions—pauses, facial expression, altered vocal pitch or speaking rate, and movement—to indicate when you are moving from one idea to the next.
- Use nonverbal cues, such as pausing, slowing your rate of speech, and letting your vocal inflection fall, to signal that you are approaching the end of your presentation.
- Add delivery cues and reminders to your final delivery outline.

Listen and Respond

Principle Four: Listen and respond thoughtfully to others.

- As you listen to presentations, consider the cultural differences in the organization of speakers from cultures other than your own.

Adapt

Principle Five: Appropriately adapt messages to others.

- Investigate and consider using the customary organizational strategy of your audience's culture.
- Discuss last the idea that you most want your audience to remember.
- If you know your audience will be skeptical of some of your ideas, first present ideas on which you can agree.
- Provide signposts as organizational cues for your audience.
- Use your introduction and conclusion to help adapt your presentation to your audience.

SUMMARY

Once you have found supporting material, you are ready to organize your ideas and information. Depending on your topic, purpose, and audience, you can organize the main ideas of your presentation chronologically, topically, spatially, by cause and effect, or by problem and solution. You can sometimes organize supporting material according to one of these same patterns, or you can organize it according to the principles of recency, primacy, complexity, or specificity or from soft to hard evidence.

With your presentation organized, you will want to add signposts—previews, transitions, and summaries—to make your organization clearly apparent to your audience. A carefully planned introduction will get your audience's attention, introduce your topic, give the audience a reason to listen, establish your credibility, and preview your main ideas. In an equally carefully planned conclusion, you can summarize your presentation, reemphasize the central idea in a memorable way, motivate your audience to respond, and provide closure.

A final step before beginning to rehearse your presentation is to prepare a detailed preparation outline and a delivery outline that eventually becomes your speaking notes.

DISCUSSION AND REVIEW

1. List and explain five strategies for organizing the main ideas in a presentation.

2. List and explain five strategies for organizing supporting material in a presentation.

3. List and define three types of verbal signposts.

4. How can you make a nonverbal transition?

5. List and explain five functions of a presentation introduction.

6. How can you get your audience's attention in your introduction?

7. List and explain four functions of a presentation conclusion.

8. What is included on most preparation outlines? What are such outlines used for?

9. What is included on most delivery outlines? What are such outlines used for?

PUTTING PRINCIPLES INTO PRACTICE

1. Take notes as you listen to a presentation, either live or on audiotape or videotape. Then organize your notes into an outline that you think reflects both the speaker's organization and the intended relationship among ideas and supporting material.

2. Read one of the speeches in Appendix E. Answer the following questions:

   a. How are the main ideas organized?

   b. Look closely at the supporting materials. If two or more are used to support any one main idea, what strategy do you think the speaker used to organize them?

   c. Is there an initial preview statement? If so, what is it?

   d. Is there a final summary? If so, what is it?

   e. Find at least one example of each of the following:

      A transition word or phrase
      An internal preview
      An internal summary

3. Draft an introduction for a presentation on one of the following topics:

   Strategies for surviving a tornado

   Private-school vouchers

   Mars up close

   Celebrities and the press

   In addition to introducing the topic and previewing your main ideas, be sure to plan strategies for getting your audience's attention and giving them a reason to listen. Also devise a way to establish your own credibility as a speaker on that topic.

4. Miguel, who plays guitar in a mariachi band, plans to give an informative presentation on mariachi music. He wants to talk a little about the history of mariachi bands, the kind of music they play, and their role in Mexican and Mexican-American culture. In addition, he plans to introduce the instruments most commonly used in mariachi music: trumpet, guitar, and such percussion instruments as tambourines and maracas.

   Miguel asks you to help him develop a good introduction for the presentation. How do you think he might best introduce his presentation to achieve all five functions of a presentation introduction?

Chapter 4.2 *Practice Test*

MULTIPLE CHOICE. Choose the *best* answer to each of the following questions.

1. Which of the following are considered "hard" evidence?
   a. definitions
   b. statistics
   c. analogies
   d. descriptions

2. Alexia is giving a presentation utilizing a problem-and-solution organizational pattern. What would Alexia's general purpose be?
   a. to persuade
   b. to inform
   c. to entertain
   d. to convince

3. Which of the following would *not* be considered an effective transition?
   a. enumerating the main points of the presentation
   b. a change in the pitch of your voice
   c. a phrase such as "in other words"
   d. moving from one side of the room to the other

4. When subdividing your standard outline, you should remember to
   a. have only one subdivision per level.
   b. have at least two subdivisions per level.
   c. have at least three subdivisions per level.
   d. keep subdivisions to an absolute minimum.

5. "Now we will turn our attention to the causes of higher tuition rates" is an example of a(n)
   a. internal summary.
   b. preview.
   c. transition.
   d. final summary.

6. In preparing a presentation on golf clubs, Rob came up with four main ideas: "Woods," "Irons," "Specialty Clubs," and "Putters." Rob used which organizational pattern?
   a. topical
   b. chronological
   c. spatial
   d. problem-and-solution

7. Which of the following elements should be included last in a presentation introduction?
   a. attention-getter
   b. establishment of credibility
   c. motivation for the audience to listen
   d. central idea of the presentation

8. What is the strategy used by a speaker who organizes supporting material so that the most important material is presented last?
   a. complexity
   b. primacy
   c. chronology
   d. recency

9. Melissa is preparing a presentation on Disney World's attractions and their locations. In all likelihood, she will use which organizational pattern for her main ideas?
   a. spatial
   b. problem-and-solution
   c. topical
   d. chronological

10. An effective conclusion should accomplish all of the following *except*
    a. motivating the audience to respond.
    b. reemphasizing the main idea.
    c. introducing a new key idea.
    d. summarizing the presentation.

11. Which organizational pattern would be most effective for arranging the main points of a presentation with the specific purpose "To inform my audience how to build a low-cost bookshelf"?

a. problem-and-solution

b. cause-and-effect

c. topical

d. chronological

12. In using the cause-and-effect organizational pattern, it is important that you

a. identify the cause first and then explain its effects.

b. identify the effect first and then explain its causes.

c. identify either the cause or effect first and then explain the other.

d. identify the effect first but only explain part of the cause.

13. Your delivery outline should fit neatly on

a. one note card.

b. two or three note cards.

c. four or five note cards.

d. as many note cards as it takes.

14. Which of the following organizational patterns would use the principle of complexity?

a. spatial

b. cause-and-effect

c. topical

d. chronological

15. In your delivery outline, you should remember to

a. include your purpose statement.

b. leave out your supporting material.

c. include your complete introduction.

d. leave out your purpose statement.

16. What organizational pattern is the author of this speech using?

I. Chewing gum dates back to ancient Greek and Mayan cultures.

II. Modern chewing gum was inspired by General Santa Ana and Thomas Adams.

III. In the future, chewing gum will be used as a nutraceutical product.

a. spatial

b. cause-and-effect

c. topical

d. chronological

17. When preparing a delivery outline, the speaker should

a. use complete declarative sentences.

b. include the purpose statement.

c. use standard outline format.

d. make headings grammatically parallel.

18. When preparing an informative speech about ways to increase energy efficiency in the home for her school's chapter of the Sierra Club, which organizational principle should Olivia consider?

a. recency

b. primacy

c. complexity

d. specificity

19. Which of the following topics would be best organized according to a topical organizational pattern?

a. The Apollo Space Program

b. How to Bake Banana Bread

c. The Path of Hurricane Katrina's Destruction

d. Alternative Energy Options

20. Jesse states the central idea of his speech as follows: "Behavioral problems are on the rise in our schools, and clothing has the ability to affect behaviors; therefore, I propose that all public schools require school uniforms." Which type of organizational pattern does this central idea suggest?

a. chronological

b. topical

c. cause-and-effect

d. problem-and-solution

TRUE/FALSE. Indicate whether the following statements are *true* or *false*.

1. T or F   "My second point" is an example of an internal summary.

2. T or F   Referring back to the introduction in the conclusion of a presentation is a

good way to provide closure to the presentation.

3. T or F   The introduction is written before the main points of a presentation.

4. T or F   The preparation outline is the outline from which you will speak.

5. T or F   It is important to use words or short phrases in your delivery outline.

6. T or F   A speaker should provide closure to a presentation by saying "Thank you" to the audience.

7. T or F   When giving evidence, speakers should always move from "soft" evidence to "hard" evidence.

8. T or F   A quote from U.S. Secretary of Labor Elaine Chao stating that an increase in the minimum wage would be bad for economic growth is an example of "hard" evidence.

9. T or F   Unless you are introduced by another person, you should begin your presentation by telling your audience your name and what your speech is about.

10. T or F   The specific purpose of your speech should be included on the preparation outline but not the delivery outline.

FILL IN THE BLANK. Complete the following statements.

1. The topical organizational pattern of moving from simple ideas to ideas that are more difficult is based on the _____ principle.

2. In her biology presentation, Amanda focused first on widespread disease in underdeveloped parts of the country and then explained different way that disease could be stopped. Amanda used _____ organization.

3. The condensed version of your preparation outline that you use while giving your presentation is known as the _____ _____.

4. A presentation that first describes global warming and then details why global warming occurs is using _____ organization.

5. Supporting materials such as hypothetical illustrations or analogies are _____ evidence.

6. An example of _____ evidence would be factual examples.

7. If the main ideas of your presentation move from one location to another, then you are using _____ organization.

8. A speaker uses a(n) _____ to let the audience know he or she is moving from one point to the next.

9. The first time you state your main ideas to the audience is typically in the _____ _____.

10. Ordering a presentation by the sequence in which something happens is _____ organization.

Delivering Your Presentation

CHAPTER OUTLINE

Methods of Delivery

Effective Verbal Delivery

Effective Nonverbal Delivery

Effective Presentation Aids

Some Final Tips for Rehearsing and Delivering
   Your Presentation

Summary

CHAPTER OBJECTIVES

After studying this chapter, you should be able to

1. List and describe the four methods of delivery and provide suggestions for effectively using each one.
2. List and explain five criteria for using words well.
3. List and define three types of figurative language that can be used to make a presentation memorable.
4. Explain ways to create verbal drama and cadence in a presentation.
5. Identify and illustrate characteristics of effective delivery.
6. List 11 types of visual aids from which a speaker might select, and provide suggestions for using each type effectively.
7. Offer four general guidelines for preparing and using effective presentation aids.

O the orator's joys! To inflate the chest, to roll the thunder of the voice out from the ribs and throat, to make the people rage, weep, hate, desire . . .

Walt Whitman

Jacob Lawrence, The Life of Harriet Tubman, #21: Every antislavery convention held within 500 miles of Harriet Tubman found her at the meeting. She spoke in words that brought tears to the eyes and sorrow to the hearts of all who heard her speak of the suffering of her people. 1940. Casein tempera on hardboard, 17 7/8 × 12". Hampton University Museum. Photo credit: The Jacob and Gwendolyn Lawrence Foundation/Art Resource, NY. © 2007 The Jacob and Gwendolyn Lawrence Foundation, Seattle/Artists Rights Society (ARS), New York.

W hich is more important: the content of a presentation or the way it is delivered? Speakers and speech teachers have argued about the answer to this question for thousands of years. In the fourth century BC, the Greek rhetorician Aristotle declared delivery "superfluous." On the other hand, when his contemporary and fellow Athenian Demosthenes was asked to name the three most important elements for a speaker to master, he is reported to have replied, "Delivery, delivery, delivery."

Nonverbal

The debate continues. Which is more important: content or delivery? It is clear that the way you deliver a speech influences the way listeners respond to you and to your message. In a now-classic study, Alan H. Monroe found that audience members equate effective presentational speaking with such nonverbal factors as direct eye contact, alertness, enthusiasm, a pleasant voice, and animated gestures.[1] Another researcher concluded that delivery was almost twice as important as content when students gave self-introduction presentations, and three times as important when students gave persuasive presentations.[2] Other scholars have found that delivery provides important information about a speaker's feelings and emotions and will in turn affect listeners' emotional responses to the speaker.[3] Most speech teachers today believe that both content and delivery contribute to the effectiveness of a presentation. As a modern speechwriter and communication coach suggests,

> In the real world—the world where you and I do business—content and delivery are always related. And woe be to the communicator who forgets this.[4]

**Aware
Verbal
Nonverbal
Listen and Respond
Adapt**

In this chapter, we will discuss how you can apply the five communication principles for a lifetime to delivery. We will talk about both verbal and nonverbal delivery skills. We will consider how important it is to be aware of the words you use and of such nonverbal cues as gestures, eye contact, and facial expression. We will discuss how to determine what presentation aids might be effective for your audience, and we'll offer guidelines for both the preparation and the use of various types of presentation aids.

Methods of Delivery

Audiences today generally expect speakers to use clear, concise, everyday language and conversational delivery style, as opposed to the flowery language and dramatic, choreographed gestures used by speakers a century ago. However, different audiences expect and prefer variations of this delivery style. For example, if you are using a microphone to speak to an audience of 1000 people, your listeners may expect a relatively formal delivery style. On the other hand, your communication class would probably find it odd if you delivered a formal oration to your 25 classmates.

People from different cultures also have different expectations of speakers' delivery. Listeners from Japan and China, for example, prefer subdued gestures to a more flamboyant delivery style. British listeners expect a speaker to stay behind a lectern and use relatively few gestures.

Speakers should consider and adapt to their audience's expectations, their topic, and the speaking situation as they select from four basic methods of delivery: manuscript speaking, memorized speaking, impromptu speaking, and extemporaneous speaking. Each is more appropriate to some speaking contexts and audiences than to others, and each requires a speaker to use a slightly different delivery style. Let's consider each of these four delivery methods in more detail.

Adapt

Manuscript Speaking

Perhaps you remember the first presentation you ever had to give—maybe as long ago as elementary school. Chances are that you wrote your speech out and read it to your audience.

Unfortunately, **manuscript speaking, or reading a presentation from written text,** is rarely done well enough to be interesting. Most speakers who rely on a manuscript read it in either a monotone or a pattern of vocal inflection that makes the presentation sound as if it were being read. They are so afraid of losing their place that they keep their eyes glued to the manuscript and seldom look at the audience. These challenges are significant enough that most speakers should avoid reading from a manuscript most of the time.

However, there are some exceptions. Sometimes effective verbal messages depend on careful and exact phrasing. For example, because an awkward statement made by the U.S. Secretary of State could cause an international crisis, he or she usually has remarks on critical issues carefully scripted. A company manager or administrator presenting a new, potentially controversial company policy to employees or customers might also deliver that announcement from a manuscript.

Verbal

If you ever have to speak on a sensitive, critical, or controversial issue, you too might need to deliver a manuscript presentation. If so, consider the following suggestions:[5]

- Type your manuscript in short, easy-to-scan phrases on the upper two-thirds of the paper so that you do not have to look too far down into your notes.
- Use appropriate nonverbal messages. Try to take in an entire sentence at a time so that you can maintain eye contact throughout each sentence.
- Do not read the manuscript too quickly. Use a slash mark (/) or some other symbol to remind you to pause in strategic places.
- Vary the rhythm, inflection, and pace of your delivery so that the presentation does not sound like it is being read.
- Use gestures and movement to add further nonverbal interest and emphasis to your message.

Nonverbal

Memorized Speaking

After that first speech you read in elementary school, you probably became a more savvy speaker, and the next time you had to give a speech, you decided to write it out and memorize it. You thought that no one would be able to tell you had written it out first. What you didn't know then, but probably do now, is that **delivering a presentation word for word from memory without using notes, called memorized speaking,** sounds stiff and recited. In addition, you run the risk of forgetting parts of your speech and having to search awkwardly for words in front of your audience. And you forfeit the ability to adapt to your audience while you are speaking.

However, speaking from memory is occasionally justifiable. Memorized speaking might be appropriate in the same instances as manuscript speaking, when exact wording is critical to the success of the message, and when the speaker has time to commit the speech to memory. If you must deliver a short presentation within narrowly proscribed time limits, memorizing and rehearsing it will allow you to time it more accurately. Three guidelines can help you use nonverbal messages effectively when you deliver a presentation from memory:

Nonverbal

- Do not deliver your memorized speech too rapidly.
- Avoid patterns of vocal inflection that make the speech sound recited. Focus on what you are saying, and let your voice rise and fall to emphasize key words and phrases and to reflect the structures of your sentences. Consider recording your presentation and listening to it to ensure that your vocal delivery sounds like a conversation rather than a recitation.
- Use gestures and movement to add interest and emphasis to your message.

Impromptu Speaking

In September 1993, then-President Bill Clinton stood before a joint session of Congress to deliver an important speech about health-care reform. What happened during the first 9 minutes of that presentation has become what political advisor and commentator Paul Begala calls "part of the Clinton legend":

> The teleprompter screens are whizzing forward and backwards with last year's speech, trying to find it, and finally, they killed it all together and reloaded it. Nine minutes the guy went without a note, and no one could tell.[6]

Although you can usually plan your presentations, there are times—as illustrated by Clinton's experience—when the best plans go awry. In other, more likely instances, you may be asked to answer a question or respond to an argument without advance warning or time to prepare a presentation. At such times, you will have to call on your skills in **impromptu speaking, or speaking "off the cuff" with no advance preparation.** Five guidelines can help you avoid fumbling for words or rambling:

Adapt

- Consider your audience. A quick mental check of who your audience members are and what their interests, expectations, and knowledge are can help ensure that your impromptu remarks are audience-centered.

- Be brief. As one leadership consultant points out,

  > You're not the star—not this time, anyway. If you were the luminary, they would not have asked you to speak without warning. You're merely expected to hit a theme, say a few nice words, and then depart.[7]

  One to three minutes is probably a realistic time frame for most impromptu presentations.
- Organize. Think quickly about an introduction, body, and conclusion. If you want to make more than one point, use a simple organizational strategy such as chronological order—past, present, and future. Or construct an alphabetical list, in which your main ideas begin with the letters A, B, and C.[8]
- Draw on your personal experience and knowledge. Audiences almost always respond favorably to personal illustrations, so use any appropriate and relevant ones.
- Use gestures and movement that arise naturally from what you are saying.
- Be aware of the potential impact of your communication. If your subject is at all sensitive or your information is classified, be noncommittal in what you say.

Aware
Nonverbal

Extemporaneous Speaking

We have saved for last the method of speaking that is the most appropriate choice for most circumstances: **extemporaneous speaking. This is the speaking style taught today in most public speaking classes and preferred by most audiences. When you speak extemporaneously, you develop your presentation according to the various stages of the audience-centered public speaking model, stopping short of writing it out.** Instead, you speak from an outline and rehearse the presentation until you can deliver it fluently. Your audience will know that you have prepared, but will also have the sense that the presentation is being created as they listen to it—and to some extent, it is. In short, the extemporaneous presentation is a well-developed and well-organized message delivered in an interesting and vivid manner. It reflects your understanding of how to use both verbal and nonverbal messages effectively and your ability to adapt these messages to your audience.

Aware
Verbal
Nonverbal
Adapt

Although the presentational speaking chapters in this book offer numerous guidelines for extemporaneous speaking, consider these four when you reach the rehearsal and delivery stages:

- Use a full-content preparation outline when you begin to rehearse your extemporaneous presentation. Be aware of your growing confidence in delivering it, and continue to decrease your reliance on your notes.
- Prepare an abbreviated delivery outline and speaking notes. Continue to rehearse, using this new outline.
- Even as you become increasingly familiar with your message, do not try to memorize it word for word. Continue to vary the ways in which you express your ideas and information.

- As you deliver your presentation, adapt it to your audience. Use gestures and movement that arise naturally from what you are saying.

RECAP

Methods of Delivery

Manuscript	Reading a presentation from a written text
Memorized	Giving a presentation word for word from memory without using notes
Impromptu	Delivering a presentation without advance preparation
Extemporaneous	Speaking from a written or memorized outline without having memorized the exact wording of the presentation

QUICK REVIEW

Effective Verbal Delivery

While you will not write out most presentations word for word, you will want to think about and rehearse words, phrases, and sentences that accurately and effectively communicate your ideas. At the same time, you will want to give your message a distinctive and memorable style. Let's examine some guidelines for effectively using and understanding words and word structures in a presentation.

EXPLORE

Verbal

Using Words Well

The most effective words are specific and concrete, unbiased, vivid, simple, and correct. Building on our discussion in Chapter 1.3 of the power of verbal messages, we'll examine each of these characteristics in turn.

Specific, Concrete Words   **A specific word refers to an individual member of a general class**—for example, *ammonite* as opposed to the more general term *fossil,* or *sodium* as opposed to *chemical.* Specific words are often **concrete words, appealing to one of the five senses and clearly communicating an image.** For example, which of the following pairs of words creates a more specific mental picture: *dog* or *poodle, utensil* or *spatula, toy* or *Lego?* In each case, the second word is more specific and concrete than the first and better communicates the image the speaker intends. For maximum clarity in your communication, use more specific, concrete words than general, abstract ones in your presentations.

Unbiased Words   **Unbiased words are those that do not offend, either intentionally or unintentionally, any sexual, racial, cultural, or religious group—or any audience member who may belong to one of these groups.** Although a speaker can fairly easily avoid overtly offensive language, it is more difficult to avoid language that more subtly stereotypes or discriminates. As we noted in Chapter 1.3, the once-acceptable usage of a masculine noun (*man, mankind*) to refer generically to all people may now be offensive to many audience members. Other words that reflect gender bias include *chairman, waiter,* and *congressman.* Even if you yourself do not consider these terms offensive, a member of your audience might. When possible, you should adapt to your audience by choosing instead such unbiased gender-neutral alternatives as *chairperson* or *chair, server,* and *member of Congress.*

Vivid Words   **Vivid words add color and interest to your language.** Like concrete words, they help you communicate mental images more accurately and interestingly. Most speakers who try to make their language more vivid think first of adding adjectives to nouns—for example, *distressed oak table* instead of *table,* or *scruffy tabby cat* instead of *cat.* And certainly the first phrase of each example is more vivid. However, speakers less frequently consider the potential power of substituting vivid verbs for "blah" verbs—for example, *sprout* instead of *grow,* or *devour* instead of *eat.* When searching for a vivid word, you might want to consult **a thesaurus, or collection of synonyms.** But do not feel that the most obscure or unusual synonym you find will necessarily be the most vivid. Sometimes a simple word can evoke a vivid image for your audience.

Simple Words   **Simple words** are generally an asset to a speaker. **They will be immediately understandable to an audience.** In his essay "Politics and the English Language," George Orwell includes this prescription for simplicity:

> Never use a long word where a short one will do. If it is possible to cut a word out, always cut it out. Never use a foreign phrase, a scientific word, or a jargon word if you can think of an everyday English equivalent.[9]

Selected thoughtfully, simple words can communicate with both accuracy and power.

Aware

Correct Words   Finally, and perhaps most obviously, you should use correct words when you speak. **A correct word means what the speaker intends and is grammatically correct in the phrase or sentence in which it appears.** Grammatical and usage errors communicate a lack of preparation and can lower your credibility with your audience. Be aware of any errors you make habitually. If you are uncertain of how to use a word, look it up in a dictionary or ask someone who knows. If you are stumped by whether to say "Neither the people nor the president *knows* how to solve the problem" or "Neither the people nor the president *know* how to solve the problem," seek assistance from a good English handbook. (By the way, the first sentence is correct!)

RECAP

Using Words Well

Use specific, concrete words to communicate clearly and specifically.

Use unbiased words to avoid offending any sexual, racial, cultural, or religious group.

Use vivid words to add color and interest to your language.

Use simple words to be understood readily.

Use correct words to enhance your credibility.

Crafting Memorable Word Structures

Verbal

We have discussed the importance of using words that are concrete, unbiased, vivid, simple, and correct. Now we will turn our attention to word structures— phrases and sentences that create the figurative language, drama, and cadences needed to make a presentation memorable.

Figurative Language   One way to make your presentation memorable is to use **figurative language, or figures of speech**, including **metaphors (implied comparisons)**, **similes (overt comparisons using *like* or *as*)**, and **personification (the attribution of human qualities to nonhuman things or ideas). Such language is memorable because it is used in a way that is a little different from ordinary, expected usage.** Nineteenth-century Missouri Senator George Graham Vest used all three types of figurative language to good advantage in his short but memorable "Tribute to the Dog" (delivered in Warrensburg, Missouri, in 1870, and nominated by columnist William Safire as one of the greatest speeches of the Second Millennium).[10] Vest makes the abstract concept of malice more concrete with the metaphor "the stone of malice." He uses a simile to compare the dog's master to a prince: "He guards the sleep of his pauper master as if he were a prince." And he personifies death, which "takes [the dog's] master in its embrace." Vest's speech is memorable at least in part because of the figurative language he employs.

Drama   Another way in which you can make your word structures more memorable is to use language to create **drama** in your presentation by **phrasing something in an unexpected way**. Three specific devices that can help you achieve verbal drama are omission, inversion, and suspension.

When you strip a phrase or sentence of nonessential words that the audience expects or with which they are so familiar that they will mentally fill them in, you are using omission. A captain of a World War II Navy destroyer used omission to inform headquarters of his successful efforts at finding and sinking an enemy submarine. He cabled back to headquarters:

> Sighted sub—sank same.

Inversion—reversing the normal order of words in a phrase or sentence—can also create drama in a presentation. John F. Kennedy inverted the usual subject–verb–object sentence pattern to object–subject–verb to make this brief declaration memorable:

> This much we pledge. . . . [11]

A third way to create drama through sentence structures is to employ verbal **suspension, saving a key word or phrase for the end of a sentence, rather than placing it at the beginning.** Speaking to the Democratic National Convention in July 2004, former U.S. President Jimmy Carter used suspension to dramatize the importance of America's global role:

> At stake is nothing less than our nation's soul.[12]

Advertisers use this technique frequently. Instead of saying "Coke goes better with everything," one copywriter some years ago decided to make the slogan more memorable by suspending the product name until the end of the sentence. He wrote,

> Things go better with Coke.

Old Drum, the dog made famous by George Graham Vest's use of figurative language.

Cadence   A final way to create memorable word structures is to create **cadence, or language rhythm.** A speaker does this not by speaking in a singsong pattern, but by using such stylistic devices as parallelism, antithesis, repetition, and alliteration.

Parallelism occurs when two or more clauses or sentences have the same grammatical pattern. After the bitterly contested U.S. presidential election of 2000, George W. Bush used simple parallel structures to emphasize the importance of finding common ground and building consensus:

> Our future demands it, and our history proves it.[13]

Maya Angelou mesmerizes her audiences with her extraordinary skill in the effective use of language.

Antithesis is similar to parallelism, except that the two structures contrast in meaning. Nobel Laureate Elie Wiesel used antithesis in his 1999 Millennium Lecture on "The Perils of Indifference":

> Indifference . . . is not only a sin, it is a punishment.[14]

Repetition of a key word or phrase can add emphasis to an important idea and memorability to your message. Note the repetition of the key phrase "It is a violation of human rights" in this excerpt from a speech by Hillary Rodham Clinton:

> It is a violation of human rights when babies are denied food, or drowned, or suffocated, or their spines broken, simply because they are born girls.
> It is a violation of human rights when women and girls are sold into the slavery of prostitution.
> It is a violation of human rights when women are doused with gasoline, set on fire, and burned to death because their marriage dowries are deemed too small.[15]

A final strategy for creating cadence is to use **alliteration, the repetition of an initial consonant sound several times in a phrase, clause, or sentence.** Kicking off the "space race" in 1962, John F. Kennedy coined this alliterative phrase:

> hour of change and challenge[16]

The repetition of the *ch* sound added cadence—and memorability—to the passage.

RECAP

Crafting Memorable Word Structures

To make your message memorable, use . . .

Figurative Language

Metaphor	Making an implied comparison
Simile	Making a comparison using *like* or *as*
Personification	Attributing human qualities to nonhuman things or ideas

Drama

Omission	Leaving nonessential words out of a phrase or sentence
Inversion	Reversing the normal order of words in a phrase or sentence
Suspension	Withholding the key words in a phrase or sentence until the end

Cadence

Parallelism	Using two or more clauses or sentences with the same grammatical structure
Antithesis	Using a two-part parallel structure in which the second part contrasts in meaning with the first
Repetition	Using a key word or phrase more than once
Alliteration	Repeating a consonant sound

Effective Nonverbal Delivery

At this point, you know how important it is to deliver your presentation effectively and what delivery style most audiences today prefer. You are familiar with the four methods of delivery and know how to maximize the use of each one. And you have some ideas about how to use effective and memorable language. But you may still be wondering, "What do I do with my hands?" "Is it all right to move around while I speak?" "How can I make my voice sound interesting?" To help answer these and other similar questions, and to help you use nonverbal messages more effectively, we will examine five major categories of

By walking up close to her audience, this speaker establishes a connection with her listeners.

nonverbal delivery: eye contact, physical delivery, facial expression, vocal delivery, and personal appearance. This discussion further develops the fundamental principle of using and interpreting nonverbal messages that we introduced in Chapter 1.4.

Eye Contact

Of all the nonverbal delivery variables discussed in this chapter, the most important one in a presentational speaking situation for North Americans is **eye contact. Looking at your audience during your presentation** lets them know that you are interested in them and ready to talk to them. It also permits you to determine whether they are responding to you. And most listeners will think that you are more capable and trustworthy if you look them in the eye. Several studies document a relationship between eye contact and speaker credibility, as well as between eye contact and listener learning.[17]

How much eye contact do you need to sustain? One study found that speakers with less than 50% eye contact are considered unfriendly, uninformed, inexperienced, and even dishonest by their listeners.[18] Is there such a thing as too much eye contact? Probably not, for North American audiences. Be aware, though, that not all people from all cultures prefer as much eye contact as North Americans do. Asians, for example, generally prefer less.

The following suggestions can help you use eye contact effectively when you speak in public:

Adapt

Nonverbal

- Establish eye contact with your audience before you say anything. Eye contact sends the message, "I am interested in you. I have something I want to say to you. Tune me in."

- Maintain eye contact with your audience as you deliver your opening sentence without looking at your notes.
- Try to establish eye contact with people throughout your audience, not just with the front row or only one or two people. Briefly look into the eyes of an individual, then transfer your eye contact to someone else. Do not look over your listeners' heads! They will notice if you do so and may even turn around to try to find out what you are looking at.

Physical Delivery

Gestures, movement, and posture are the three key elements of physical delivery. A good speaker knows how to use effective gestures, make meaningful movements, and maintain appropriate posture while speaking to an audience.

"Hang him, you idiots! Hang him! ... 'String him up' is a figure of speech!"

Gestures   **The hand and arm movements you use while speaking are called gestures.** Nearly all people from all cultures use some gestures when they speak. In fact, research suggests that gesturing is instinctive and that it is intrinsic to speaking and thinking.[19] Yet even if you gesture easily and appropriately in the course of everyday conversation, you may feel awkward about what to do with your hands when you are in front of an audience. To minimize this challenge, consider the following guidelines:

EXPLORE

- Focus on the message you want to communicate. As in ordinary conversation, when you speak in public, your hands should help to emphasize or reinforce your verbal message. Your gestures should coincide with what you are saying.
- Again, as in conversation, let your gestures flow with your message. They should appear natural, not tense or rigid.
- Be definite. If you want to gesture, go ahead and gesture. Avoid minor hand movements that will be masked by the lectern or that may appear to your audience as accidental brief jerks.
- Vary your gestures. Try not to use the same hand or one all-purpose gesture all the time. Think of the different gestures you can use, depending on whether you want to enumerate, point, describe, or emphasize ideas.
- Don't overdo your gestures. You want your audience to focus not on your gestures, but on your message.
- Make your gestures appropriate to your audience and situation. When you are speaking to a large audience in a relatively formal setting, use bolder,

Nonverbal

Adapt

more sweeping, and more dramatic gestures than when you are speaking to a small audience in an informal setting. Consider, too, the culture-based expectations of your audience. Americans in general tend to use more gestures than do speakers from other cultures. If you are speaking to a culturally diverse audience, you might want to tone down your gestures.

Nonverbal

Movement   Another element of physical delivery is **movement, or a change of location during a presentation.** You may have wondered, "Should I walk around during my presentation, or should I stay in one place?" "Should I stay behind the lectern, or could I stand beside or in front of it?" "Can I move around among the audience?" The following criteria may help you to determine the answers to these questions:

- Like gestures, any movement should be purposeful. It should be consistent with the verbal content of your message; otherwise it will appear to be aimless wandering. You might signal the beginning of a new idea or major point in your speech with movement. Or you might move to signal a transition from a serious idea to a more humorous one. The bottom line is that your use of movement should make sense to your listeners. No movement at all is better than random, distracting movement.
- If such physical barriers as a lectern, a row of chairs, or an overhead projector make you feel cut off from your audience, move closer to them. Studies suggest that physical proximity enhances learning.[20]
- Adapt to the cultural expectations of your audience. British listeners, for example, have commented to your authors that American lecturers tend to stand too close to an audience when speaking. If you think that movement will make your audience uncomfortable, stay in one carefully chosen spot to deliver your presentation.

Adapt

Nonverbal

Posture   **Posture (your stance)** is the third element of physical delivery you should consider when delivering a presentation. One study suggests that your posture may reflect on your credibility as a speaker.[21] Another study suggests that "fear contagion," the spread of fear throughout a crowd, is largely a response to posture cues.[22] Certainly, slouching lazily across a lectern does not communicate enthusiasm for or interest in your audience or your topic. On the other hand, you should adapt your posture to your topic, your audience, and the formality or informality of the speaking occasion. For example, it may be perfectly appropriate, as well as comfortable and natural, to sit on the edge of a desk during a very informal presentation. In spite of the fact that few speech teachers or texts attempt to advocate specific speaking postures, speakers should observe some basic commonsense guidelines about their posture:

Adapt

- Avoid slouching, shifting from one foot to the other, or drooping your head.
- Unless you are disabled, do not sit while delivering a presentation. The exception might be perching on the edge of a desk or stool (which would still elevate you slightly above your audience) during a very informal presentation.

Diversity and Communication

The Academic Quarter

When speaking at a Polish university a few years ago, one of your authors expected to begin promptly at 11:00 AM, as announced in the program and on posters. By 11:10 it was clear that the speech would not begin on time, and your author began to despair of having any audience at all.

In Poland, it turns out, both students and professors expect to adhere to the "academic quarter." This means that most lectures begin at least 15 minutes, or a quarter of an hour, after the announced starting time.

If your author had asked a Polish professor about the audience's expectations, he would have known about this custom in advance. One way to avoid such misunderstandings is to talk with people you know who are familiar with the cultural expectations. Try to observe other speakers presenting to similar audiences. And ask specific questions, including the following:

1. Where does the audience expect me to stand while speaking?
2. Do listeners expect direct eye contact?
3. When will the audience expect me to start and stop my talk?
4. Will listeners find movement and gestures distracting or welcome?
5. Do listeners expect presentation aids?

Keep cultural differences in mind as you rehearse and deliver presentations to diverse audiences.

Like your gestures and movement, your posture should not call attention to itself. It should reflect your interest in and attention to your audience and your presentation.

Facial Expression

Your facial expression plays a key role in expressing your thoughts, emotions, and attitudes.[23] Your audience sees your face before they hear what you are going to say, giving you the opportunity to set the tone for your message even before you begin speaking.

Social psychologist Paul Ekman has found that facial expressions of primary emotions are virtually universal, so even a culturally diverse audience will be able to read your facial expressions clearly.[24]

Throughout your presentation, your facial expression, like your body language and eye contact, should be appropriate to your message. Present somber news wearing a serious expression. Relate a humorous story with a smile. To communicate interest in your listeners, keep your expression alert and friendly. Consultants criticized both George W. Bush and John Kerry for their inappropriate facial expressions during the 2004 U.S. presidential debates, noting specifically that Bush needed to control his grimaces and smirks and Kerry needed to develop a more natural, authentic smile.[25]

On the Web

There are several sites on the Web where you can both see and hear famous speeches from the past and today.

C-SPAN Online: www.c-span.org/watch
History Channel Archive of Speeches:
www.historychannel.com/speeches/index.html
U.S. Presidential Inaugural Speeches:
www.bartleby.com/inaugural
Michigan State University Vincent Voice Library:
vvl.lib.msu.edu/index.cfm

Can you guess by his facial expression what message Bill Clinton may have been communicating to the graduating class?

Nonverbal

Adapt

To help ensure that you are maximizing your use of this important nonverbal delivery cue, rehearse your presentation in front of a mirror; or better yet, videotape yourself rehearsing your presentation. Consider as objectively as possible whether your face is reflecting the emotional tone of your ideas.

Vocal Delivery

We have already discussed the importance of selecting words and word phrases that will most effectively communicate your ideas, information, and images. We referred to this element of delivery as verbal delivery. **Vocal delivery,** on the other hand, **involves nonverbal vocal cues—not the words you say, but the way you say them.** Effective vocal delivery requires that you speak so that your audience can understand you and will remain interested in what you are saying. Nonverbal vocal elements include volume, pitch, rate, and articulation.

Volume   Volume is the softness or loudness of your voice. It is the most fundamental determinant of audience understanding. If you do not speak loudly enough, even the most brilliant presentation will be ineffective, because the audience simply will not hear you. In addition, volume can signal important ideas in your presentation; you can deliver a key idea either more loudly or more softly than the level at which you have been speaking. Consider these guidelines to help you appropriately adapt the volume of your voice to your audience's needs:

- Speak loudly enough that the members of your audience farthest from you can hear you without straining. This will ensure that everyone else in the room can hear you, too.
- Vary the volume of your voice in a purposeful way. Indicate important ideas by turning your volume up or down.
- Be aware of whether you need a microphone to amplify your volume. If you do and one is available, use it.

There are three kinds of microphones, only one of which demands much technique. The *lavaliere microphone* is the clip-on type often used by news reporters and interviewees. Worn on the front of a shirt or a jacket lapel, it requires no particular care other than not thumping it or accidentally knocking it off.

The *boom microphone* is used by makers of movies and TV shows. It hangs over the heads of the speakers and is remote controlled, so the speakers need not be particularly concerned with it.

Developing Your Presentation

Rehearse Your Presentation

Ben begins to rehearse his presentation. From the beginning, he stands and speaks aloud, practicing gestures and movement that seem appropriate to his message.

At first, Ben uses his preparation outline (pp. 62–65). These early rehearsals go pretty well, but the speech runs a little long. Ben needs to edit it.

He wonders whether he can cut any of his plentiful supporting material. Examining his preparation outline again, he notes that he has two statistics to support the widespread abuse of Coricidin, one from the American Association of Poison Control Centers and another from the Scripps Howard News Service. The statistic from the American Association of Poison Control Centers seems more credible. He decides to cut the other statistic before he prepares his speaking notes and continues with his rehearsals.

The third kind of microphone, and the most common, is the *stationary microphone.* This is the type that is most often attached to a lectern, sitting on a desk, or standing on the floor. Generally, the stationary microphones used today are multidirectional. You do not have to remain frozen behind a stationary mike while speaking. However, you will have to keep your mouth about the same distance from the mike at all times to avoid distracting fluctuations in the volume of sound. You can turn your head from side to side and use gestures, but you will have to limit other movements.

Under ideal circumstances, you will be able to practice before you speak with the type of microphone you will use. If you have the chance, figure out where to stand for the best sound quality and how sensitive the mike is to extraneous noise. Practice will accustom you to any voice distortion or echo that might occur so that these sound qualities do not surprise you during your presentation.[26]

Pitch   While volume is the loudness or softness of your voice, **pitch refers to how high or low your voice is.** To some extent, pitch is determined by physiology. The faster the folds in your vocal cords vibrate, the higher the habitual pitch of your voice. In general, female vocal folds vibrate much faster than do those of males. However, you can raise or lower your habitual pitch within a certain range. **Variation in pitch, called inflection,** is a key factor in communicating the meaning of your words. You know that a startled "Oh!" in response to something someone has told you communicates something quite different than a lower-pitched, questioning "Oh?" Your vocal inflection indicates your emotional response to what you have heard. Vocal inflection also helps to keep an audience interested in your presentation. If your pitch is a monotone, the audience will probably become bored quickly. To help you monitor and practice your pitch and inflection as you prepare to speak, record and play back your presentation at least once as you rehearse. Listen carefully to your pitch and inflection. If you think you are speaking in too much of a monotone, practice the presentation again with exaggerated variations in pitch.

Rate   Another vocal variable is **rate, or speed**. How fast do you talk? Most speakers average between 120 and 180 words per minute but vary their rate to add interest to their delivery and to emphasize key ideas. To determine whether your speaking rate is appropriate and purposeful, become consciously aware of your speaking rate. Record your presentation during rehearsal and listen critically to your speech speed. If it seems too fast, make a conscious effort to slow down. Use more **pauses (a few seconds of silence during a presentation)** after questions and before important ideas. If you are speaking too slowly, make a conscious effort to speed up.

Articulation   **Articulation is the enunciation of speech sounds.** As a speaker, you want to articulate distinctly to ensure that your audience can determine what words you are using. Sometimes we fall into the habits of mumbling or slurring—saying *wanna* instead of *want to,* or *chesterdrawers* instead of *chest of drawers.* Some nonstandard articulation may be part of a speaker's **dialect, a speech style common to an ethnic group or a geographic region.** One dialect with which most of us are probably familiar is the dialect of the southern United States, characterized by a distinctive drawl. Although most native speakers of English can understand English dialects, studies have shown that North American listeners assign more favorable ratings to, and can recall more information presented by, speakers with dialects similar to their own.[27] If your dialect is significantly different from that of your

Technology *and* Communication

Rehearsing on Videotape

There is no feedback more total or more objective than feedback provided by videotape. First, it reproduces your total image, both visual and aural; and second, it lets you see for yourself. If friends or colleagues tell you that you are a good speaker, you may not respect their judgment, you may think they're being nice rather than honest, or you may think they're biased in your favor. Bruce, a pharmaceutical salesman, simply couldn't believe it when people told him he was a good speaker because an unpleasant high school speaking experience had convinced him he would never be able to speak well. Seeing himself on videotape was a revelation: He saw for himself how good he was. Another person could never have convinced him of it.

By the same token, if someone tells you your voice is too high, that you slouch, or that you need to loosen up your body, you may not be convinced. A videotape has the inherent reassurance of a machine: It has no ulterior motive, and it lets you see what others see.

People are constantly amazed when they see themselves on videotape—it's as if they were seeing and hearing themselves for the first time. They really see the extra 20 pounds they've been lugging for 10 years; they see the stiff way they stand; they hear the lack of energy in their voices, the *um*'s, the *you see*'s, the *you know*'s, the *like*'s.

Becoming aware of the kind of image you project is the first step toward controlling it or altering it.[28]

listeners or if you suspect that it could be potentially distracting, you may want to work to improve or standardize your articulation. To do so, be aware of key words or phrases that you have a tendency to drawl, slur, or chop. Once you have identified them, practice saying them distinctly and correctly.

Appearance

What would you wear to deliver a presentation to your class? To address your city council? The fact that you probably would wear something different for these two occasions suggests that you are already aware of the importance of a speaker's **appearance, both dress and grooming.** There is considerable evidence that your personal appearance affects how your audience will respond to you and your message. If you violate your audience's expectations, you will be less successful in achieving your purpose. The following guidelines might help make your wardrobe selection a bit easier the next time you are called on to speak:

Aware

- Never wear anything that would be potentially distracting—for example, a T-shirt with writing on it. You want your audience to listen to you, not read you.

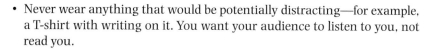

RECAP

Characteristics of Effective Nonverbal Delivery

- *Gestures* should be relaxed, definite, varied, and appropriate to your audience and the speaking situation.
- *Movement* should be purposeful.
- *Posture* should feel natural and be appropriate to your topic, your audience, and the occasion.
- *Eye contact* should be established before you say anything and sustained as much as possible throughout your presentation.
- *Facial expression* should be alert, friendly, and appropriate to your message.
- *Volume* should be loud enough that you can be easily heard and should be purposefully varied.
- *Pitch* should be varied so that the inflection in your voice helps to sustain your audience's interest.
- *Rate* should be neither too fast nor too slow and can be varied to add interest and emphasize key ideas.
- *Articulation* should be clear and distinct.
- *Appearance* should conform to what the audience expects.

QUICK REVIEW

Nonverbal

Adapt

- Consider wearing appropriate clothing as a presentation aid. For example, if you are a nurse or emergency technician, wear your uniform when you speak about your profession. (We will discuss presentation aids in more detail shortly.)
- Take cues from your audience. If you know that they will be dressed in business attire, dress similarly. If anything, you want to be a bit more dressed up than members of your audience.
- When in doubt about what to wear, select something conservative.

Effective Presentation Aids

We have already discussed two elements of delivery: verbal delivery and non-verbal delivery. A third element used with increasing frequency in this era of sophisticated computer presentation software is the presentation aid. The term **presentation aid refers to anything your audience can listen to or look at to help them understand your ideas.** Charts, photographs, posters, drawings, graphs, videos, and CDs are some of the types of presentation aids frequently used by speakers.

Presentation aids can be invaluable to a speaker. They help you gain and maintain your audience's attention.[29] They communicate your organization of ideas. They illustrate sequences of events or procedures. And they help your audience understand and remember your message. In addition, chances are that, for at least one of the assignments in your communication class, you will be required to use a presentation aid. Because presentation aids are valuable supplements to your speeches and because students of communication are so often required to use them, let's discuss first the types of presentation aids that are available to you, including computer-generated ones. Then we will discuss guidelines for preparing presentation aids, and finally provide some general suggestions for using your presentation aids effectively.

Types of Presentation Aids

If you are required to use a presentation aid for an assignment or if you think a presentation aid might enhance your message, you have a number of options from which to select. You might decide to use an object or a model; a person; such two-dimensional presentation aids as drawings, photographs, maps, charts, or graphs; or a videotape, CD-ROM, DVD, audiotape, or audio CD.

Objects   The first type of presentation aid you ever used—perhaps as long ago as preschool "show and tell"—was probably an object. You took to school your favorite teddy bear or the new remote-control car you got for your birthday. Remember how the kids crowded around to see what you had brought? Objects add interest to a talk because they are real. Whether the members of your audience are in preschool or college, they like tangible, real things. If you use an object as a presentation aid, consider these guidelines:

- Make certain the object can be handled easily. If it is too large, it may be unwieldy; if it is too small, your audience won't be able to see it.
- Don't use dangerous or illegal objects as presentation aids. They may make your audience members uneasy or actually put them at risk.

Models   If it is impossible to bring an object to class, you may be able to substitute a model. You cannot bring a 1965 Ford Thunderbird into a classroom, but you may be able to construct and bring a model. You could probably not acquire a dog's heart to bring to class, but you might be able to find a model to use for your explanation of how heartworms damage that vital organ. If you use a model as a presentation aid, be sure that the model is large enough to be seen by all members of your audience.

People   You might not think of people as potential presentation aids, but they can be. President George W. Bush has used ordinary people as visual aids for some of his most important speeches, "asking them to stand and then telling stories of their sacrifices or heroism . . . a way of coming down from the stage, as it were, and mingling with the crowd."[30] In other instances, people can model costumes, play a sport with you, or demonstrate a dance. Consider the following guidelines if you are going to ask someone to assist you by acting as a presentation aid for a speech:

- Rehearse with the person who will be helping you.
- Don't have the person stand beside you doing nothing. Wait until you need your presentation aid to have him or her come to the front.
- Don't let your presentation aid steal the show. Make his or her role specific and fairly brief. As the speaker, you should remain the "person of the hour."

Drawings   You can use simple drawings to help illustrate or explain ideas that you are talking about. For example, you could sketch the tunnels of a fire ant mound to show your audience why it is so difficult to eradicate an entire colony. You could sketch the plants and animals crucial to the life cycle of the Florida Everglades. If you use a drawing as a visual aid, consider these suggestions:

- Keep your drawings large and simple. Line drawings are often more effective than more detailed ones.
- Consider drawing or photocopying your drawing onto a sheet of overhead transparency film and using an overhead projector to show the drawing to your audience.
- Your drawing does not have to be original artwork. If you need help, you could ask a friend to help you prepare a drawing or you could utilize computer software to generate a simple image. Just be sure to credit your source if you use someone else's sketch.

Photographs   If you are giving a speech on urban forestry, you might want to show your audience good color pictures of trees appropriate for urban sites in your area. In this case, photographs would show color and detail that would be nearly impossible to achieve with drawings. The biggest challenge to using photographs as presentation aids is size; most photos are simply too small to be seen clearly from a distance. If you want to use a photograph, you will usually have to enlarge it. Consider the following options for making photographs into viable presentation aids:

- Many copy centers or photo shops can produce poster-size color photocopies.
- Transfer your photograph to a slide and project it onto a screen.
- Store digital photos on a computer disk. Then, when you want the photos, you can bring them up on your computer screen and use a video projection system to enlarge them for your audience.

Maps   Like photographs, most maps are too small to be useful as presentation aids; you must enlarge them in some way. Consider these suggestions for using maps effectively in a presentation:

- Enlarge your map by photocopying it or by transferring it to a slide. An outline map with few details can be copied or drawn on overhead transparency film.
- Highlight on your map the areas or routes you are going to talk about in your presentation.

Charts   Charts can summarize and organize a great deal of information in a small space. Consider using a chart any time you need to present information that could be organized under several headings or in several columns. The chart in Figure 4.3.1 displays 2000 United States census statistics on popula-

FIGURE 4.3.1
Chart

Population of the United States, by Age (Source: 2000 Census)	
Age	**Number**
0 to 9 years	40,000,000
10 to 19 years	41,000,000
20 to 34 years	59,000,000
35 to 54 years	83,000,000
55 to 64 years	24,000,000
over 64 years	35,000,000

tion age groups.[31] You can prepare charts quite easily by using the Table feature in your word-processing program. Keep in mind these guidelines:

- Whether you use a large flip chart, transfer your chart to an overhead transparency, or use a computer presentation program, be certain your chart is big enough to be seen easily.
- Keep your chart simple. Do not try to put too much information on one chart. Eliminate any unnecessary words.
- Print or type any lettering on a chart, instead of writing in script.

Graphs Graphs are effective ways to present statistical relationships to your audience. They help to make data more concrete. You are probably already familiar with the three main types of graphs. **A bar graph consists of bars of various lengths representing percentages or numbers.** It is useful for making comparisons. **A round pie graph shows how data are divided proportionately.** And **a line graph can show both trends over a period of time and relationships among variables.** Figure 4.3.2 illustrates all three types of graphs, displaying the statistics from the chart in Figure 4.3.1. All three graphs were generated by Microsoft Excel. The following guidelines will help you use graphs more effectively in your presentations:

- Make your graphs big, by drawing them on a large piece of paper, by drawing or copying them on an overhead transparency, or by putting them on a computer disk for projection.
- Keep your graphs simple and uncluttered.
- Remember that many computer programs will generate graphs from statistics. You don't usually need to draw your own.

Videotapes A VCR will allow you to show scenes from a movie, an excerpt from a training film, or a brief original video to an audience. Modern VCRs have good picture and sound quality and permit freeze-frame viewing. They also allow you to rewind and replay a scene several times if you want your audience to watch different specific elements of the film. If you plan to use a videotape in a presentation, consider these suggestions:

- If you have an audience of 25 to 30 people, you can use a 25-inch television screen. For larger audiences, you will need a large-screen projection TV or several monitors.
- Use only brief clips and excerpts. Video should always supplement, rather than take over for, your speech.

CD-ROMs and DVDs CD-ROMs and DVDs allow a speaker to retrieve audio and visual information easily and quickly. One CD-ROM can contain hundreds of words, pictures, or sounds. If you were talking about President Franklin Roosevelt's New Deal, you could click your mouse to let your audience hear Roosevelt speak. If you wanted to show various images of Monet's garden, you could retrieve and project those pictures with ease. Both CD-ROMs and DVDs

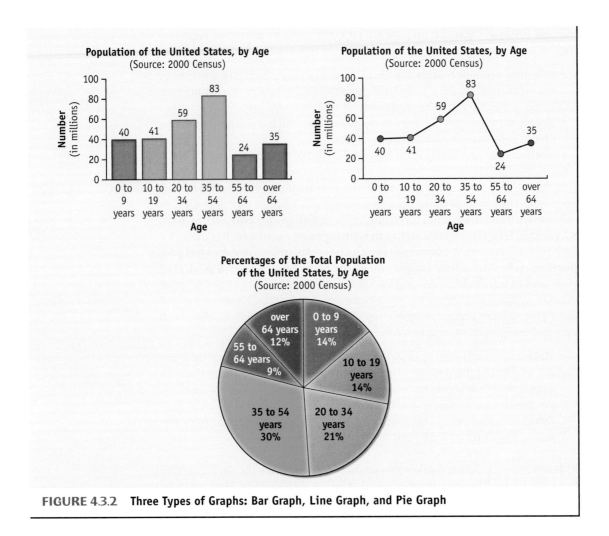

FIGURE 4.3.2   Three Types of Graphs: Bar Graph, Line Graph, and Pie Graph

can be used in combination with a large-screen video projector or a liquid crystal display (LCD) panel connected to an overhead projector. If you plan to use a CD-ROM or DVD, remember these guidelines:

- Be certain that the equipment you will need will be available in the room in which you are going to speak.
- Have the equipment set up and ready to go before you speak.

Audiotapes and Audio CDs   If you want to supplement your speech with audio presentation aids—say, music or excerpts from speeches or interviews— you might want to use cassette audiotapes or audio CDs. Both are readily available, and their sound can be amplified to fill various size rooms. The advantage of a cassette tape is that you can tape and play back original material, such as an interview you did with the dean of students. A CD has better fidelity and can be more easily cued to begin in a specific place. If you use one of these audio presentation aids, consider these suggestions:

- Be certain that your tape or CD is amplified so that your audience can hear it without straining.
- Use audio presentation aids sparingly. You do not want them to engage the audience's attention to the point that they interfere with the speech.

Computer-Generated Presentation Aids

Not too many years ago, if you wanted to use a drawing or graph as a visual aid, you had to draw it by hand on a blackboard, flip chart, or overhead transparency. If you wanted to use a photograph or map, you had to have it professionally enlarged. While speakers still use overheads, blackboards, flip charts, and posters, today they also have another option: computer graphics programs. These programs, available for both Windows and Macintosh operating systems, can both create and present professional-looking visual aids inexpensively and easily.

Using a graphics program such as Microsoft's popular PowerPoint™, you can develop a list of your main points that audience members can refer to as you speak, as illustrated in Figure 4.3.3. You can create graphs and charts. You can use clip art, or you can scan in photographs, maps, or drawings. You can even incorporate video and audio clips. If computer-projection equipment is available in the room in which you will speak, you can display your presen-

Paul Laurence Dunbar
1872–1906

- Known as the "poet laureate of his people"
- Wrote popular poetry in African–American dialect
- Wrote significant poetry in standard English: "We Wear the Mask"

FIGURE 4.3.3
PowerPoint Slide
Source: Photo of Paul Laurence Dunbar from the Ohio Historical Society, Dunbar House Web page. 14 January 2002 (9 July 2002): www.ohiohistory.org/places/dunbar

tation by connecting a computer to a special large-screen projector or an LCD panel that fits on top of an overhead projector. You can then run your program with a keyboard or mouse, or even set it to run automatically. If you do not have access to such equipment, you can transfer the images you have created to slides, overhead transparencies, or paper.

Among the advantages of learning to use computer graphics programs such as PowerPoint for classroom presentations is that they are an important way to adapt your message to audiences who increasingly expect sophisticated technical support. You will undoubtedly encounter and be expected to use these programs again in the business world. Gaining experience with them now can give you an edge in seeking employment and in making your earliest business presentation more effective.

However, such programs also have inherent risks. As one consultant points out,

> When you darken the room and give the audience a preprogrammed, oh-so-beautiful, PowerPoint presentation, the audience will say, "I'm not part of this experience. That guy up there has done it all." The result: Your colleagues will mentally go on vacation. . . .[32]

The solution? As with other presentation aids we have discussed, don't let your PowerPoint slides become your presentation—use them to supplement it. Don't use too many slides. Make certain that the ones you do use contain significant information in a simple, uncluttered style. Don't overuse bulleted text. Instead, take advantage of the ease with which you can create and show such visual elements as graphs, charts, and photos on PowerPoint slides. Finally, practice with your PowerPoint slides so that you can time them to coincide with your oral presentation.

Guidelines for Preparing Presentation Aids

In addition to the specific guidelines for preparing and using various specific types of presentation aids that we have just discussed, four general guidelines can help you prepare all types of presentation aids more effectively.

Adapt

Select the Right Presentation Aids   As is evident from the above discussion, you have a number of options for presentation aids. If you are trying to decide which to use, consider these suggestions:

1. Adapt to your audience. Let their interests, experiences, and knowledge guide your selection of presentation aids. For example, an audience of accountants would readily understand arbitrage charts that might be incomprehensible to a more general audience. If you will be speaking to a large audience, be certain that everyone will be able to see or hear your presentation aid.
2. Be constantly aware of your specific purpose. Be certain that your presentation aid contributes to its achievement.

3. Consider your own skill and experience. Use equipment with which you have had experience, or allow yourself ample time to practice. It may be better to make an overhead transparency of your PowerPoint image if the alternative is to fumble with an unfamiliar computer and LCD projector.

4. Take into account the room in which you will speak. If it has large windows and no shades, for example, do not plan to use a visual presentation aid that will require a darkened room. If you plan to run a PowerPoint presentation, be sure that both hardware and software are available and in good working order.

Make Your Presentation Aids Easy to See   You have probably experienced the frustration of squinting and straining to read a speaker's too-small presentation aid. If you are going to remember only one thing about using a presentation aid, remember this: Make it big!

Keep Your Presentation Aids Simple   Don't cram too much information on any single presentation aid. Limit text to key words or phrases. Leave plenty of white space.

Steve Jobs, chief executive officer of Apple Computer, uses a large-screen projector to make sure his audience can see his PowerPoint presentation and the product he used to create it.

Polish Your Presentation Aids   Especially in this day of readily available, professional-looking computer graphics, audiences have high expectations for the appearance of presentation aids. A sloppy, hand-drawn visual will detract from even the best verbal message. Prepare your presentation aids well in advance of your speaking date and make them as attractive and professional as possible. Even if you can't run a PowerPoint presentation in the room in which you are speaking, consider using such a program to produce your presentation aids.

Ethics *and* Communication

Profanity in an Audio Presentation Aid

Matt wants to talk to his college classmates about the use of profanity in rap music. He plans to play sound clips of several profane lyrics from current hits to illustrate his point. Should Matt play these songs, even though doing so might offend several members of his audience?

Guidelines for Using Presentation Aids

Adapt

Once you have prepared potentially effective presentation aids, you will want to utilize them effectively as well. In addition to the guidelines offered earlier in this chapter for using specific types of presentation aids, the following general suggestions will help you more effectively adapt various types of presentation aids to your audience.

Rehearse with Your Presentation Aids   The day of your speech should not be the first time you deliver your presentation while holding up your chart, turning on your projector, or cueing your CD. Practice setting up and using your presentation aids until you feel at ease with them. Consider during rehearsal what you would do at various stages of the speech if you had to carry on without your presentation aid. Electricity fails, equipment fails to show up, and bulbs burn out. Have contingency plans.

Maintain Eye Contact with Your Audience, Not with Your Presentation Aids   You can glance at your presentation aids during your talk, but do not talk to them. Keep looking at your audience.

Explain Your Presentation Aids   Always talk about and explain your presentation aids. Do not assume that the audience will understand their relevance and how to interpret them.

Time the Display of Your Presentation Aids to Coincide with Your Discussion of Them   Don't put a presentation aid in front of your audience until you are ready to use it. Likewise, remove your presentation aid after you are finished with it. Keeping presentation aids in front of an audience before or after you use them will only serve to distract from your message.

Do Not Pass Objects, Pictures, or Other Small Items among Your Audience   Passing things around distracts audience members. Either people are focused on whatever they are looking at or they are counting the number of people who will handle the object before it reaches them. If the item is too small for everyone to see it when you hold it up, it is not a good presentation aid.

Use Handouts Effectively Handing out papers during your presentation can also distract audience members. If possible, wait to distribute handouts until after you have spoken. If your audience needs to refer to the material while you're talking about it, go ahead and pass out the handouts; then, at various points in your presentation, tell audience members where in the handout they should focus.

Use Small Children and Animals with Caution Small children and even the best-trained animals are unpredictable. In a strange environment, in front of an audience, they may not behave in their usual way. The risk of having a child or animal detract from your presentation may be too great to justify their use as presentation aids.

Use Technology Thoughtfully Computer-generated graphics, LCDs, and DVDs have become increasingly common components of presentations as more and more classrooms and seminar rooms are equipped for them. However, resist the temptation to use them just because they are glitzy. One speechwriter and presentation coach warns against this bleak but all-too-common scenario:

> The presenter says, "And now, I'd like to talk about quality." And lo and behold . . . the word *quality* flashes on a screen. Now, folks, does this slide offer any new information? Does it clarify a complex point? Does it strengthen the bond between presenter and audience? You know the answer: a resounding "no."[33]

Be sure that the technology you use helps you communicate your message. And be sure that you know how to operate the hardware and that you rehearse with it.

Some Final Tips for Rehearsing and Delivering Your Presentation

Throughout this chapter, we have described and offered suggestions for effective verbal and nonverbal delivery and use of presentation aids. In addition to the tips offered throughout the chapter, the following suggestions will help you make the most of your rehearsal time and ultimately deliver your presentation successfully.

- Finish your preparation outline several days before you must deliver the presentation. Begin to rehearse from the preparation outline. Revise the presentation as necessary so that you can deliver it within your given time limits. Prepare your delivery outline and speaking notes. Continue to rehearse and to modify your speaking notes as necessary.
- Practice, practice, practice. Rehearse aloud as often as possible. Only by rehearsing will you gain confidence in both the content of the presentation and your delivery.
- Practice good delivery skills while rehearsing. Rehearse your presentation

Listen and Respond

RECAP

Preparing and Using Presentation Aids

Tips for Preparing and Using Specific Types of Presentation Aids

- Use *objects* that you can handle easily and that are safe and legal.
- Be sure that any *models* you use are large enough to be seen easily.
- Rehearse with *people* who will serve as presentation aids, and don't let them steal the show.
- Keep *drawings* simple and large.
- Be sure *photographs* are large enough to be seen easily.
- Highlight on a *map* the geographic areas you will discuss.
- Limit the amount of information you put on any single *chart*.
- Keep *graphs* simple and uncluttered.
- Use only brief excerpts and clips from *videotapes*.
- Have *CD-ROM, DVD,* or *VCR* equipment set up and ready to go before you speak.
- Amplify any *audiotapes* and *CDs* so that they can be heard easily.

General Tips for Preparing and Using Presentation Aids

Preparing Presentation Aids

- Select the right presentation aid.
- Make your presentation aids easy to see.
- Keep your presentation aids simple.
- Polish your presentation aids.

Using Presentation Aids

- Rehearse with your presentation aids.
- Maintain eye contact with your audience, not with your presentation aids.
- Explain your presentation aids.
- Time the display of your presentation aids to coincide with your discussion of them.
- Do not pass objects, pictures, or other small items among your audience.
- Use handouts effectively.
- Use small children and animals with caution.
- Use technology thoughtfully.

QUICK
REVIEW

Developing Your Presentation
STEP BY STEP

Deliver Your Presentation

The long-awaited day of Ben's presentation has arrived at last. He got a full night's sleep last night and ate a light breakfast before setting out for class.

As he waits to speak, Ben visualizes himself delivering his speech calmly and confidently. When his name is called, he rises, walks to the front of the room, and establishes eye contact with his audience before he begins to speak.

During his speech, Ben focuses on adapting his message to his listeners. He looks at individual members of his audience, uses purposeful and well-timed gestures, and speaks loudly and clearly.

Even before he hears his classmates' applause, Ben knows that his presentation has gone well.

standing up. Pay attention to your gestures, posture, eye contact, facial expression, and vocal delivery, as well as the verbal message. Rehearse with your presentation aids.

- If possible, practice your presentation for someone. Seek and consider feedback from someone about both the content and your delivery.
- Tape record or videotape your presentation. Becoming more aware of your delivery can help you make necessary adjustments.
- Re-create the speaking situation in your final rehearsals. Try to rehearse in a room similar to the one in which you will deliver the presentation. Use the speaking notes you will use the day you deliver the presentation. Give the presentation without stopping. The more realistic the rehearsal, the more confidence you will gain.
- Get plenty of rest the night before you speak. Being well rested is more valuable than frantic, last-minute rehearsal.
- Arrive early. If you don't know for certain where your room is, give yourself plenty of time to find it. Rearrange any furniture or equipment and check and set up your presentation aids.
- Review and apply the suggestions offered in Chapter 4.1 for becoming a more confident speaker. As the moment for delivering your presentation nears, remind yourself of the effort you have spent preparing it. Visualize yourself delivering the presentation effectively. Silently practice your opening lines. Think about your audience. Breathe deeply, and consciously relax.
- After you have delivered your presentation, seek feedback from members of your audience. Use the information you gain to improve your next presentation.

Aware

QUICK
REVIEW

PRINCIPLES FOR A LIFETIME: Enhancing Your Skills

Aware

Principle One: Be aware of your communication with yourself and others.

- If your subject is sensitive or your information classified, be cautious and noncommittal in any impromptu remarks you might be asked to make.
- As you feel increasingly comfortable rehearsing an extemporaneous presentation, you can decrease your reliance on your notes.
- Grammatical and usage errors communicate a lack of preparation. If you are uncertain of how to use a word or phrase, look it up or ask someone.
- Use a microphone if you need one and one is available. Be sure to rehearse with it.
- Be aware of your speaking rate, and adjust it if necessary.
- Identify key words or phrases that you have a tendency to drawl, slur, or chop. Practice saying them distinctly and clearly.
- Be certain that your presentation aids, including those that utilize technology, contribute to your specific purpose.
- Pay attention to your nonverbal delivery when you rehearse your presentation.
- During rehearsal, tape record or videotape your presentation; objectively and critically observe your gestures, posture, eye contact, facial expression, and vocal delivery, as well as your verbal message; and make necessary adjustments.
- When you deliver your presentation, apply the suggestions offered in Chapter 4.1 for becoming a more confident speaker.

Verbal

Principle Two: Effectively use and interpret verbal messages.

- Give a manuscript or memorized speech when exact wording is critical.
- Phrase your ideas so that they will be clear, accurate, and memorable.
- Do not try to memorize an extemporaneous presentation word for word; vary the ways in which you express ideas and information.
- Use words that are concrete, unbiased, vivid, simple, and correct.
- Make your presentation memorable with figurative images, drama, and cadence.

Nonverbal

Principle Three: Effectively use and interpret nonverbal messages.

- When you deliver a manuscript speech, try to look at an entire sentence at a time so that you can maintain eye contact throughout the sentence.
- Do not read a manuscript speech too rapidly; vary the rhythm, inflection, and pace of delivery so that the speech does not sound as though it were being read.
- Do not deliver a memorized speech too rapidly, and avoid patterns of vocal inflection that make the speech sound recited.
- Use gestures and movement to add interest and emphasis to both manuscript and memorized speeches.
- Use gestures to emphasize or reinforce your verbal message.
- Move during your presentation to signal the beginning of a new idea or major point or to signal a transition from a serious idea to a humorous one or vice versa.
- To heighten your credibility and to increase listener learning, use eye contact to let your audience know that you are interested in them and ready to talk to them.
- Speak loudly enough to be heard easily by all members of your audience.
- Vary the volume of your voice to emphasize ideas and sustain the audience's interest.

- Vary your speaking rate to add interest to your delivery and to emphasize key ideas.
- Articulate your words clearly.

Listen and Respond

Principle Four: Listen and respond thoughtfully to others.

- Use eye contact to help you determine how your audience members are responding to you.
- If possible, rehearse your presentation for someone and seek feedback about both your content and your delivery.

Adapt

Principle Five: Appropriately adapt messages to others.

- Although audiences today generally expect speakers to use everyday language and a conversational delivery style, you will need to adapt your delivery to audiences of different sizes and from different cultures.
- Consider your audience and speaking context when you select a method of delivery.
- Consider your audience's interests, expectations, and knowledge to ensure that your impromptu presentation is audience centered.
- As you deliver an extemporaneous presentation, adapt it to your audience.
- Avoid any language that might be offensive to a member of your audience.
- Adapt your gestures to your audience. Use bolder, more sweeping, and more dramatic gestures with large audiences. Tone down gestures if you are speaking to a culturally diverse audience who might prefer a more subdued style.
- Adapt your movement during a presentation to the cultural expectations of your audience. Better to stay in one carefully chosen spot than to make your audience uncomfortable.
- Assume a posture that seems natural to you in light of your topic, your audience, and the formality of the occasion.
- Adapt the amount of eye contact you use to the expectations of your audience. North Americans prefer as much eye contact as possible; Asians generally prefer less.
- To communicate your interest in your listeners, keep your facial expression alert and friendly.
- Adapt the volume of your voice to your audience's needs.
- Adapt to your audience's expectations for your appearance.
- Let your audience's interests, experiences, and knowledge guide your preparation and selection of presentation aids.

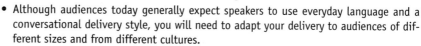

SUMMARY

Once you have developed, supported, and organized your presentation, you are ready to begin to rehearse aloud in preparation for delivering it. The way in which you deliver your presentation will in large part determine your success as a speaker.

As you begin to consider how you will deliver your presentation, you will select from four methods of delivery: manuscript speaking, memorized speaking, impromptu speaking, or extemporaneous speaking. Extemporaneous speaking is the style taught today in most presentational speaking classes and preferred by most audiences.

Once you know what method of delivery you will use, you should begin to think about and rehearse words, phrases, and sentences that will best communicate your intended message and give it a distinct and memorable style. The most effective language is concrete, unbiased, vivid, simple, and correct. You can also make your presentation memorable by using figurative language and language that creates drama and cadence.

Nonverbal variables are also critical to effective delivery. Physical delivery includes a speaker's gestures, movement, and posture. Eye contact is perhaps the most important delivery variable, determining to a large extent your credibility with your audience. Facial expression plays a key role in expressing thoughts, emotions, and attitudes. Vocal delivery includes such elements as volume, pitch, rate, and articulation. And finally, your personal appearance can also affect how your audience responds to you and your message.

Presentation aids may not always be necessary, but they are used with increasing frequency. Presentation aids may include objects or models, people, drawings, photographs, maps, charts, graphs, videotapes, CD-ROMs, DVDs, audiotapes, and audio CDs. Today, many presentation aids can be created and displayed by computer graphics programs such as PowerPoint. Guidelines for using any type of presentation aid include selecting the right one for the audience, occasion, and room and making the presentation aid simple, easy to see or hear, and polished. As you prepare to use any presentation aid, be sure that you rehearse with it, maintain eye contact with your audience, explain your presentation aid, time your use of your presentation aid, refrain from passing things around or using handouts indiscriminately, remember that small children and animals are unpredictable presentation aids, and use technology thoughtfully.

Final suggestions for rehearsing your presentation include allowing ample time for and conducting realistic rehearsals, audiotaping or videotaping your presentation, and practicing your presentation for someone who will offer feedback. Final tips for delivering your presentation include getting plenty of rest the night before you speak, arriving early, and applying the suggestions offered in Chapter 4.1 for becoming a more confident speaker.

DISCUSSION AND REVIEW

1. In what way(s) does delivery contribute to the success of a presentation?
2. What delivery method is most commonly taught and used today?
3. Give an example of how culture can influence audience expectations for speaker delivery.
4. Under what circumstances might a speaker want to deliver a manuscript or memorized speech?
5. How does an extemporaneous presentation differ from an impromptu presentation?
6. List and explain five criteria for effectiveness of words in a presentation.
7. List and define three types of figurative language that can be used to make a presentation memorable.

8. How might you create verbal drama in a presentation?

9. What is cadence? Describe briefly four strategies for achieving it in a presentation.

10. List and define the three key elements of physical delivery and provide suggestions for effectively using each one.

11. What is the most important nonverbal delivery variable for most North American audiences?

12. What can facial expression communicate during a presentation?

13. List and define four nonverbal elements of vocal delivery, and provide suggestions for using each one effectively.

14. How should you dress when you are going to deliver a presentation?

15. List 11 types of presentation aids from which a speaker might select, and provide suggestions for effectively using each type.

16. Offer four general guidelines for preparing effective presentation aids.

17. Provide eight general guidelines for using presentation aids effectively in a presentation.

18. Offer nine general guidelines for rehearsing and delivering a presentation.

PUTTING PRINCIPLES INTO PRACTICE

1. Consult either a print thesaurus or the electronic thesaurus that is part of your word-processing program and find a more concrete or specific word to express each of the following:

go	happy
say	green
big	cat
dark	street
good	car

2. Listen to a political campaign speech in person or on television. Pay particular attention to the politician's delivery. Critique his or her use of gestures, movement, posture, eye contact, facial expression, vocal delivery, and appearance. What advice would you give this politician?

3. Videotape one of your presentations, during either rehearsal or delivery to your class. Analyze your strengths and weaknesses based on the principles and suggestions offered in this chapter.

4. You are a speech consultant to the superintendent of your local school district. She is about to begin working on her annual "State of the District" address, which she gives to an audience of about 250 teachers, parents, and community members. This year, she wants to enliven her presentation of enrollment statistics, student achievement facts, and the state of the physical plant with some presentation aids. Write an advisory memo to the superintendent in which you suggest types of presentation aids she might employ and ways of using each one effectively.

5. You will need the following materials to complete this assignment:

One or two pieces of paper or poster board measuring at least 15 by 20 inches

Felt-tipped markers or a set of marking pens in at least two different colors

A ruler or straightedge

A pencil with an eraser

Three speech topics are listed below, each with a brief description and information that could be communicated with the help of a presentation aid. Design one or more presentation aids for one of the three speeches.

a. A speech about various kinds of organizing tools that college students could use to help them keep track of assignments and projects. These tools include paper wall calendars, paper daytimers, personal information-management software, handheld electronic organizers, and Internet-based calendars.[34]

b. A speech about the spread of AIDS. The number of new cases of HIV infection in 2004 on various continents are listed below.[35]

North America: 44,000
Caribbean: 53,000

Latin America: 240,000
Europe and Central Asia: 231,000
North Africa and Middle East: 92,000
Sub-Saharan Africa: 3.1 million
East Asia: 290,000
South and Southeast Asia: 890,000
Oceania: 5,000

c. A speech that discusses Web sites offering useful information about nutrition and diet. Sites might include the following:

- www.mypyramid.gov/tips_resources/index.html provides tips and resources from the USDA to help you choose healthful food and physical activity.
- www.dietsite.com allows users to enter recipes to obtain a calorie count.
- www.mealsforyou.com offers thousands of healthful recipes.

Chapter 4.3 *Practice Test*

MULTIPLE CHOICE. Choose the *best* answer to each of the following questions.

1. Varying the rate at which you speak can help you to
   a. amplify the volume of your voice.
   b. articulate words more clearly.
   c. emphasize key ideas.
   d. avoid microphone feedback.

2. The thesaurus is a good source for finding
   a. correct words.
   b. vivid words.
   c. unbiased words.
   d. concrete words.

3. In selecting presentation aids, it is important to
   a. adapt the aid to your audience.
   b. use aids that are just slightly beyond your skill and experience.
   c. use the most current technology possible.
   d. use the type of aid with which you are most familiar, regardless of the way your room is set up.

4. Which of the following presentation styles do public speaking classes teach most often?
   a. manuscript reading
   b. memorization
   c. impromptu
   d. extemporaneous

5. Which of the following would probably be the best kind of visual aid to demonstrate the major areas of spending at your university?
   a. a line graph
   b. a diagram
   c. a pie graph
   d. a chart

6. Changes in a speaker's pitch, rate, volume, and inflection are referred to as vocal
   a. delivery.
   b. pronunciation.
   c. credibility.
   d. diction.

7. When delivering an impromptu presentation, it is best to
   a. skip the introduction and conclusion and focus on the main ideas.
   b. limit the presentation to one to three minutes.

c. keep gestures and movement to a minimum.

d. take as much time as you need to get your ideas across.

8. When using visual aids in a speech, a speaker should
   a. display the visual aids only when discussing them.
   b. maintain eye contact with the audience.
   c. avoid passing handouts to the audience during the speech, if possible.
   d. all of the above

9. Which of the following will help you establish effective eye contact with an audience?
   a. Avoid looking over your audience's heads.
   b. Refer to your notes during your opening to make sure you get it right.
   c. Focus most of your eye contact on people in the first few rows.
   d. Establish eye contact with the audience only after you have started your presentation.

10. When preparing an extemporaneous presentation, you should
    a. become familiar enough with your message that you know it word for word.
    b. rehearse only with your full-content preparation outline.
    c. vary the ways you express your ideas and information.
    d. keep gestures and movement to a minimum.

11. Creating interest with your voice is particularly important with which of the following methods of speech delivery?
    a. manuscript
    b. impromptu
    c. extemporaneous
    d. memorized

12. The rhythm with which you speak is your
    a. drama.
    b. omission.
    c. parallelism.
    d. cadence.

13. During a presentation, you should do all of the following *except*
    a. vary your gestures.

b. use conversational-type gestures.

c. use gestures that will capture the attention of the audience.

d. use strong and definite gestures.

14. When speaking from a manuscript, you should do all of the following *except*
    a. use gestures and movement to add interest.
    b. read the speech quickly so that it does not sound "read."
    c. maintain eye contact as much as possible.
    d. type your manuscript on only two-thirds of a sheet of paper.

15. If you are giving a presentation in a room that has a large desk between you and the audience, it is best to
    a. leave the desk where it is and speak from behind it.
    b. incorporate the desk into your visual aids.
    c. move in front of the desk to be closer to the audience.
    d. postpone your presentation until you can find a more suitable room.

16. Tabitha naturally speaks at a rate of 185 words per minute. The average speaker delivers a presentation at a rate of 120–180 words per minute. Tabitha should
    a. stand still so as not to overstimulate the audience when speaking fast.
    b. be careful to pause after questions and important ideas.
    c. use more visual aids than normal so that her audience can keep up.
    d. all of the above

17. At the beginning of Diego's presentation about how to choose a diamond, the overhead projector he is using dies. Diego should
    a. postpone the speech until the projector can be fixed or replaced.
    b. continue with the speech, but pass the pictures around instead.
    c. continue with the speech, but use concrete language to describe the images instead.
    d. tape the slides to white paper and have a classmate hold them up for the audience.

18. Benjamin is giving a eulogy for his dog. He says, "Winston cared deeply for each and every one of us. He always greeted everyone with a smile and thanked them for their attention with slobbery kisses. He would constantly engineer escapes from the back yard to go entertain the school children." What literary technique is Benjamin using?

    a. inversion

    b. metaphor

    c. personification

    d. simile

19. In a recent speech, Kaden stated, "Opponents of gay marriage have aligned and formed a new 'Reich' more subtle and devious than those that preceded it." What literary technique is he employing in this quote?

    a. inversion

    b. metaphor

    c. personification

    d. simile

20. In a speech, Julius Caesar once said, "Veni, vidi, vici." This is an example of

    a. repetition.

    b. suspension.

    c. omission.

    d. alliteration.

TRUE/FALSE.   Indicate whether the following statements are *true* or *false*.

1. T or F   Visual aids speak for themselves and so require no explanations.

2. T or F   Concrete words are usually clearer to the audience than abstract words.

3. T or F   The use of figurative language is appropriate for novelists and poets, but not for public speakers.

4. T or F   "We are like two ships passing in the night" is an example of a metaphor.

5. T or F   When used effectively, repetition in a speech helps to create a strong cadence.

6. T or F   When possible, use straightforward words like *run* instead of *scamper, bolt,* or *whisk.*

7. T or F   The degree to which gestures should be bold, sweeping, and dramatic is related to the size of the audience.

8. T or F   Practicing in front of a mirror helps you to apply Principle Two more effectively.

9. T or F   When speaking to an audience with a dialect different from your own, it is best to minimize your dialect.

10. T or F   When using visual aids, look at your visual aids, not your audience, to help focus the audience's attention.

FILL IN THE BLANK.   Complete the following statements.

1. _____ speaking is delivering a presentation that you have rehearsed but not memorized.

2. _____ _____ include any object used to help an audience understand your message.

3. _____ is the repeating of a consonant sound several times in a sentence.

4. Metaphors, similes, and other figures of speech are all examples of _____ language.

5. Describing an automobile as being "thirsty for gas" is an example of _____.

6. Reading your presentation word for word from a written text is called _____ speaking.

7. If you are unexpectedly asked to say a few words at a meeting, you will be engaging in _____ speaking.

8. The statement "United we stand, divided we fall" is a special type of parallelism known as _____.

9. If you needed to deliver a brief, but very accurate, presentation, you would probably select _____ speaking as your delivery style.

10. A speaker's _____ is a result of variations in his or her vocal pitch.

Speaking to Inform

CHAPTER OUTLINE

CHAPTER OBJECTIVES

After studying this chapter, you should be able to

1. Explain the purpose of speaking to inform.

2. Describe and illustrate five types of informative presentations.

3. Identify and use appropriate strategies for organizing informative presentations.

4. Identify and use strategies for making informative presentations clear.

5. Identify and use strategies for making informative presentations interesting.

6. Identify and use strategies for making informative presentations memorable.

If you think knowledge is expensive,

try ignorance.

Derek Bok

Diana Ong, The Defense. © Diana Ong/SuperStock, Inc.

T his is the information age. With the help of today's technology, we are immersed in facts, data, and words. The Internet is an overflowing fount of information on every conceivable topic. Information is a good thing: It is necessary to help us live our lives. But the volume of information may create a problem. There is often too much of a good thing. Trying to use and interpret all the information we encounter can be like trying to take a drink from a fire hose; the volume of information makes this nearly an overwhelming task.

Countless times each day, you are called on to share information with others. Whether it's directions to your house, the answer to a question from a teacher, or an update on a project at work, your competence as a communicator is often based on how clearly you can present information to others. One survey of both speech teachers and students who had taken a communication course found that the single most important skill taught in a presentational speaking class is how to give an informative presentation.[1] This is not surprising, given the importance of sending and receiving information in our lives.

The purpose of a message to **inform is to share information with others to enhance their knowledge or understanding of the information, concepts, and ideas you present.** When you inform someone, you assume the role of a teacher by defining, illustrating, clarifying, or elaborating on a topic.

Speaking to inform others can be a challenging task. The information you communicate to someone else is rarely, if ever, understood exactly as you intend it. As we have noted, we're each different from one another. We literally experience the world in different ways. As a student, you have firsthand experience that just because a teacher presents information, you don't always soak up knowledge like a sponge. Informing or teaching others is a challenge because of a simple fact: *Presenting information does not mean that communication has occurred.* Communication happens when listeners make sense of the information.

Another challenge of speaking to inform is to keep your informative message from becoming a persuasive one. It cannot be denied that informing and persuading are interrelated. Information alone may persuade someone to think or do something in a different way. However, if you intentionally try to change or reinforce your listeners' feelings, ideas, or behavior, your speech may become more persuasive than informative.

In this chapter, we will suggest ways to build on your experience and enhance your skill in informing others. We will examine different types of informative tasks and identify specific strategies to help you organize your messages and make them clear, interesting, and memorable. Throughout our discussion we will remind you of the five communication principles for a lifetime.

Aware
Verbal
Nonverbal
Listen and Respond
Adapt

Types of Informative Presentations

When preparing an informative presentation, your first task, after considering the needs and backgrounds of your audience, is to select a topic. Although you may be assigned a topic based on your job, experience, or expertise, there are

Ethics and *Communication*

Confidential or Potentially Dangerous Information

Mike, a computer engineering major, understands how a computer hacker recently accessed confidential personal information files on faculty members at his university. The procedure is actually simple enough that even people without sophisticated technical ability could understand and replicate it. Mike thinks the procedure might be a good topic for an interesting informative presentation. Meanwhile Mike's classmate Paul, a chemistry major, considers whether to give an informative presentation on how to create homemade explosives. If you are privy to confidential or potentially dangerous information, is it ethical to share it with others in an informative presentation?

times (such as in a communication class) when you are given a free hand in determining what you will talk about. Identifying the type of informative presentation you will deliver can help you select and narrow your topic, organize your message, and select appropriate supporting material.

Presentations about Objects

A speech about an object might be about anything tangible—anything you can see or touch. You may or may not show the actual object to your audience while you are talking about it. Objects that could form the basis of an interesting presentation might include these:

Objects from your own collection (antiques, compact discs, baseball cards)
The Eiffel Tower
Cellos
Digital cameras
The Roosevelt Memorial
Toys

The time limit for your speech will determine the amount of detail you can share with your listeners. Even in a 30- to 45-minute presentation, you cannot talk about every aspect of any of the objects listed. So you will need to focus on a specific purpose.

Presentations about Procedures

A presentation about a procedure discusses how something works (for example, how blood travels through the human circulatory system), or describes a process that produces a particular outcome (such as how grapes become wine). At the close of such a presentation, your audience should be able to describe, understand, or perform the procedure you have described. Here are some examples of procedures that could be the topics of effective informative presentations:

> How to surf the Internet
> How state laws are made
> How to refinish furniture
> How to select a personal digital assistant (PDA)
> How to plant an organic garden
> How to select and purchase a stock

Notice that all of these examples start with the word *how*. A presentation about a procedure usually focuses on how a process is completed or how something can be accomplished. Presentations about procedures are often presented in workshops or other training situations in which people learn skills. One good way to teach people a skill is to follow the acronym T-E-A-C-H, which stands for Tell-Example-Apply-Coach-Help.[2]

- *Tell.*   Describe what you want your listeners to know.
- *Example.*   Show them an example of how to perform the skill.
- *Apply.*   Give them an opportunity to apply the knowledge by performing the skill.
- *Coach.*   Provide positive coaching to encourage them.
- *Help.*   Help them learn by correcting mistakes.

Many presentations about procedures include visual aids. Whether you are teaching people how to install a computer modem or how to give a presentation, showing them how to do something is almost always more effective than just telling them how to do it.

Presentations about People

A biographical presentation could be about someone famous or about someone you know personally. Most of us enjoy hearing about the lives of real people, whether famous or not, living or dead, who have some special quality. The key to making an effective biographical presentation is to be selective. Don't try to cover every detail of your subject's life. Relate the key elements in the person's career, personality, or other significant life features so that you build to a particular point, rather than just recite facts about an individual. Perhaps your grandfather was known for his generosity, for example. Mention some notable examples of his philanthropy. If you are talking about a well-known personality, pick information or a period that is not widely known, such as the person's private hobby or childhood. One speaker gave a memorable presentation about his friend:

> To enter Charlie's home was to enter a world of order and efficiency. His den reflected his many years as an Air Force officer; it was orderly and neat. He always knew exactly where everything was. When he finished reading the morning paper, he folded it so neatly by his favorite chair that you would

hardly know that it had been read. Yet for all of his efficiency, you knew the minute you walked into his home that he cared for others, that he cared for you. His jokes, his stories, his skill in listening to others drew people to him. He never met a stranger. He looked for opportunities to help others.

Note how these details capture Charlie's personality and charm. Presentations about people should give your listeners the feeling that the person is a unique, authentic individual.

One specific type of presentation about a person is an introduction of another speaker and his or her topic. There are two cardinal rules for introducing another speaker: Be brief, and be accurate. Remember that the audience has come to hear the main speaker, not to listen to you. And be certain that you know how to pronounce the speaker's name and that you have accurate information about him or her.

Presentations about Events

Where were you on September 11, 2001, the day terrorists attacked the World Trade Center and the Pentagon? Chances are that you clearly remember where you were and what you were doing on that and other similarly fateful days. Major events punctuate our lives and mark the passage of time.

A major event can form the basis of a fascinating informative presentation. You can choose to talk about an event that you have either witnessed or researched. Your goal is to describe the event in concrete, tangible terms and to bring the experience to life for your audience. Have you experienced a major disaster such as a hurricane or a tornado? Have you witnessed the inauguration of a president, governor, or senator? Or you may want to re-create an event that your parents or grandparents lived through. What was it like to be at Pearl Harbor on December 7, 1941? How did people react when Neil Armstrong took his first steps on the moon on July 20, 1969?

You may have heard a recording of the famous radio broadcast of the explosion and crash of the dirigible *Hindenburg.* The announcer's ability to describe both the scene and the incredible emotion of the moment has made that broadcast a classic. As that broadcaster was able to do, your purpose as an informative speaker describing an event is to make that event come alive for your listeners and to help them visualize the scene.

Presentations about Ideas

Presentations about ideas are by nature more abstract than the other types of presentations. The following principles, concepts, and theories might be topics of idea presentations:

Principles of time management
Freedom of speech
Evolution
Theories of communication
Buddhism
Animal rights

Verbal

As you look at this list, you may think, "Those topics sure look boring." The key to gaining and maintaining interest in your presentation about an idea lies in your selection of supporting material. A good speaker selects illustrations, examples, and anecdotes that make an otherwise abstract idea seem both exciting and relevant to the audience.

Strategies for Organizing Your Informative Presentation

As with any presentation, your audience will more readily understand your informative presentation if you organize your ideas logically. Regardless of the length or complexity of your message, you must follow a logical pattern in order to be understood.

Organizing Presentations about Objects

Presentations about objects may be organized topically; a topical pattern is structured around the logical divisions of the object you're describing. Here's a sample topical outline for a speech about an object—a nuclear power plant:

I. The reactor core
   A. The nuclear fuel in the core
   B. The placement of the fuel in the core

II. The reactor vessel
   A. The walls of a reactor vessel
   B. The function of the coolant in the reactor vessel

III. The reactor control rods
   A. The description of the control rods
   B. The function of the control rods

Presentations about objects may also be organized chronologically. A speaker might, for example, focus on the history and development of nuclear power plants; such a presentation would probably be organized chronologically. Or, depending on the speaker's specific purpose, the presentation could be organized spatially, describing the physical layout of a nuclear power plant.

Organizing Presentations about Procedures

Speeches about procedures are usually organized chronologically, according to the steps involved in the process. Anita organized chronologically her explanation of how to develop a new training curriculum in teamwork skills:

When speaking about Native American rock art in Texas, this speaker may find it helpful to organize her speech either topically, spatially, or chronologically.

I. Conduct a needs assessment of your department.
   A. Identify the method of assessing department needs.
   B. Implement the needs assessment.

II. Identify the topics that should be presented in the training.
   A. Specify topics that all members of the department need.
   B. Specify topics that only some members of the department need.

III. Write training objectives.
   A. Write objectives that are measurable.
   B. Write objectives that are specific.
   C. Write objectives that are attainable.

IV. Develop lesson plans for the training.
   A. Identify the training methods you will use.
   B. Identify the materials you will need.

Note that Anita grouped the tasks into steps. Her audience will remember the four general steps much more easily than they could have hoped to recall the curriculum development process if each individual task were listed as a separate step.

Organizing Presentations about People

One way to talk about a person's life is in chronological order—birth, school, career, family, professional achievements, death. However, if you are interested in presenting a specific theme, such as "Winston Churchill, master of English prose," you may decide instead to organize Churchill's experiences topically. You could first discuss Churchill's achievements as a brilliant orator whose words defied the German military machine in 1940, and then trace the origins of his skill to his work as a cub reporter in South Africa during the Boer War of 1899 to 1902.

Organizing Presentations about Events

Most speeches about an event follow a chronological arrangement. But a presentation about an event might also describe the complex issues or causes behind the event and be organized topically. For example, if you were to talk about the Civil War, you might choose to focus on the three causes of the war:

I. Political
II. Economic
III. Social

Adapt

Although these main points are topical, specific subpoints may be organized chronologically. However you choose to organize your speech about an event, your goal should be to ensure that your audience is enthralled by your vivid description.

Organizing Presentations about Ideas

Most presentations about ideas are organized topically (by logical subdivisions of the central idea) or according to complexity (from simple ideas to more complex ones). The following example illustrates how Thompson organized a presentation about philosophy into an informative speech:

I. Definition of philosophy
   A. Philosophy as viewed in ancient times
   B. Philosophy as viewed today

II. Three branches of the study of philosophy
   A. Metaphysics
      1. The study of ontology
      2. The study of cosmology
   B. Epistemology
      1. Knowledge derived from thinking
      2. Knowledge derived from experiencing
   C. Logic
      1. Types of reasoning
      2. Types of proof

Thompson decided that the most logical way to give an introductory talk about philosophy was first to define it and then to describe three branches of philosophy. Because of time limits, he chose only to describe three branches or types of philosophy. He used a topical organizational pattern to organize his message.

RECAP

Organizing Informative Presentations

Presentation Type	Description	Typical Organizational Patterns	Sample Topics
Presentations about objects	Present information about tangible things	Topical Spatial Chronological	The Rosetta Stone MP3 players Space shuttle The U.S. Capitol
Presentations about procedures	Review how something works or describe a process	Chronological Topical Complexity	How to . . . Clone an animal Operate a nuclear power plant Use a computer Trap lobsters
Presentations about people	Describe either famous people or personal acquaintances	Chronological Topical	Rosa Parks Nelson Mandela Indira Gandhi Your grandmother Your favorite teacher
Presentations about events	Describe an actual event	Chronological Topical Complexity Spatial	Chinese New Year Inauguration Day Cinco de Mayo
Presentations about ideas	Present abstract information or information about principles, concepts, theories, or issues	Topical Complexity	Communism Economic theory Tao-Te Ching

QUICK REVIEW

Strategies for Making Your Informative Presentation Clear

Think of the best teacher you ever had. He or she was probably a great lecturer with a special talent for making information clear, interesting, and memorable. Like teachers, some speakers are better than others at presenting information clearly. In this section, we will review some of the principles that can help you become the kind of speaker whose presentations are memorable.[3]

Aware
Verbal
Nonverbal
Listen and Respond
Adapt

A message is clear when the listener understands it in the way the speaker intended. Phrased in baseball terminology, a message is clear when what I threw is what you caught. How do you make your messages clear to others? First, be aware (mindful) of what you intend to communicate. Is the message clear to you? Say to yourself, "If I heard this message for the first time, would it make sense to me?"

If the message makes sense to you, select appropriate words that are reinforced with appropriate nonverbal cues to express your ideas. If you detect that your listeners are puzzled by what you say, stop and try another way to express your ideas.

Adapt your message to your audience. Be audience centered. Keep your listeners in mind as you select and narrow a topic, fine-tune your purpose, and complete each preparation and presentation task. Here are several additional specific strategies to make your message clear.

Simplify Ideas

Verbal

Your job as a presentational speaker is to get your ideas over to your audience, not to see how much information you can cram into your speech. The simpler your ideas and phrases, the greater the chance that your audience will remember them.

Let's say you decide to talk about state-of-the-art personal computer hardware. Fine—but just don't try to make your audience as sophisticated as you are about computers in a 5-minute presentation. Discuss only major features and name one or two leaders in the field. Don't load your presentation with details. Edit ruthlessly.

Pace Your Information Flow

Verbal
Adapt

Arrange your supporting material so that you present an even flow of information, rather than bunch up a number of significant details around one point. If you present too much new information too quickly, you may overwhelm your audience. Their ability to understand may falter.

You should be especially sensitive to the flow of information if your topic is new or unfamiliar to your listeners. Make sure that your audience has time to process any new information you present. Use supporting material to regulate the pace of your presentation.

Again, do not try to see how much detail and content you can cram into a presentation. Your job is to present information so that the audience can grasp it, not to show off how much you know.

Relate New Information to Old

Most of us learn by building on what we already know. We try to make sense out of our world by associating the new with the old. When you meet someone for the first time, you may be reminded of someone you already know. Your understanding of calculus is based on your knowledge of algebra.

Diversity and Communication

Using an Interpreter

*I*t is quite possible that you may at some time be asked to speak to an audience that does not understand English. In such a situation, you will need an interpreter to translate your message so that your audience can understand you. When using an interpreter, consider the following tips:

1. Realize that a presentation that may take you 30 minutes to deliver without an interpreter will take at least an hour to present with an interpreter. Edit your message to make sure it fits within the time limit.

2. Even with an experienced interpreter, you'll need to slow your speaking rate a bit. Also, be sure to pause after every two or three sentences to give the interpreter time to translate your message.

3. Don't assume that your audience doesn't understand you just because you are using an interpreter. Don't say anything that you don't want your audience to hear.

4. If you have many facts, figures, or other detailed data, write this information down before you speak, and give it to your interpreter.

5. Humor often doesn't translate well. Be cautious of using a joke that was a real knee-slapper when

you told it to your colleagues in your office; it may not have the same effect on people with a different cultural background and different language. Also, even a very skilled interpreter may have difficulty communicating the intended meaning of your humor.

6. Avoid using slang, jargon, or any terms that will be unfamiliar to your listeners or interpreter.

7. When possible, talk with your interpreter before you deliver your presentation. Tell him or her the general points you will present. If possible, give the interpreter an outline or a transcript if you are using a manuscript.

When presenting new information to a group, help your audience associate your new idea with something that is familiar to them. Use an analogy. Tell bewildered college freshmen how their new academic life will be similar to high school and how it will be different. Describe how your raising cattle over the summer was similar to taking care of any animal; they all need food, water, and shelter. By building on the familiar, you help your listeners understand how your new concept or information relates to their experience.

Verbal

QUICK REVIEW

Strategies for Making Your Informative Presentation Interesting

He had them. Every audience member's eyes were riveted on the speaker. It was as quiet as midnight in a funeral home. Audience members were also leaning forward, ever so slightly, not wanting to miss a single idea or brilliant illustration. No one moved. They hung on every word. How can you create such interest when *you* speak? Here are several strategies that can help you keep your audiences listening for more.

Relate to Your Listeners' Interests

Adapt

Your listeners may be interested in your topic for a variety of reasons. It may affect them directly; it may add to their knowledge; it may satisfy their curiosity; or it may entertain them. These reasons are not mutually exclusive. For example, if you were talking to a group of businesspeople about the latest changes in local tax policies, you would be discussing something that would affect them directly, add to their knowledge, and satisfy their curiosity. But your listeners' primary interest would be in how the taxes would affect them. By contrast, if you were giving a lecture on 15th-century Benin sculpture to a middle-class audience at a public library, your listeners would be interested because your talk would add to their knowledge, satisfy their curiosity, and entertain them. Such a talk can also affect your listeners directly by making them more interesting to others. If your audience feels that they will benefit from your presentation in some way, your presentation will interest them.

Throughout this book, we have encouraged you to adapt to your communication partners—to develop an audience-centered approach to presentational speaking. Being an audience-centered informative speaker means that you are aware of information that your audience can use. Specifically, what factors help maintain audience interest? Consider the following strategies.[4]

- *Activity and movement.*   We are more likely to listen to a story that is action-packed than to one that listlessly lingers on an idea too long.
- *Issues and events close to an audience.*   To capture your listeners' attention, relate your information to what is happening in your school, community, or state. Not surprisingly, most people are interested in themselves. Therefore, one of the secrets to making a presentation interesting is to use examples to which your audience can relate. Make it personal. When appropriate, mention specific audience members' names.
- *Conflict.*   Clashes of ideas; stories that pit one side against another; or opposing forces in government, religion, or interpersonal relationships grab attention. The Greeks learned long ago that the essential ingredient of any play, be it comedy or tragedy, is conflict.

Another way you can make your message interesting is to think about why you are interested in the topic. Once you are aware of your own interests and background, you can often find ways to establish common bonds with your audience.

Use Attention-Catching Supporting Material

Supporting material is effective if it both clarifies your ideas and keeps your listeners' attention. One classic type of supporting material often used in informative speaking is definition. But if you are trying to tell your listeners about a complex or abstract process, you will need more than definitions to explain what you mean. When describing abstract ideas or processes, it's usually more difficult to hold listeners' attention. Research suggests that you can demystify a complex process and increase audience interest if you first provide a simple overview of the process with an analogy, model, picture, or vivid description.[5]

Before going into great detail, first give listeners the "big picture" or convey the gist of the process. Analogies (comparisons) are often a good way to do this. For example, if you are describing how a personal computer works, you could say that it stores information the way a filing cabinet does or that computer software works like a piano roll on an old-fashioned player piano. In addition to using an analogy, consider using a model or other visual aid to show relationships among the steps of a complex process.

You can also describe the process, providing more detail than you do when you just define something. Descriptions answer questions about the *who, what, where, why,* and *when* of the process. Who is involved in the process? What is the process, idea, or event that you want to describe? Where and when does the process take place? Why does it occur, or why is it important to the audience? (Of course, not all of these questions apply to every description.)

Establish a Motive for Your Audience to Listen to You

Most audiences will probably not be waiting breathlessly for you to talk to them. You will need to motivate them to listen to you.

Some situations have built-in motivations for listeners. A teacher can say, "There will be a test covering my lecture tomorrow. It will count as 50% of your semester grade." Such threatening methods may not make the teacher popular, but they certainly will motivate the class to listen. Similarly, a boss might say, "Your ability to use these sales principles will determine whether you keep your job." Your boss's statement will probably motivate you to learn the company's sales principles. However, unlike a teacher or a boss, you will rarely have the power to motivate

The 5th Wave   By Rich Tennant

©RICHTENNANT

"...which reminds me of a story about a dyslexic mathematician..."

Oh no. Not the perturbation of transient time-independent theory joke again!

QUANTUM FEST

© The 5th Wave, www.the5thwave.com

On the Web

The Internet is a vast resource of material for informative speeches. In addition to using search engines to perform keyword searches, you may want to take advantage of such resources as Web-based encyclopedias, almanacs, and statistical databases. Take a look at the following:

www.infoplease.com provides access to a number of informative resources, including *The Columbia Electronic Encyclopedia,* 6th ed., and the *Information Please Almanac.*

factfinder.census.gov is a user-friendly site that offers population, housing, economic, and geographic data from the U.S. Census Bureau.

www.fedstats.gov offers official statistical information from more than 100 federal government agencies.

Colin Powell's use of memorable word pictures helps his audience visualize the images he talks about.

your listeners with such strong-arm tactics, and you will therefore need to find more creative ways to get your audience to listen to you.

One way to arouse the interest of your listeners is to ask them a question. Speaking on the high cost of tuition, you might ask, "How many of you are interested in saving tuition dollars this year?" You'll probably have their attention. Then proceed to tell them that you will talk about several approaches to seeking low-cost loans and grants. "Who would like to save money on their income taxes?" "How many of you would like to have a happier home life?" "How many of you would like to learn an effective way of preparing your next speech?" These are other examples of questions that could stimulate your listeners' interest and motivate them to give you their attention. Besides using rhetorical questions, you can begin with an anecdote, a startling statistic, or some other attention-grabbing device.

Don't assume that your listeners will be automatically interested in what you have to say. Pique their interest with a question. Capture their attention. Motivate them to listen to you. Tell them how the information you present will be of value to them. As the British writer G. K. Chesterton once said, "There is no such thing as an uninteresting topic; there are only uninterested people."

Use Word Pictures

Verbal

Words have the power to create powerful images that can gain and hold an audience's attention. Consider using a word picture to make your message vivid and interesting. **Word pictures are lively descriptions that help your listeners form a mental image by appealing to their senses of sight, taste, smell, sound, and touch.** The following suggestions will help you construct effective word pictures:

- Form a clear mental image of the person, place, or object before you try to describe it.
- Describe the appearance of the person, place, or object. What would your listeners see if they were looking at it? Use lively language to describe the flaws and foibles, bumps and beauties of the people, places, and things you want your audience to see. Make your description an invitation to the imagination—a stately pleasure dome into which your listeners can enter and view its treasures with you.
- Describe what your listeners would hear. Use colorful, onomatopoetic words, such as *buzz, snort, hum, crackle,* or *hiss.* These words are much more descriptive than the more general term *noise.* Imitate the sound you want

Technology *and* *Communication*

Using an Electronic Thesaurus

*M*ost word-processing programs include an electronic thesaurus. To use this tool in Microsoft Word, highlight a word in your text for which you would like to find a synonym. Then click on "Thesaurus" under the "Tools" menu. You will get a pop-up box with several alternatives for your highlighted word. If one of these synonyms creates a better word picture, you might want to replace your original word with the new one.

A word of caution, however, about using any thesaurus, whether electronic or traditional: Be sure that you know the alternative word well enough to understand its connotations and how to use it in a grammatically correct way. A thesaurus should remind you of a word with which you are already familiar, not launch you into an uncharted adventure in diction!

your listeners to hear with their "mental ear." For example, instead of saying "When I walked in the woods, I heard the sound of twigs breaking beneath my feet and wind moving the leaves above me in the trees," you might say, "As I walked in the woods, I heard the *crackle* of twigs underfoot and the *rustle* of leaves overhead."

- Describe smells, if appropriate. What fragrance or aroma do you want your audience to recall? Such diverse subjects as Thanksgiving, nighttime in the tropics, and the first day of school all lend themselves to olfactory imagery. No Thanksgiving would be complete without the rich aroma of roast turkey and the pungent, tangy odor of cranberries. A warm, humid evening in Miami smells of salt air and gardenia blossoms. And the first day of school evokes for many the scents of new shoe leather, unused crayons, and freshly painted classrooms. In each case, the associated smells greatly enhance the overall word picture.

- Describe how an object feels when touched. Use words that are as clear and vivid as possible. Rather than saying that something is rough or smooth, use a simile, such as "the rock was rough as sandpaper" or "the pebble was as smooth as a baby's skin." These descriptions appeal to both the visual and tactile senses.

- Describe taste, one of the most powerful of the senses, if appropriate. Thinking about your grandmother may evoke for you memories of her rich, homemade noodles; her sweet, fudgy, nut brownies; and her light, flaky, buttery pie crust. Descriptions of these taste sensations would be welcome to almost any audience, particularly your fellow college students subsisting mainly on dormitory food or their own cooking! More important, such description can help you paint an accurate, vivid image of your grandmother.

- Describe the emotion that a listener might feel if he or she were to experience the situation you relate. If you experienced the situation, describe your own emotions. Use specific adjectives rather than general terms such as *happy* or *sad*. One speaker, talking about receiving her first speech assignment, described her reaction with these words: "My heart stopped. Panic began to rise up inside. Me? . . . For the next five days I lived in dreaded anticipation of the forthcoming event."[6]

Note how effectively such words and phrases as "my heart stopped," "panic," and "dreaded anticipation" describe the above-mentioned speaker's terror at the prospect of giving a speech—much more so than if she had said simply, "I was scared." The more vividly and accurately you can describe emotion, the more intimately involved in your description the audience will become. One final word of caution: Don't describe horrific events too explicitly. You will risk alienating your audience, rather than engaging them.

Create Interesting Presentation Aids

Nonverbal

Research about learning styles suggests that many of your listeners are more likely to remember your ideas if you can reinforce them with presentation aids. Pictures, graphs, posters, and computer-generated graphics can help you gain and maintain audience members' attention, as well as increase their retention of the information you present. Today's audiences are exposed daily to a barrage of messages conveyed through highly visual electronic media—CD-ROM, DVD, the World Wide Web, and video. They have grown to depend on more than words alone to help them remember ideas and information. When you present summaries of data, a well-crafted line graph or colorful pie chart can quickly and memorably reinforce the words and numbers you cite.

Use Humor

"Humor is the spice of speeches," says comedian Michael Klepper. "Too little and your message may be bland or lifeless, too much and it can burn the mouth."[7] The challenge is to use just the right kind of humor in the right amounts. Use humor wisely by considering the following ideas:[8]

- *Use humor to make a point.*   Don't just tell jokes for the sake of getting a laugh. Make sure your story or punch line relates to your message. Here's an example of how a brief joke was used to make a point about the value of teamwork:

    I read recently about a veterinarian and a taxidermist who decided to share a shop in a small town in Ohio. The sign in the front window read: "Either way, you get your dog back."

    There is an important lesson there. We need to work together to solve our problems. People from marketing need to work with operations people. Designers need to work with engineers. Then, when we find a problem that one part of the organization can't solve, someone else may suggest a solution. It doesn't matter who comes up with the solution. The important thing is to "get your dog back."[9]

- *Make yourself the butt of the joke.*   Audiences love it when you tell a funny or embarrassing story about yourself. And if the joke's on you, you don't have to worry about whether you will offend someone else.
- *Use humorous quotations.*   You don't have to be a comedy writer to be funny. Quote humorous lines of proverbs, poetry, or sayings from others. But remember, what may be funny to you may not be funny to your audience. Some people love the humor of George Carlin; some don't. Try out your quotes and jokes on others before you present them from behind the lectern. Also, don't try to pass off a quotation from someone else as one of your own; always give credit for quotations you use.
- *Use cartoons.*   Using an overhead projector to display a cartoon or scanning a cartoon into your computer presentation may be just the right way to make your point. Make sure your cartoon is large enough to be seen by everyone in the audience. As with any humor, don't overdo your use of cartoons.

Strategies for Making Your Informative Presentation Memorable

If you've made your message clear and interesting, you're well on your way to ensuring that your audience members remember what you say. The goal is for your ideas to stick in your listeners' minds as if they were made of Velcro, rather than slide off as if they were made of Teflon. When you inform or teach, your job is to ensure as much retention of what you have conveyed as possible, by presenting the information as effectively as you can. People remember what is important to them. So one of the keys to making a message memorable is, again, to adapt your message to your listeners. Presenting a well-organized message will also go a long way toward helping your listeners remember what you say. Here are several strategies for making your presentation memorable.

Adapt

Build In Redundancy

It is seldom necessary for writers to repeat themselves. If readers don't quite understand a passage, they can go back and read it again. When you speak, however, it is useful to repeat key points. As we have noted before, audience members generally cannot stop you if a point in your presentation is unclear or if their minds wander; you need to build in redundancy to make sure that the information you want to communicate will get across. Most speech teachers advise their students to structure their presentations as follows:

1. *Tell them what you're going to tell them.*   In the introduction of your presentation, provide a broad overview of the purpose of your message. Identify the major points you will present.
2. *Tell them.*   In the body of your presentation, develop each of the main points mentioned during your introduction.

Verbal

3. *Tell them what you've told them.*   Finally, in your conclusion, summarize the key ideas discussed in the body.

Use Adult Learning Principles

If your audience consists of adult listeners, you will need to ensure that you deliver your message in the way that adults learn best. **Adult learners prefer the following:**[10]

- **To be given information they can use immediately**
- **To be involved actively in the learning process**
- **To connect their life experiences with the new information they learn**
- **To know how the new information is relevant to their busy lives**
- **To receive information that is relevant to their needs**

Adapt

Most people who have office jobs have in-baskets (or simply "in-piles") on their desks, where they place work that needs to be done. Similarly, adult learners tend to have "mental in-baskets"; as audience members, they have mental agendas of what they want or need to gain from listening to a presentation. Remember the characteristics of adult learners, and don't forget about the important principle of adapting your message to others. You will make your message memorable and also have more success in informing your audience if you tailor your information to address *their* agenda.

Reinforce Key Ideas Verbally

Verbal

You can reinforce an idea by using such phrases as "This is the most important point" or "Be sure to remember this next point; it's the most compelling one." Suppose you have four suggestions for helping your listeners chair a meeting, and your last suggestion is the most important. How can you make sure your audience knows that? Just tell them: "Of all the suggestions I've given you, this last tip is the most important one. Here it is: Never fail to distribute an agenda before you chair any meeting." Be careful not to overuse this technique. If you claim that every other point is a key point, soon your audience will not believe you.

Reinforce Key Ideas Nonverbally

Nonverbal

You can also signal the importance of a point with nonverbal emphasis. Gestures serve the purpose of accenting or emphasizing key phrases, as italics do in written communication.

A well-placed pause can provide emphasis and reinforcement for a point. Pausing just before or just after you make an important point will focus attention on your thought. Raising or lowering your voice can also reinforce a key idea.

Movement can help emphasize major ideas. Moving from behind the lectern to tell a personal anecdote can signal that something special and more intimate is about to be said. Remember that your movement and gestures should be meaningful and natural, rather than seeming arbitrary or forced. Your need to emphasize an idea can provide the motivation to make a meaningful movement.

RECAP

Strategies for Making an Informative Presentation Clear, Interesting, and Memorable

Make Your Presentation Clear
Simplify ideas.
Pace the information flow.
Relate new information to old.

Make Your Presentation Interesting
Relate to your listeners' interests.
Use attention-catching supporting material.
Establish a motive for your audience to listen to you.
Use word pictures.
Use interesting presentation aids.
Use humor.

Make Your Presentation Memorable
Build in redundancy.
Use adult learning principles.
Reinforce key ideas verbally.
Reinforce key ideas nonverbally.

SAMPLE INFORMATIVE PRESENTATION

Alton Tisino
Texas State University–San Marcos

The Power of Music[11]

When I woke up this morning, one thing on my mind was music. I'm sure everyone wakes up with a certain tune or a favorite song in their head. Music is a treasured art form that we all share. Sometimes we can hear a song, and it will take us back to a significant time in our lives; or other times, a song can give us inspiration or motivate us to continue whatever it is we are doing. Whether it is in a car or at home, or at a restaurant or even in an elevator, music plays a big part in our daily lives and can bring us together like no other art form.

Alton establishes a motive for his audience to listen by referring to music experiences common to all people.

Alton further arouses the interest of his listeners by asking two rhetorical questions.

Alton previews the two main ideas of his presentation.

Alton uses both a definition and an explanation to clarify the role of rhythm in music.

So why is music so powerful? What are the elements that make music so special? Some people say they like the beat of a song, some people say they like the melody in a song, while others simply enjoy the lyrics in a song. Well, according to world-famous composer Duke Ellington, there are three major elements in music: rhythm, melody, and harmony. In order for us to discover what makes music so special, we must first understand these terms, and then see how music itself is beneficial to us in our daily lives.

The *Dictionary of Music* defines *rhythm* as "the division of impulses, sound, and accents or movement in musical time." There are many theories on how rhythm was transformed into music. But, I'd like to cite poet Langston Hughes and his explanation on how rhythm was transformed into music:

> The rhythm of the heart is the first and most important rhythm in human life. Thousands of years ago men transformed the rhythm of the heartbeat into a drumbeat. And the rhythm of music began. They made a slow steady drumbeat to walk to or march to, a faster beat to sing to, and a changing beat to dance to. Rhythm is something we share in common. You and I, with all the plants and animals and people in the world and with all the stars and moon and sun and all the vast universe beyond this wonderful earth which is our home.[12]

Alton provides a signpost to summarize his first subpoint and preview the next one.

Now that we have found our rhythm, we must look further into the foundation of music and discover melody.

Melody is defined as "an arrangement of single tones in a meaningful sequence." A melody gives life to a song and is the root for every tune you will ever hear. We have now found our melody and now we're only missing one piece to the puzzle of music.

Harmony is defined as "the sound resulting from the simultaneous sounding of two or more tones consonant with each other." Rhythm and melody would not be complete without harmony.

This signpost signals Alton's move from his first main idea to his second main idea.

Now that we discovered the foundations of music, let me now explain to you how music is beneficial to us.

Many health experts believe music is good for the digestive system. According to researchers at the *Continuous Music Network*, slow music is better for your digestive system than no music at all. Clinical studies show that people take on average three mouthfuls when there's soothing music in the background, versus four mouthfuls when no tunes are played at all.

Having offered statistical evidence that music is beneficial to exercise, Alton relates a brief personal anecdote.

While music can help us relax at the dinner table, it can also help us go that extra mile when exercising. The music network *Galaxie* program director Mike Guinta stated that "Studies show men increase their workout time by 30 percent and women by 25 percent...." Scientific studies have shown that music keeps your mind off the physical discomfort of a straining activity. I can personally recall a time I felt I could no longer go on with the strenuous activity of a workout. But somehow by listening to music on my headphones, it gave me an extra boost of energy.

Studies also have shown that unborn babies who listen to classical music in the mother's womb become smarter. Many therapists and psychiatrists have their patients listen to music to help them relax and deal with stress and depression. These are just a few of the many benefits that music has for us.

We have discovered the three major elements in music: rhythm, melody, and harmony. Whether it be the hard-hitting drums of rock, the melodic tunes of our favorite pop songs, or the harmonic, complex style of jazz, music is the universal language of the world because it can generate the feelings of human emotions—joy, sorrow, love, and pain—thus making it beneficial in our daily lives.

The fact of the matter is we make our own music all the time. Now let me explain to you how we do this. Just by being alive, our heartbeat makes its own rhythm. We make melody by arranging our thoughts in a meaningful sequence. And we make the final stage of music, harmony, simply by interacting with each other. We all have rhythm, and we all have music, and with music we have good times.

As part of the necessary built-in redundancy of informative presentations, Alton briefly summarizes his main ideas.

By explaining how the elements of music apply to everyone's life, Alton draws on the principles that adult learners prefer to connect their life experiences with the new information they have learned and that they prefer relevant information.

Alton closes his presentation with a reference to George Gershwin's famous song "I Got Rhythm."

PRINCIPLES FOR A LIFETIME: Enhancing Your Skills

Principle One: Be aware of your communication with yourself and others.

Aware

- Be conscious of the type of informative message you are developing (presentation about an object, a procedure, a person, an event, or an idea), to help you determine how best to organize your message.
- Be consciously aware of using strategies that will make your informative messages clear, interesting, and memorable.

Principle Two: Effectively use and interpret verbal messages.

Verbal

- Use supporting material such as stories, examples, and illustrations to gain and maintain attention.
- Use word pictures to make images and stories interesting and memorable.
- Pace the flow of the information you present to enhance message clarity.
- Relate new information to old information to increase clarity and retention.
- Verbally reinforce ideas to help make your message memorable.
- Use simple ideas rather than complex ideas to make your message clear.
- Build in message redundancy to enhance message retention.

Principle Three: Effectively use and interpret nonverbal messages.

Nonverbal

- Use presentation aids to make messages clear, interesting, and memorable.
- Observe the nonverbal behavior of your audience to help you determine whether your message has been communicated clearly.
- Nonverbally reinforce ideas to make your message memorable.

Listen and Respond

Adapt

Principle Four: Listen and respond thoughtfully to others.

- Before you deliver you presentation to an audience, talk and listen to audience members to help you customize your message for them.

Principle Five: Appropriately adapt messages to others.

- Adapt the structure and flow of your presentation to your listeners to enhance message clarity.
- Adapt your examples and illustrations to your listeners to help gain and maintain interest and attention.
- Develop a motivation for your audience to listen to you.

SUMMARY

To inform is to teach someone something you know. In this chapter, you have studied the goals, principles, and strategies that presentational speakers use to inform others.

There are five basic types of informative presentations. Messages about ideas are often abstract and generally discuss principles, concepts, or theories. Messages about objects discuss tangible things. Messages about procedures explain a process or describe how something works. Messages about people can be about either the famous or the little known. Messages about events describe major occurrences or personal experiences.

Strategies for organizing your informative presentation will vary according to the type of informative presentation and your specific purpose. A presentation about an object may be organized topically, chronologically, or spatially. A presentation about a procedure will usually be organized chronologically. Presentations about either people or events are also usually organized chronologically but can be organized topically. And a presentation about an idea will probably be organized topically.

To make your message clear, use simple rather than complex ideas, pace the flow of your information, and relate new information to old ideas. In order to increase interest in your presentation, relate information to your listeners, find and use attention-catching supporting material, establish a motive for your audience to listen to you, use vivid word pictures, use humor appropriately, and create intriguing and clear presentation aids. Finally, to make messages memorable, build in some redundancy (tell them what you're going to tell them; tell them; tell them what you've told them), use principles of adult learning, and reinforce key ideas both verbally and nonverbally.

DISCUSSION AND REVIEW

1. What is informative speaking?
2. What is the purpose of speaking to inform?
3. Describe the five types of informative speaking.
4. Explain how to organize each type of informative presentation.
5. What are three strategies to make your informative message clear?
6. Identify six strategies that can enhance interest in your informative talk.
7. What are four strategies that can make your presentation memorable?

PUTTING PRINCIPLES INTO PRACTICE

1. From the following list of suggested topics for an informative presentation, select five and develop a specific-purpose sentence for each. For one of those topics, identify two to four major ideas. Organize them topically, chronologically, or according to some other logical pattern of organization.

   How to get a better grade in your communication class

   The spread of terrorism in the world

   How the U.S. Constitution was written

   A historical person I wish I could meet

   What makes a good teacher

   The best way to lose weight

   How to buy a digital camera

   Surrogate parenthood

   Safe-driving principles

   How the stock market works

   Social Security

2. Replace each of the following words with a livelier one:

cat	work
airplane	light
house	eat
walk	study

3. Look up the origin of the following words in a comprehensive dictionary, such as the *Oxford English Dictionary* or the *Etymological Dictionary of Modern English*.

logic	teacher
pillow	dance
love	amateur
communication	disciple

4. Write a word picture—a vivid, colorful description that appeals to the senses—of one of the following scenes:

   Your first day learning how to drive

   Visiting your father or mother at work

   A holiday when you were six

   A visit to your grandparents' house

   Your first day at college

   Your most frightening experience

   Your most memorable birthday celebration

Chapter 4.4   *Practice Test*

MULTIPLE CHOICE. Choose the *best* answer to each of the following questions.

1. Linda is preparing a presentation on how to cook lasagna. Which of the following strategies will work best in capturing her audience's attention?

   a. Share an award-winning recipe from a local Italian restaurant.

   b. Show a video from Italy of chefs making lasagna.

   c. Find out ahead of time if any of her classmates have made lasagna and mention them by name during the presentation.

   d. Show pictures of baked lasagna from *Bon Appetite* magazine.

2. When using humor in a presentation, you should do all of the following *except*

   a. quote others' humorous sayings.

   b. make yourself the butt of your own jokes.

   c. not worry about making a point with humor—just use it to relax the audience.

   d. use visuals such as cartoons.

3. Asking your audience "How many of you are interested in doubling your income in one year?" helps to

   a. build redundancy in your message.

   b. reinforce your key ideas.

   c. establish a motive for the audience to listen to you.

   d. alienate a number of audience members.

4. Presentations about ideas are usually arranged in a _____ manner.

   a. causal

   b. topical

   c. chronological

   d. spatial

5. Which of the following is a good strategy when sharing something unfamiliar with the audience?

   a. Give them plenty of details about the new idea.

   b. Challenge them to find out more information about the new idea.

   c. Relate the new information to something they already know.

   d. Gloss over it quickly to get back to more familiar territory.

6. During an informative presentation, communication between you and the audience occurs when

   a. you prepare the presentation.

   b. you present the information to the audience.

   c. the audience makes sense of the information you give them.

   d. the presentation is over.

7. Christie gave a presentation on the Gateway Arch in St. Louis. Christie's presentation was about

   a. an object.

   b. a procedure.

   c. an event.

   d. an idea.

8. The selection and narrowing of your topic will be easier if you

   a. consider the needs and backgrounds of your audience.

   b. consider your knowledge of and experience with the topic.

   c. identify the type of presentation you will deliver.

   d. all of the above

9. Creating a word picture will do all of the following *except*

   a. be too abstract for most audiences.

   b. help to gain the audience's attention.

   c. appeal to the audience's senses.

   d. help the audience remember your message.

10. Adult listeners prefer all of the following *except*

   a. being observers, rather than active participants, in the learning process.

   b. knowing how the information relates to their busy lives.

   c. receiving information they can use immediately.

   d. connecting new information to their life experiences.

11. If you are speaking on a topic that is new or unfamiliar to your audience, you should

   a. put as much information as you can at the beginning of the presentation.

   b. maximize the amount of information throughout the presentation.

   c. use supporting material to control the flow of information throughout the presentation.

   d. wait until the end of the speech to give the audience as much information as you can.

12. According to the T-E-A-C-H acronym, the first step in teaching people a skill is to

   a. give them an opportunity to perform the skill.

   b. describe what it is you want them to know.

   c. provide positive encouragement.

   d. show them an example of how to perform the skill.

13. A presentation about the day John F. Kennedy was assassinated would more than likely be organized

   a. spatially.

   b. chronologically.

   c. topically.

   d. according to complexity.

14. When trying to create interest in your presentation, it is important to remember that

   a. most audiences are interested in what you are interested in.

   b. audiences are usually interested in a particular topic for just one reason.

   c. there are a number of reasons an audience may be interested in a given topic.

   d. you need to focus on connecting to your audience only at the beginning of the presentation.

15. When you are describing an abstract or complex idea to your audience, it is best to

   a. describe it first, then provide a model or picture as a summary.

   b. give them as many details as possible about the idea.

   c. cover it quickly, especially if the audience appears to be confused.

   d. provide a model or picture first, then describe the idea.

16. When giving a presentation about a person, you should give your audience the impression that the person is a _____ and _____ individual.

   a. trustworthy; competent

   b. distinguished; significant

   c. worthy; intelligent

   d. unique; authentic

17. *Hiss, tick, hum, whoosh,* and *gush* are all examples of _____ words.

   a. concrete

   b. onomatopoetic

   c. apoplectic

   d. metaphoric

18. Seonaid is giving a presentation on nanotechnology. Based on the principles of adult learning, she should

   a. focus on how nanotechnology will revolutionize medicine in the future.

   b. explain how nanotechnology is affecting the audience members' lives today.

   c. discuss the theories behind nanotechnology.

   d. review the key pioneers in the field of nanotechnology.

19. According to the principles of adult learning, which of the following techniques would help make your presentation more memorable?

   a. analogy

   b. onomatopoeia

   c. inversion

   d. humor

20. Tristan has a lot of information in his presentation that is new to his audience. He should arrange that information so that it is
    a. mostly in the first third of the body.
    b. mostly in the second third of the body.
    c. mostly in the last third of the body.
    d. spread evenly throughout the body.

TRUE/FALSE. Indicate whether the following statements are *true* or *false*.

1. T or F   When speaking informatively, it is best to use simple ideas rather than complex ones.
2. T or F   Your supportive material does *not* influence your audience's interest in your presentation.
3. T or F   Previewing, stating, and reviewing your main points makes your presentation more memorable.
4. T or F   A presentation about how to make cheese enchiladas is a presentation about an object.
5. T or F   A preacher's urging the members of his church to contribute to the new building fund is an example of an informative presentation.
6. T or F   Adult learners prefer to explore novel and abstract ideas for the sake of learning.
7. T or F   Including phrases such as "The main point of this all is that . . ." helps reinforce ideas for the audience.
8. T or F   To preserve credibility, effective speakers avoid being the butt of their own jokes.

9. T or F   Word pictures should appeal to as many senses as possible.
10. T or F   Presentations about procedures should typically be organized in a chronological fashion.

FILL IN THE BLANK. Complete the following statements.

1. A comparison between a known idea and an unknown idea is a(n) _____.
2. If your presentation describes how something works, it is a presentation about a(n) _____.
3. When you _____ an audience, you enhance their knowledge or understanding of something.
4. A presentation on the life of Rosa Parks or any other civil rights activist is a presentation about a(n) _____.
5. Phil gave a speech on "The Best Super Bowl Ever Played." His was a presentation about a(n) _____.
6. A _____ _____ describes something in vivid words.
7. Karen's presentation on artificial intelligence is more than likely a presentation about a(n) _____.
8. Asking an audience a direct question about their interest in your topic is one way of establishing a _____ for your audience to listen to you.
9. Presentations about _____ may focus on anything that is tangible—anything that can be seen or touched.
10. You build _____ into your presentation by telling the audience what you are going to tell them, telling them, and then telling them what you told them.

Speaking to Persuade

CHAPTER OUTLINE

CHAPTER OBJECTIVES

After studying this chapter, you should be able to

1. Define persuasion and describe four strategies for motivating listeners.

2. Define attitudes, beliefs, and values and explain why a speaker should know which one he or she is targeting in a persuasive message.

3. Define and provide examples of propositions of fact, value, and policy.

4. Define credibility; analyze its three factors; and describe how to enhance initial, derived, and terminal credibility.

5. Define and provide an example of inductive, deductive, and causal reasoning and reasoning by analogy.

6. List and explain eight logical fallacies.

7. Explain three ways to make emotional appeals in a persuasive presentation.

8. List and explain four ways to organize a persuasive message.

9. List and explain the five steps of the motivated sequence.

10. Provide specific suggestions for adapting to receptive audiences, neutral audiences, and unreceptive audiences.

Give me the right word and the right accent and I will move the world.

Joseph Conrad

Edouard Pignon, The Meeting. 1936. Oil on canvas. 130 × 95 cm. Inv.D.97-8-1; AM1997-142. Photo: R. G. Ojeda. Musee des Beaux-Arts, Lille, France. Photo credit: Reunion des Musées Nationaux/Art Resource, NY. © 2007 Artists Rights Society (ARS), New York/ADAGP, Paris.

From ancient times to the present, the skill of persuasion has been highly valued. Consider:

- In ancient Greece, citizens accused of crimes would spend a tidy sum to hire skilled orators to argue their cases before a judge in hopes of gaining their freedom; today, skilled trial lawyers are still well paid, both for their knowledge of the law and for their persuasive skill.
- During the Super Bowl, advertisers spend thousands of dollars per second on TV commercials to persuade you to buy their products.
- It is estimated that, during the 2004 U.S. presidential election, George W. Bush spent more than $345 million to persuade the citizens of the United States to vote for him.

But you don't have to be an attorney, an advertiser, or a politician to draw on the highly valued skill of persuasion. Whether you're asking your roommate to help you clean the kitchen, seeking an extension on your term paper, or trying to convince the school board not to raise taxes, you too will need to wield the power to persuade.

In 333 BC, Aristotle was among the first to write a comprehensive guide to persuasion. His work, *The Rhetoric*, was used by other Greek and Roman writers who sought to summarize principles and strategies of persuasion. The chapter you are reading draws on some of that more-than-2000-year-old classic advice and updates it with contemporary research. We first define persuasion, noting how it is similar to and different from informing others, and then describe how persuasion works by explaining how to motivate an audience. We'll also offer suggestions for developing a persuasive speech; present ideas to help you organize your persuasive message; and provide methods to help you move an audience with your credibility, use of logic, and use of emotional appeals. Finally, although we hope that all of the audiences you face are receptive to your persuasive speeches, we'll help you adapt your message not only to receptive audiences but also to those who are neutral or unreceptive.

Persuasion Defined

Persuasion is the process of attempting to change or reinforce attitudes, beliefs, values, or behavior. When we persuade, we are inviting someone to modify or maintain the way he or she thinks, feels, or behaves.

In the previous chapter, we described strategies for informing others—presenting new information so that others will understand and remember what is communicated. Because informative speaking and persuasive speaking are related, we will build on the suggestions we offered for informing others. Like an informative presentation, a persuasive presentation needs to be well organized; to have a clear beginning, middle, and end; to use interesting supporting mate-

Ethics and Communication

Hidden Agendas

David is trying to get business people to invest in the new Internet company he works for. He told a group of people at a Chamber of Commerce meeting that he wanted to inform them about some of the new and exciting ideas his company was developing. His real purpose, however, was to get people to invest in his company. Was it ethical of David not to tell his listeners that he really wanted them to become investors?

rial; to have smooth transitions; and to be skillfully delivered. As a persuasive speaker, you will need to develop arguments supported with evidence. But in a persuasive presentation, the speaker invites the listener to make an explicit choice, rather than just offering information about the options. Also, when you persuade, you will do more than teach; you will ask your audience to respond thoughtfully to the information you present. Persuasive speakers intentionally try to change or reinforce their listeners' feelings, ideas, or behavior.

Coercive communication, unlike persuasive communication, takes away an individual's free choice. In the opening pages of this book we suggested that an effective communicator not only is understood and achieves his or her goal, but also is ethical. **Using force to achieve your goal is coercion,** not persuasion. **Using weapons, threats, and other unethical strategies may momentarily achieve what you want, but it certainly is not appropriate or ethical to use such means.** Efforts to persuade should be grounded in giving people options rather than forcing them to respond in a certain way. To be ethical, the persuader has an obligation to be honest and forthright in crafting messages.

Now that you have an understanding of what persuasion is and isn't, you undoubtedly have questions about how to begin to develop a persuasive message. You start your preparation for a persuasive presentation as you begin preparing for any speech, by considering the needs, interests, and background of your audience. Ethically adapting to listeners is important in any communication situation, but is especially important when persuading others.

EXPLORE

The audience-centered model of public speaking, introduced in Chapter 4.1 and shown again in Figure 4.5.1, can help you design and deliver a persuasive presentation just as it can an informative one. Audience analysis is at the heart of the speech-making process; it affects every choice you make as a speaker. Before we talk about the nuts and bolts of developing a persuasive presentation, we'll describe the psychology of persuasion—what motivates an audience to respond to your persuasive appeal. Understanding how an audience is likely to respond to your message not only can help you to develop your

FIGURE 4.5.1
An Audience-Centered Model of the Presentational Speaking Process

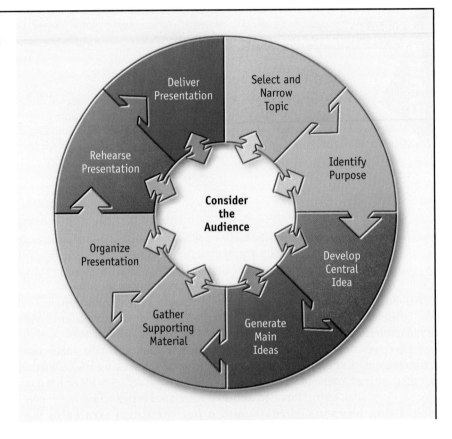

presentation but also can help you be a smarter consumer of persuasive messages that come your way.

Motivating Your Audience: The Psychology of Persuasion

How does persuasion work? What makes you dial the phone to have a piping hot cheese-and-pepperoni pizza delivered to your door after watching a television commercial for pizza? What motivates people to do things that they wouldn't do unless they were persuaded to do so? Let's look at four explanations of why people respond to efforts to persuade.

Motivating with Dissonance

When you are presented with information that is inconsistent with your current thinking or feelings, you experience a kind of mental

What can you do to motivate your audience to act in a certain way? You might try to create cognitive dissonance, appeal to their needs or fears, or promise a positive result if they follow your advice.

discomfort called cognitive dissonance. For example, if you frequently drive while you are drowsy and then you learn that drowsy driving is a major contributor to traffic accidents, dissonance theory predicts that you will experience cognitive dissonance. The incompatibility between your behavior and your new knowledge will make you feel uncomfortable. And your discomfort may prompt you to change your thoughts, likes or dislikes, feelings, or behavior so that you can restore your comfort level or sense of balance—in this case, by not driving when drowsy.

Skilled persuasive speakers know that creating dissonance and then offering their listeners a way to restore balance is an effective persuasive strategy. For example, Sean wants to persuade his listeners to take greater safety precautions in preparing food. He begins by focusing on the health threat posed by bacteria in even the cleanest kitchens:

Verbal

> Right now, as you sit and listen to me speak about kitchen bacteria, millions of them are probably reproducing in your kitchen, simply waiting for the perfect opportunity to join you for lunch.[1]

Sean is deliberately creating dissonance. He knows that his audience members value their health and that they have always assumed their kitchens to be relatively clean. His next task is to restore the audience's sense of balance. He assures them that solutions exist and that "they are simple and you can start them as early as today."[2] If the audience implements such simple actions as washing hands frequently, using paper towels, and washing sponges and dishcloths along with the dishes, then they can resolve their dissonance and once again feel secure about their kitchen safety. The need to resolve dissonance provides one explanation of why people may respond to a speaker's attempts to persuade.

Adapt

EXPLORE

Motivating with Needs

Need is one of the best motivators. When you go shopping for a new pair of shoes because the heel has come off your old pair, you are much more likely to buy shoes than is someone who is just browsing. As a speaker, the better you understand what your listeners need, the better you can adapt to them and the greater the chances that you can persuade them to change an attitude, belief, or value or get them to take some action.

The classic theory that outlines our basic needs was developed by Abraham Maslow.[3] If you've taken a psychology course, you have undoubtedly encountered this theory, which has important applications for persuasion. Maslow suggested that **a hierarchy of needs motivates the behavior of all people. Basic physiological needs (such as needs for food, water, and air) have to be satisfied before we attend to any other concern.** Once our physiological needs are met, we think next about safety needs. We need to feel safe and to be able to protect those we love. Comfortable and secure, we attend next to social needs, including the needs to be loved and to belong to a group. The next level of need is the need for self-esteem, or to think well of ourselves. Finally, if these first four levels of need have been satisfied, we may attend to the need for self-actualization, or achieving our highest potential. Figure 4.5.2 illustrates Maslow's classic five levels of needs, with the most basic at the bottom.

As a persuasive speaker, understanding and applying the hierarchy of needs helps you to adapt to your audience. One practical application is to do everything in your power to ensure that your audience's physiological needs are met. For example, if your listeners are sweating and fanning themselves, they are unlikely to be very interested in whether Bigfoot exists or whether the

FIGURE 4.5.2
Maslow's Hierarchy of Needs

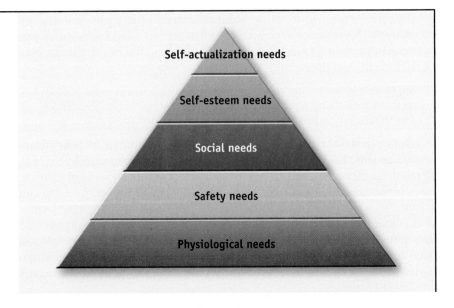

city should re-open River Park. If you can turn on the air-conditioning or fans, you will stand a greater chance to persuade them.

Another way in which you can apply the need hierarchy is to appeal to an audience's basic needs. For example, Mike knows that most of his audience members have young friends or family members who routinely ride school buses. As he begins to talk about the problem of safety hazards on school buses, he appeals to the audience's need to protect those they love. Similarly, at one time the U.S. Army used the recruiting slogan "Be all that you can be" to tap into the need for self-actualization, or achievement of one's highest potential.

Motivating with Fear Appeals

One of the oldest ways to convince people to change their minds or their behavior is by scaring them into compliance. Fear works. The appeal to fear takes the form of a verbal message—an "if-then" statement. *If* you don't do X, *then* awful things will happen to you. "If you don't get a flu shot, then you will probably catch the flu." "If you don't wear a seatbelt, then you are more likely to die in an automobile accident." "If you don't vote for me, then my opponent in this election will ruin the country." These are examples of fear appeals. A variety of research studies support the following strategies for effectively using fear as a motivator.[4]

Verbal

- *A strong threat to a family member or someone whom members of the audience care about will often be more successful than a fear appeal directed at the audience members themselves.*   Here's an example: "If your parents don't have a smoke alarm in their house, they are ten times more likely to die in a house fire."
- *The more respected the speaker, the greater the likelihood that the appeal to fear will work.*   If you're trying to motivate your audience with fear, you may not have the credibility to convince them that the threat will harm them, but you could use the opinion of someone who is highly believable, competent, and trustworthy. Quoting a doctor if you're talking about a health issue, or an award-winning teacher if you're talking about an education issue, will probably be more effective than just stating your own opinion when trying to motivate with fear.
- *Fear appeals are more successful if you convince your audience that the threat is real and will affect them unless they take action.*   In trying to convince her audience to eat less fat and exercise more, Doreen said, "An overly fatty diet coupled with lack of exercise is the primary cause of heart disease in the United States. Eat less fat and get more exercise, or you may die prematurely."
- *Increasing the intensity of a fear appeal increases the likelihood that the fear appeal will be effective; this is especially true if the listener can take the action the persuader is suggesting.*[5]   Research findings suggest that the more fear and anxiety produced by a message, the more likely it is that the listener will respond. Strong, credible fear appeals seem to work better than mild fear appeals if evidence exists to support the claim.

Fear appeals work based on the theory of cognitive dissonance and Maslow's need theory. The fear aroused creates dissonance. Taking action reduces the fear and can meet a need—such as to live a long life, to be safe from harm, to have good friends, or to have a fulfilling career.

Of course, you have an ethical responsibility not to overstate your case or fabricate evidence when using a fear appeal. The persuader always has an ethical responsibility to be truthful when trying to arouse fear in the listener.

Motivating with Positive Appeals

Verbal

From a political candidate's TV ad: "Vote for me and you'll have lower taxes and higher wages, and your children will be better educated." Does this politician's promise have a familiar ring to it? It sounds like what most politicians offer—better days ahead if you'll vote for the person you see on your TV screen. Politicians, salespeople, and most other successful persuaders know that one way to change or reinforce your attitudes, beliefs, values, or behavior is to use a positive motivational appeal. Positive motivational appeals are verbal messages promising that good things will happen if the speaker's advice is followed. The key to using positive motivational appeals is to know what your listeners value. Most Americans value a comfortable, prosperous life; stimulating, exciting activity; a sense of accomplishment; world, community, and personal peace; and overall happiness and contentment. In a persuasive presentation, you can motivate your listeners to respond to your message by describing what good, positive things will happen to them if they follow your advice.

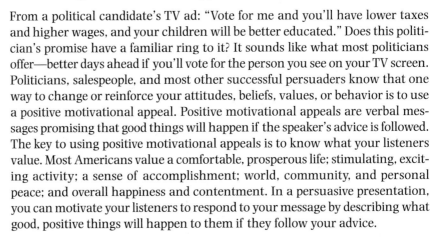

Selecting and Narrowing Your Persuasive Topic

Aware
Adapt

With a basic understanding of how persuasion works, we're ready to focus on the specifics of developing a persuasive talk. As with any presentation, after you've thought about your audience, the next step is to select and narrow your topic. In a communication class, you may be given some latitude in selecting your topic. The best persuasive topic is one about which you feel strongly. If your listeners sense that you are committed to and excited about your topic, the chances are greater that they will be interested and involved as well. In most nonclassroom persuasive-speaking situations, you probably won't be asked to pick a persuasive topic; your topic will stem from your personal convictions. When you have the flexibility of selecting your own topic, the principle of appropriately adapting messages to others can guide your choice. Know the local, state, national, and international issues that interest and affect your listeners. Should the city build a new power plant? Should convicted child molesters be permitted to live in any neighborhood they like? Should the United States drop economic sanctions against Cuba? These and other controversial issues make excellent persuasive speech topics. Avoid frivolous topics, such as "why you should make your own potholders," when so many important issues challenge the world and your listeners.

Pay particular attention to print and electronic media so that you remain informed about important issues of the day. Daily newspapers and national weekly news magazines such as *Time, Newsweek,* and *U.S. News & World Report* can suggest potential persuasive topics. Another interesting source of controversial issues is talk radio; both local and national programs can provide ideas for persuasive topics. Chat rooms on the Internet and home pages of print and broadcast media can also provide ideas for persuasive presentations.

After you have chosen a topic for your persuasive message, keeping up with the media can give you additional ideas for narrowing your topic and for finding interesting and appropriate supporting material for your presentation.

Verbal

QUICK REVIEW

Identifying Your Persuasive Purpose

Once you have a topic for your persuasive presentation, your next step is to identify both a general and a specific purpose. The general purpose is easy—to persuade. The specific purpose requires more thought. The way you word your specific purpose will help you focus your message. When your general purpose is to persuade, your specific purpose will target your audience's attitudes, beliefs, values, or behavior. You can, as you recall from our definition of persuasion, try to *reinforce* attitudes, beliefs, values, and behavior the audience already holds; or you can try to *change* their attitudes, beliefs, values, or behavior. Reinforcing what an audience already knows or thinks is relatively easy, but it is more of a challenge to change their minds. To increase your chances for success, it is important to be aware of the differences among attitudes, beliefs, and values and to know which one you are targeting in your specific purpose statement. Let's examine the terms *attitude, belief,* and *value* in more detail.

Aware

An attitude is a learned predisposition to respond favorably or unfavorably to something. In other words, attitudes represent likes and dislikes. Because many attitudes are formed quickly and often with little evidence, they are relatively susceptible to change if the person who holds them is exposed to additional evidence or gains more experience. For example, we may like a song we hear on the radio, then decide after we buy the single that we don't really like it so well after all. We may think that we don't like spinach, then discover that a friend's Florentine dip is delicious. As a persuasive speaker, you would probably have a good chance to succeed if your specific purpose targeted audience attitudes about the following issues:

- At the end of my presentation, the audience will favor making downtown streets one way to regulate traffic flow.
- At the end of my presentation, the audience will agree that the community needs a new elementary school.

A belief is the way in which we structure our perception of reality—our sense of what is true or false. Perhaps you believe that the earth is round, that God exists, and that your local bank is a financially sound institution. We base our beliefs on our own past experiences and on the experiences of other people. Beliefs are more difficult to alter than attitudes. If your audience were skeptical, you would need a great deal of evidence to succeed with these specific purpose statements:

- At the end of my presentation, the audience will testify that ghosts exist.
- At the end of my presentation, the audience will acknowledge that the increase in highway traffic deaths is related to the increase in the speed limit for large trucks.

A value is an enduring conception of right or wrong, good or bad. If you value something, you classify it as good or desirable and its opposite or its absence as bad or wrong. If you do not value something, you are indifferent to it. Values determine your behavior and goals. For example, because you value honesty, you refuse to cheat on a test. Because you value freedom, you support asylum for political refugees. Values are stable and deeply ingrained. Although it is not impossible to change the values of an audience, it is much more difficult than trying to change attitudes or beliefs. Political and religious points of view are especially difficult to modify. If you were speaking to a right-wing conservative Republican audience, you would find it difficult to achieve these specific purposes:

- At the end of my presentation, the audience will campaign for the Democratic ticket in the upcoming election.
- At the end of my presentation, the audience will support the right of art museums to show whatever kinds of art the museum directors deem appropriate.

Figure 4.5.3 illustrates that attitudes lie fairly close to the surface of our convictions, with values the most deeply ingrained in the center of the model. Be aware of whether your specific purpose aims to change or reinforce an attitude, a belief, a value, or a behavior, and be realistic in assessing what you will need to do in your presentation to effect change.

Developing Your Central Idea as a Persuasive Proposition

Verbal

After clarifying their specific purpose, most persuasive speakers find it useful to cast their central idea as **a proposition, or statement with which they want their audience to agree.** A well-worded proposition is a verbal message that can help you further fine-tune your persuasive objective and develop strategies for convincing your audience that your proposition is true. There are

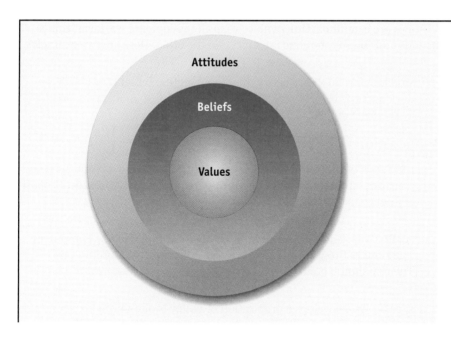

FIGURE 4.5.3
Comparing Attitudes, Beliefs, and Values
Attitudes—our likes and dislikes—are more likely to change than are our beliefs or values. Our sense of what is right and wrong—our values—are least likely to change.

three categories of propositions: propositions of fact, propositions of value, and propositions of policy. Let's examine each of these types in more detail.

Propositions of Fact

Propositions of fact are claims that something is or is not the case or that something did or did not happen. A speaker who used a proposition of fact as the central idea of a persuasive presentation would focus on changing or reinforcing an audience's beliefs—what they think is true. Propositions of fact can become central ideas for persuasive speeches. Here are some examples:

> U.S. foreign embassies and consulates are vulnerable to terrorist attacks.
> Nuclear power plants are safe and efficient.
> People who were abused by their parents are more likely to abuse their own children.

A speech based on one of these propositions would need to include credible evidence to support the accuracy of the conclusion.

Propositions of Value

As the word *value* suggests, **propositions of value call for the listener to judge the worth or importance of something.** A simple example would be

"Tattoos are beautiful." Other value propositions compare two ideas, things, or actions and suggest that one is better than the other. Here are two examples:

> Small high schools are better than large high schools.
> Rock music is better than classical music.

Propositions of Policy

The third type of proposition, **the proposition of policy, advocates a specific action—changing a regulation, procedure, or behavior.** Propositions of policy include the word *should*. Here are some examples:

> All first-year college students should have their own laptop computers.
> The Honors Program should have a full-time faculty coordinator.
> The city should build a new public library.

The speaker who develops a proposition of policy is often likely to go one step beyond influencing an audience's attitudes, beliefs, and values, and urge them to take action.

With your specific purpose and central idea in hand, you are ready to move to the next stages in the presentational speaking process. In most cases, you can draw your main ideas from several *reasons* the persuasive proposition is true. Then you will be ready to begin gathering supporting material.

RECAP

Persuasive Propositions

Type of Proposition	Definition	Example
Proposition of Fact	A claim that something is or is not the case or that it did or did not happen	Asbestos exists in our elementary school.
Proposition of Value	A claim that calls for the listener to judge the worth or importance of something	Using calculators for elementary math is a good idea.
Proposition of Policy	A claim advocating a specific action to change a policy, procedure, or behavior	Casino gambling should be legalized in all states.

QUICK
REVIEW

Supporting Your Presentation with Credibility, Logic, and Emotion

Aristotle defined *rhetoric* as the process of "discovering the available means of persuasion."[6] What are those "available means"? They are the various strategies you can use to support your message. Aristotle suggested three: (1) **emphasizing the credibility or ethical character of a speaker (ethos);** (2) **using logical arguments (logos);** and (3) **using emotional appeals to move an audience (pathos).**

Ethos: Establishing Your Credibility

If you were going to buy a new computer, to whom would you turn for advice? Perhaps you would consult your brother, the computer geek, or your roommate, the computer science major. Or you might seek advice from *Consumer Reports*, the monthly publication of studies of various consumer products. In other words, you would turn to a source that you consider knowledgeable, competent, and trustworthy—a source you think is credible.

Credibility **is an audience's perception of a speaker's competence, trustworthiness, and dynamism.** It is not something a speaker inherently possesses or lacks; rather, it is based on the listeners' attitude toward the speaker. Your listeners, not you, determine whether you have credibility.

Teachers and researchers have for centuries sought to understand the factors audiences consider in deciding whether a speaker is credible. Aristotle thought that a public speaker should be ethical, possess good character, display common sense, and be concerned for the well-being of his audience. Quintilian, a Roman teacher of public speaking, advised that a speaker should be "a good man speaking well." These ancient speculations about the elements that enhance a speaker's credibility have been generally supported by modern research.

One clear factor in credibility is **competence. A speaker should be informed, skilled, or knowledgeable about the subject he or she is discussing.** You will be more persuasive if you can convince your listeners that you know something about your topic. How? You can use verbal messages effectively by talking about relevant personal experience with the topic. If you have taken and enjoyed a cruise, you can tell your audience about the highlights of your trip. You can also cite evidence to support your ideas. Even if you have not taken a cruise yourself, you can be prepared with information about what a good value a cruise is—how much it costs and what is included, versus how much the same tour would cost if one were to travel by air and stay and eat in hotels.

A second factor in credibility is **trustworthiness. While delivering a speech, you need to convey honesty and sincerity to your audience.** You can't do this simply by saying, "Trust me." You have to earn trust. You can do so by demonstrating that you are interested in and experienced with your

Bono uses his charismatic speaking style to help persuade his audience to support his cause.

topic. Again, speaking from personal experience makes you seem a more trustworthy speaker. Conversely, having something to gain by persuading your audience may make you suspect in their eyes. That's why salespeople and politicians often lack credibility. If you do what they say, they will clearly benefit by earning sales commissions or being elected to public office.

A third factor in credibility is a speaker's **dynamism, or energy.** Dynamism is often projected through delivery. Applying the communication principle of effectively using and understanding nonverbal messages, a speaker who maintains eye contact, has enthusiastic vocal inflection, and moves and gestures purposefully is likely to be seen as dynamic. **Charisma is a form of dynamism. A charismatic speaker possesses charm, talent, magnetism, and other qualities that make the person attractive and energetic.** President Franklin Roosevelt and Diana, Princess of Wales, were considered charismatic speakers by many people.

Nonverbal

A speaker has opportunities throughout a presentation to enhance his or her credibility. The first such opportunity results in **initial credibility. This is the impression of your credibility listeners have even before you begin speaking.** They grant you initial credibility based on such factors as your appearance and your credentials. Dressing appropriately and having a brief summary of your qualifications and accomplishments ready for the person who will introduce you are two strategies for enhancing your initial credibility.

Adapt

The second credibility-building opportunity yields **derived credibility. This is the perception your audience forms as you deliver your presentation.** If you appropriately adapt your message to your audience, you will enhance your derived credibility. Specific strategies include establishing common ground with your audience, supporting your arguments with evidence, and presenting a well-organized message.

Diversity and *Communication*

"Elementary Reasoning, My Dear Watson"

Although we often use the word *diversity* to refer to readily discernible differences in sex, race, culture, and age, *diversity* can also refer to differences in perspective or point of view. As the following narrative shows, people may draw different conclusions from the same evidence.

Sherlock Holmes and Dr. Watson went on a camping trip. After a good meal and a bottle of wine, they lay down for the night and went to sleep. Some hours later, Holmes awoke and nudged his faithful friend.

"Watson, look up at the sky and tell me what you see."

Watson replied, "I see millions and millions of stars."

"What does that tell you?" inquired Holmes.

Watson pondered for a minute. "Astronomically, it tells me that there are millions of galaxies and potentially billions of planets. Astrologically, I observe that Saturn is in Leo. Horologically, I deduce that the time is approximately a quarter past three. Theologically, I can see that God is all powerful and that we are small and insignificant. Meteorologically, I suspect that we will have a beautiful day tomorrow. What does it tell you?"

Holmes was silent for a minute, then spoke. "Watson, you idiot! Someone has stolen our tent!"

The last form of credibility, called **terminal credibility, is the perception of your credibility your listeners have when you finish your presentation.** A thoughtfully prepared and well-delivered conclusion can enhance your terminal credibility, as can maintaining eye contact through and even after your closing sentence. Also, apply the communication principle of listening and responding thoughtfully to others. Be prepared to answer questions after your presentation, regardless of whether a question-and-answer period is planned.

Verbal
Nonverbal
Listen and Respond

RECAP

Enhancing Your Credibility

Enhancing Your Initial Credibility: Before You Speak

- Dress appropriately.
- Have a brief summary of your qualifications and accomplishments ready for the person who will introduce you.

Enhancing Your Derived Credibility: As You Speak

- Establish common ground with your audience.
- Support your arguments with evidence.
- Present a well-organized message.

Enhancing Your Terminal Credibility: After You Speak

- Prepare your conclusion, and deliver it well.
- Maintain eye contact through and even after your closing sentence.
- Be prepared to answer questions after your presentation.

Logos: Using Evidence and Reasoning

In addition to being considered a credible speaker, you will gain influence with your audience if you can effectively use logically structured arguments supported with evidence. As we noted earlier, Aristotle called logical arguments *logos*, which, translated from Greek, means "the word." Using words effectively to communicate your arguments to your listeners is vital to persuading thoughtful and informed listeners. The goal is to provide logical proof for your arguments. **Proof consists of both evidence and reasoning. Evidence is another word for the illustrations, definitions, statistics, and opinions that are your supporting material. Reasoning is the process of drawing conclusions from your evidence.** There are three major ways to draw logical conclusions: inductively, deductively, and causally.

Verbal

Inductive Reasoning   **Reasoning that arrives at a general conclusion from specific instances or examples is known as inductive reasoning.** You reason inductively when you claim that a conclusion is probably true because of specific evidence. For example, if you were giving a speech attempting to convince your audience that Hondas are reliable cars, you might use inductive reasoning to make your point. You have a 1994 Honda Civic that has 140,000 miles on it and has required little repair other than routine maintenance. Your brother has a Honda Accord and has driven it twice as long as any other car he has ever owned. Your mom just returned from a 3000-mile road trip in her Honda Odyssey minivan, which performed beautifully. Based on these specific examples, bolstered by statistics from many other Honda owners, you ask your audience to agree that your general conclusion is probable: Hondas are reliable cars.

Reasoning by analogy is a special type of inductive reasoning. An analogy demonstrates how an unfamiliar idea, thing, or situation is similar to something the audience already understands. If you develop an original analogy, rather than quote one you find in a printed source, you are reasoning inductively. Here's an example of reasoning by analogy: The new mandatory rear seatbelt laws that were enacted in Missouri saved lives; Kansas should also develop mandatory rear seatbelt laws. The key to arguing by analogy is to claim that the two things you are comparing (such as driving habits in Missouri and Kansas) are similar, so that your argument is a sound one. Here's another example: England has a relaxed policy toward violence being shown on television and has experienced no major

Holocaust survivor, author, and human rights activist Elie Wiesel uses the rhetorical devices of evidence and reasoning to appeal to his audiences.

rise in violent crimes; the United States should therefore relax its policy on showing violence on TV.

Deductive Reasoning   **Reasoning from a general statement or principle to reach a specific conclusion is called deductive reasoning.** Deductive reasoning can be structured as **a syllogism, a three-part argument that consists of a major premise, a minor premise, and a conclusion.** In a message in which you are attempting to convince your audience to vote for an upcoming school bond issue, your syllogism might look like this:

MAJOR PREMISE: Keeping schools in good repair extends the number of years that the buildings can be used.

MINOR PREMISE: The proposed school bond issue provides money for school repairs.

CONCLUSION: The proposed school bond issue will extend the number of years that we can use our current buildings.

Contemporary logicians note that when you reason deductively, your conclusion is certain rather than probable. The certainty of the conclusion rests primarily on the validity of the major premise and secondarily on the truth of the minor premise. If you can prove that keeping schools in good repair extends the useful life of the buildings and if it is true that the proposed bond issue provides money for school repairs, then your conclusion will be certain.

Causal Reasoning   **You use causal reasoning when you relate two or more events in such a way as to conclude that one or more of the events probably caused the others.** For example, you might argue that public inoculation programs during the twentieth century eradicated smallpox.

As we noted when we discussed cause-and-effect as a persuasive organizational strategy, there are two ways to structure a causal argument. One is by reasoning from cause to effect, or predicting a result from a known fact. You know that you have had an inch of rain over the last few days, so you predict that the aquifer level will rise. The inch of rain is the cause; the rising aquifer is the effect. The other way to structure a causal argument is by reasoning from a known effect to the cause. National Transportation Safety Board accident investigators reason from effect to cause when they reconstruct airplane wreckage to find clues to the cause of an air disaster.

The key to developing any causal argument is to be certain that a causal relationship actually exists between the two factors you are investigating. A few summers ago, a young science student was involved in a project involving counting chimney swifts in a given area just before sunset. He counted the most swifts on the Fourth of July. However, it would not have been valid to argue that fireworks (or watermelon or hot dogs or anything else connected with the Fourth of July) caused an increase in the number of chimney swifts seen in the area. The Fourth of July holiday and the bird count were not related by cause and effect.

Inductive, Deductive, and Causal Reasoning

Type of Reasoning	Reasoning begins with . . .	Reasoning ends with . . .	Conclusion is . . .	Example
Inductive	specific examples	a general conclusion	probable or not probable	Dell, Gateway, and IBM computers are all reliable. Therefore, PCs are reliable.
Deductive	a general statement	a specific conclusion	certain or not certain	All professors at this college have advanced degrees. Tom Bryson is a professor at this college. Therefore, Tom Bryson has an advanced degree.
Causal	something known	a speculation about causes or effects of what is known	likely or not likely	The number of people with undergraduate degrees has risen steadily since 1960. This increasing number has caused a glut in the job market for people with degrees.

Aware

Trying to establish a causal link where none exists is one type of **logical fallacy—false reasoning that occurs when someone attempts to persuade without adequate evidence or with arguments that are irrelevant or inappropriate.** To be a better-informed consumer, as well as a more ethical persuasive speaker, you should be aware of some of the following common logical fallacies.

Causal Fallacy   **Making a faulty cause-and-effect connection between two things or events,** such as trying to link the Fourth of July with the chimney swift count, is **a causal fallacy,** or, to use its Latin name, *post hoc, ergo propter hoc* ("after this; therefore, because of this"). Simply because one event follows another does not mean that the two are related.

Bandwagon Fallacy   "Jumping on the bandwagon" is a colloquial expression for thinking or doing something just because everybody else is. **Someone who argues that "everybody thinks that, so you should too" is using the bandwagon fallacy.** Speakers using the bandwagon fallacy often use the word *everybody:*

> Everybody knows that taxes are too high.
> Everybody agrees that the government should support a strong military.

Either-Or Fallacy   "Either we support the bond issue or we end up busing our students to another school district!" shouts Lupe in a moment of heated debate among the members of the school board. **This either-or fallacy oversimplifies the issue by offering only two choices and ignores the fact that there may be other solutions** to the district's problem of dilapidated buildings (for example, purchasing portable classroom buildings or drawing new attendance zones within the district).

Hasty Generalization   **A person who tries to draw a conclusion from too little evidence or nonexistent evidence is making a hasty generalization.** For example, one person's failing a math test does not necessarily mean that the test was too difficult or unfair.

Personal Attack   **Making a personal attack on someone connected with an idea, rather than addressing the idea itself, is a logical fallacy.** This approach is also known as an *ad hominem* argument, a Latin phrase that means "to the man." "The HMO bill is a bad idea because it was proposed by that crazy senator" is an example of a personal attack. Don't dismiss an idea solely because you have something against the person who presents it.

Red Herring   **Someone who argues against an issue by bringing up irrelevant facts or arguments to distract others from the issue is using a red herring.** This fallacy takes its name from the old trick of dragging a red herring across a trail to distract dogs who are following a scent. Speakers use a red herring when they want to distract an audience from certain issues. For example, a congressional representative who has been indicted for misuse of federal funds calls a press conference and spends most of the time talking about a colleague's sexual indiscretions.

Appeal to Misplaced Authority   When advertisers trot out baseball players to endorse breakfast cereal and movie stars to pitch credit cards, they are guilty of an **appeal to misplaced authority—using someone without the**

appropriate credentials or expertise to endorse an idea or product.
Although baseball players may know a great deal about the game of baseball,
they are no more expert than most of us about cereal. Movie stars may be
experts at acting but probably not in the field of personal finance.

Non Sequitur   If you argue that students should give blood because it is
nearly time for final exams, you are guilty of **a non sequitur** (Latin for "it
does not follow")—**your idea or conclusion does not logically follow from
the previous idea or conclusion.**

Persuasive speakers who provide logical proof (evidence and reasoning)
for their arguments and who avoid logical fallacies heighten their chances for
success with their audience. But good speakers know that evidence and reasoning are not their only tools. Emotion is another powerful strategy for moving
an audience to support a persuasive proposition.

Pathos: Using Emotion

People often make decisions based not on logic but on emotion. Advertisers
know this. Think of the soft-drink commercials you see on television. There is
little rational reason that people should spend any part of their food budget on
soft drinks. They are "empty calories." So soft-drink advertisers turn instead
to emotional appeals, striving to connect feelings of pleasure with their product. Smiling people, upbeat music, and good times are usually part of the for-
mula for selling soft drinks.

Verbal

One way to make an emotional appeal is with emotion-arousing verbal
messages. Words such as *mother, flag, freedom*, and *slavery* trigger emotional
responses in listeners. Patriotic slogans, such as "Remember the Alamo" and
"Give me liberty, or give me death," are examples of phrases that have successfully aroused emotions in their listeners.

Another way to appeal to emotions is by using concrete illustrations and
descriptions. Although illustrations and descriptions are themselves types of
evidence or supporting material, their impact is often emotional, as in the following example:

> Michelle Hutchinson carefully placed her three-year-old daughter into her
> child safety seat. She was certain that Dana was secure. Within minutes
> Michelle was involved in a minor accident, and the seat belt that was never
> designed to hold a child safety seat allowed the seat to lunge forward, crush-
> ing the three-year-old's skull on the dash. Dana died three days later. . . . [7]

Nonverbal

Effective use of nonverbal messages can also appeal to an audience's emotions. Visual aids—pictures, slides, or video—can provide emotion-arousing
images. A photograph of a dirty, ragged child alone in a big city can evoke sad-
ness and pain. A video clip of an airplane crash can arouse fear and horror. A
picture of a smiling baby makes most of us smile, too. As a speaker, you can use
visual aids to evoke both positive and negative emotions.

When you use emotional appeals, you do have an obligation to be ethical
and forthright. Making false claims, misusing evidence or images, or relying

exclusively on emotion without any evidence or reasoning violates standards of ethical presentational speaking.

RECAP

Tips for Using Emotion to Persuade

- Use emotion-arousing words.
- Use concrete illustrations and descriptions to create emotional images.
- Use visual aids to evoke both positive and negative emotions.
- Be ethical and forthright. Avoid making false claims, misusing evidence or images, or relying exclusively on emotion.

QUICK REVIEW

Organizing Your Persuasive Message

WATCH

You already know that how you organize a presentation can have an impact on your listeners' response to your message. Some speakers gather stories, examples, facts, and statistics to achieve their persuasive goal and then develop an organizational structure for these materials. Other speakers organize the presentation first and then collect supporting material. In reality, the organization of your presentation usually emerges after you have done at least some initial research and thinking about both your message and your audience. An audience-centered speaker adapts the organizational structure of the presentation based on the needs, attitudes, beliefs, behaviors, and background of the audience. Most persuasive presentations are organized according to one of four strategies: problem and solution, cause and effect, refutation, or the motivated sequence—a special variation of the problem-and-solution format.

Adapt

Problem and Solution

Problem-and-solution organization is the most basic organizational pattern for a persuasive presentation. The problem-and-solution strategy works best when a problem can be clearly documented and a solution or solutions proposed to deal with the evils of the problem.

When you use problem-and-solution organization, apply the principle of appropriately adapting messages to others. If you are speaking to an apathetic audience or one that is not even aware that a problem exists, you can emphasize the problem portion of the message. If your audience is already aware of the problem, you can emphasize the solution or solutions. In either case, your challenge will be to provide ample evidence that your perception of the problem is accurate and reasonable. You'll also need to convince your listeners that

Adapt

the solution or solutions you advocate are the most appropriate ones to solve the problem.

Note how Nicholas organizes his presentation, "The Death of Reading," in a problem-and-solution pattern:[8]

I. PROBLEM: Reading is a dying activity.
   A. Each year more than 500 courts hear arguments to ban books.
   B. Since 1990, more than 2000 libraries across America have closed.
   C. Leisure reading has decreased more than 50% since 1975.

II. SOLUTIONS:
   A. Teach children that reading as an activity has worth and beauty.
   B. Teach children that books in and of themselves only express ideas and should not be banned.
   C. Support programs such as "One City, One Book" that encourage community involvement and literary discussion.
   D. Give books as gifts.
   E. Allow others to see you read.

The persuasive presentation at the end of this chapter offers an example of a message organized by first stating the problem and then presenting some specific solutions.

Cause and Effect

Aware

A speaker who employs **cause-and-effect organization can either identify a situation and then discuss the resulting effects (cause–effect) or present a situation and then explore its causes (effect–cause).**

Regardless of which variation you choose, you should apply the fundamental principle of being aware of your communication with yourself and others. Specifically, you must analyze and then convince your listeners of the critical causal link. An effect may have more than one cause. For example, standardized test scores may be low in your state both because of low per-pupil expenditures and because of a lack of parental involvement in the schools. To argue that only one of the two factors causes the low test scores would not be accurate. It is also possible for two situations to coexist but not be causally related. Perhaps standardized test scores are indeed low in your state, and your state has a lottery. Both situations exist, but one does not cause the other. However, if two or more situations are causally related, a cause-and-effect strategy can work well for a persuasive presentation. Here is an example of a persuasive outline organized from cause to effect:[9]

I. CAUSE: The foster care system is in crisis.
   A. Since 1987, there has been a 90% increase in the number of children placed in foster care nationally.
   B. During that same time, there has been a 3% decrease in the number of licensed foster homes.

II. EFFECT: Children in foster care are at risk.

A. Children in the foster care system are five times more likely to die as a result of abuse than children in the general population.
B. 80% of federal prisoners spent time in the nation's foster care system as children.

Refutation

A third way to organize your efforts to persuade an audience is especially useful when you are facing an unreceptive audience—one that does not agree with your point of view or your specific proposition. **Refutation is an organizational strategy by which you identify objections to your proposition and then refute those objections with arguments and evidence.** You will be most likely to organize your persuasive message by refutation if you know your listeners' chief objections to your proposition. In fact, if you do not acknowledge such objections, the audience will probably think about them during your presentation anyway. Credible facts and statistics will generally be more effective than emotional arguments in supporting your points of refutation.

Suppose, for example, that you plan to speak to a group of junior high school teachers, advocating a school reconfiguration that would eliminate the junior high and send the teachers either to middle school or to high school. They would undoubtedly have some concerns about their own welfare and that of their students, as well as issues of loyalty to their present administrators. You could organize your presentation to this group according to those three issues. Your major points could be as follows:

I. The school reconfiguration will not jeopardize any of your jobs or programs.
II. The school reconfiguration will actually benefit students by requiring fewer changes in schools during their critical pre-adolescent years.
III. Principals and lead teachers will be reassigned at their same levels in the schools to which they will move.

Utilizing refutation as your organizational strategy is one way to adapt your message to your audience.

Adapt

The Motivated Sequence

The **motivated sequence,** devised by Alan Monroe, **is a five-step organizational plan that integrates the problem-and-solution organizational method with principles that have been confirmed by research and practical experience.**[10] **The five steps involved are attention, need, satisfaction, visualization, and action.**

Attention   Your first task in applying the motivated sequence, and the first stage in appropriately adapting your message to others, is to get your listeners' attention. You already know attention-getting strategies for introductions: rhetorical questions, illustrations, startling facts or statistics, quotations,

Adapt

humorous stories, and references to historical or recent events. The attention step is, in essence, your application of one of these strategies.

Sherry begins her presentation about reforming sex offender registries with this attention-catching illustration:

> Maureen Kanka felt her neighborhood was like any other. She never knew danger lurked across the street from her house until her 7-year-old daughter, Megan, disappeared. Megan's body was later found dumped in a nearby park. A puppy had been used to lure Megan into a neighbor's house where she was raped, strangled, and suffocated.[11]

Need   After getting your audience's attention, establish why your topic, problem, or issue should concern your listeners. Tell your audience about the problem. Adapt your message to them by convincing them that the problem affects them directly. Argue that there is a need for change. During the need step (which corresponds to the problem step in a problem-and-solution strategy), you should develop logical arguments backed by evidence. It's during the need step that you create dissonance or use a credible fear appeal to motivate listeners to respond to your solution. Sherry develops her need step as follows:

> State and local authorities are dismally failing to keep track of convicted child molesters, meaning that thousands of perpetrators like Megan's killer are unidentified, putting millions of children at risk. Problems in sex offender registries are allowing thousands of sexual predators to roam unchecked.[12]

Satisfaction   After you explain and document a need or problem, identify your plan (or solution) and explain how it will satisfy the need. You need not go into painstaking detail. Present enough information so that your listeners have a general understanding of how the problem may be solved. Sherry suggests two legislative solutions in her satisfaction step:

> At the government level, federal coordination is a must. A truly national registry needs to be created. However, a national registry alone will not fix the problem. Thus, a second piece of legislation should put coded notations onto sex offenders' driver's licenses and require the licenses to be presented for annual routine automobile registration. Furthermore, license bureaus would be required to contact police when offenders change addresses.[13]

Verbal

Visualization   Now you need to give your audience a sense of what it would be like if your solution were adopted or, conversely, if it were not adopted. **Visualization—a word picture of the future—**applies the fundamental principle of effectively using and understanding verbal messages. An appropriate presentation aid can also help your audience visualize the implications of your persuasive message. **With a positive visualization approach, you paint a rosy picture of how wonderful the future will be if your satisfaction step is implemented. With a negative visualization approach, you paint a bleak picture of how terrible the future will be if nothing is done; you use a fear appeal to motivate your listeners to do what you suggest to avoid further problems.** Or you might combine both approaches:

The problem will be solved if your solution is adopted, but things will get increasingly worse if it is not. An ethical speaker takes care to ensure that the positive or negative visualization message is accurate and not overstated. Sherry offers negative visualization to drive home the urgency of her message:

> It is too late to save Megan Kanka. Her parents will never again be met by the joy of her smile and the contributions she could have made to our society will never be fulfilled.[14]

Action   The final step of the motivated sequence requires that you adapt your solution to your audience. Offer them some specific action they can take to solve the problem you have discussed. Identify exactly what you want them to do. Give them simple, clear, easy-to-follow steps. Provide a phone number to call for more information, an address to which they can

In the final step of Monroe's motivated sequence, the speaker calls for the audience to take action.

write a letter of support, or a petition to sign at the end of your presentation. Sherry suggests a specific action step her listeners can take to solve the problem she has identified:

> On a personal level, we can help police follow up on offenders missing from the registry by being on guard and watching for signs of abuse among children in our families and neighborhoods.[15]

Adapt

The action step is your conclusion. You remind your audience of the problem (need step), give them the solution (satisfaction step), and remind them what great things will happen if they follow your advice (positive visualization) or what bad things will happen if they don't do what you say (negative visualization). Finally, unless they are unreceptive to your ideas, tell them what they need to do next (action step).

You can adapt the motivated sequence to your topic and the needs of your audience. For example, if you are speaking to a knowledgeable, receptive audience, you do not need to spend a great deal of time on the need step. Your listeners already know that the need is serious. They may, however, feel helpless to do anything about it. Clearly, you would want to emphasize the satisfaction and action steps.

Adapt

On the other hand, if you are speaking to a neutral or apathetic audience, you will need to spend time getting their attention and proving that a problem exists, that it is significant, and that it affects them personally. You will emphasize the attention, need, and visualization steps. In the final section of this chapter, we will offer additional strategies for persuading receptive, unreceptive, and neutral audiences.

Is there one best way to organize a persuasive message? The answer is no. The organizational strategy you select must depend on your audience, your

RECAP

Organizational Patterns for Persuasive Presentations

Organizational Pattern	Definition	Example
Problem and Solution	Organization by discussing a problem and then its various solutions	I. Tooth decay threatens children's dental health. II. Inexpensive, easy to apply sealants make teeth resistant to decay.
Cause and Effect	Organization by discussing a situation and its causes or a situation and its effects	I. Most HMOs refuse to pay for treatment they deem "experimental." II. Patients die who might have been saved by "experimental" treatment.
Refutation	Organization according to objections your listeners may have to your ideas and arguments	I. Although you may think that college football players get too much financial aid, they work hard for it, spending 20 to 30 hours a week in training and on the field. II. Although you may think that college football players don't spend much time on academics, they have 2 hours of enforced study every weeknight.
Motivated Sequence	Alan H. Monroe's five-step plan for organizing a persuasive message; the five steps are attention, need, satisfaction, visualization, and action	I. Attention: "An apple a day keeps the doctor busy." What has happened to the old adage? Why has it changed? II. Need: Pesticides are poisoning our fresh fruits and vegetables. III. Satisfaction: Growers must seek environmentally friendly alternatives to pesticides. IV. Visualization: Remember the apple poisoned by Snow White's wicked stepmother? You may be feeding such apples to your own children. V. Action: Buy fruits and vegetables raised organically.

Technology *and* *Communication*

The Motivated Sequence in Television Advertising

Strategies for organizing persuasive messages are used not just by presentational speakers but also by advertisers. Many 60-second television commercials persuade at least in part through utilizing the motivated sequence.

The next time you are watching television, pay particular attention to the commercials. How does a commercial get your attention? How does the advertiser establish a need for the product? What product is being sold? (With some contemporary advertising, the answer to that question is more difficult to discern than you might expect!) What does the commercial suggest will happen if you buy and use the product? If you don't? And what action does the advertiser advise you to take? For example, does the commercial suggest where you can go to get the product?

message, and your desired objective. What is important is that you remember that your decision can have a major effect on your listeners' response to your message.

QUICK REVIEW

How to Adapt Ideas to People and People to Ideas

Donald C. Bryant's definition of rhetoric emphasizes the principle of appropriately adapting a message to an audience: "Rhetoric" he said, "is the process of adjusting ideas to people and people to ideas."[16] And with this thought we've come full circle in the process of developing a persuasive message. As we have emphasized throughout our discussion of presentational speaking, analyzing your audience and adapting to them is at the heart of the speech-making process; it's one of the fundamental communication principles for a lifetime. In a persuasive presentation, that adaptation begins with identifying your specific purpose and understanding whether you are trying to change or reinforce attitudes, beliefs, values, or behavior. It continues with your selection of an organizational strategy. For example, if your audience members are unreceptive toward your ideas, you might choose to organize your speech by refutation, addressing the audience's objections head on. Both research studies and experienced speakers can offer other useful suggestions to help you adapt to your audience. Let's look at some specific strategies for persuading receptive, neutral, and unreceptive audiences.

The Receptive Audience

It is usually a pleasure to address an audience that already supports you and your message. You can explore your ideas in depth and can be fairly certain of a successful appeal to action if your audience is receptive.

One suggestion that may help you make the most of such a speaking opportunity is to identify with your audience. Emphasize your similarities and common interests. The introduction of your message may be a good place in which to do this.

Another suggestion is to be overt in stating your speaking objective, telling your audience exactly what you want them to do, and asking audience members for an immediate show of support. If your audience is already receptive, you need not worry that being overt will antagonize them. Rather, it will give you more time to rouse them to passionate commitment and action.

Adapt

A third suggestion for persuading a receptive audience is to use emotional appeals. If your audience already supports your position, you can spend less time providing detailed evidence. Rather, you can focus on moving your receptive audience to action with strong emotional appeals.

The Neutral Audience

Many audiences will fall somewhere between being wildly enthusiastic and being hostile. They will simply be neutral. Their neutrality may take the form of indifference: They know about the topic or issue, but they don't see how it affects them or they can't make up their minds about it. Or their neutrality may take the form of ignorance: They just don't know much about the topic. Regardless of whether your neutral audience is indifferent or ignorant, your challenge is to get them interested in your message.

One way to get a neutral audience interested is to "hook" them with an especially engaging introduction or attention step. Brian provided such an introduction to his persuasive presentation about the number of Americans who live with chronic pain:

> "I can't shower because the water feels like molten lava. Every time someone turns on a ceiling fan, it feels like razor blades are cutting through my legs. I'm dying." Meet David Bogan, financial advisor from Deptford, New Jersey; Porsche, boat, and homeowner; and a victim of a debilitating car accident that has not only rendered him two years of chronic leg pain, but a fall from the pinnacle of success. Bogan has nothing now. Life to him, life with searing pain, is a worthless tease of agony and distress.[17]

Another strategy for persuading neutral audiences is to refer to universal beliefs or common concerns. Protecting the environment and having access to good health care might fall in the latter category.

A third strategy for neutral audiences is to show how the topic affects not only them but also people they care about. For example, parents will be interested in issues and policies that affect their children.

Finally, be realistic about what you can accomplish. People who are neutral at the beginning of your presentation are unlikely to change in just a few minutes to having strong opinions. Persuasion is unlikely to occur all at once or after one presentation of arguments and issues.

The Unreceptive Audience

One of your biggest challenges as a speaker is to persuade audience members who are unreceptive toward you or your message. If they are unreceptive toward you personally, your job is to seek ways to enhance your credibility and persuade them to listen to you. If they are unreceptive toward your point of view, several strategies may help.

First, don't immediately announce your persuasive purpose. Immediately and explicitly telling your listeners that you plan to change their minds can make them defensive. Focus instead on areas of agreement. As you would with a neutral audience, refer to universal beliefs and concerns. Instead of saying to your unreceptive audience, "I'm here this morning to convince you that we should raise city taxes," you might say, "I think we can agree that we have an important common goal: achieving the best quality of life possible here in our small community."

Second, if you think your audience may be unreceptive, advance your strongest arguments first. This strategy is the principle of primacy. If you save your best argument for last (the recency principle), your audience may already have stopped listening.

Third, acknowledge the opposing points of view that members of your audience may hold. Summarize the reasons they may oppose your point of view; then cite evidence and use arguments to refute the opposition and support your conclusion. In speaking to students seeking to hold down tuition costs, a dean might say, "I am aware that many of you struggle to pay for your education. You work nights, take out loans, and live frugally." Then the dean could go on to identify how the university could provide additional financial assistance to students.

RECAP

Adapting Ideas to People and People to Ideas

Persuading the Receptive Audience	Persuading the Neutral Audience	Persuading the Unreceptive Audience
• Identify with your audience. • Emphasize common interests. • Provide a clear objective; tell your listeners what you want them to do. • Appropriately use emotional appeals.	• Gain and maintain your audience's attention. • Refer to beliefs and concerns that are important to listeners. • Show how the topic affects people your listeners care about. • Be realistic about what you can accomplish.	• Don't tell listeners that you are going to try to convince them to support your position. • Present your strongest arguments first. • Acknowledge opposing points of view. • Don't expect a major shift in attitudes or behavior.

Finally, as with a neutral audience, don't expect a major shift in attitude from an unreceptive audience. Set a realistic goal. It may be enough for an 8- to 10-minute presentation just to have your listeners hear you out and at least think about some of your arguments.

SAMPLE PERSUASIVE PRESENTATION

William Stephens
Sheridan College

Cruisin' Out of Control[18]

William captures the attention of his listeners with a startling statistic about the number of people who go on cruises annually. His use of the first person ("we") helps him establish common ground with his listeners.

Each year more than twelve million vacationers pack their bags, head for ocean ports, and embark on cruises. We love the sumptuous banquets, the impeccable service, and especially the pristine scenery. Unfortunately, as the October 2001 *Natural Life* reported, the trips we take are "endangering the very ecosystems [we're] so keen to observe." According to Ross Klein's book *Cruise Ship Blues*, pollution by hundreds of luxury liners sailing the seas is fouling the world's oceans and beaches, destroying vast food supplies on which we depend, threatening endangered species, and spreading deadly diseases.

Today we'll expose the dirty underside of the cruise ship industry, explore reasons these liners continue to pollute our oceans and coastlines, and examine some steps we must take to remedy this shameful situation. Think of a cruise ship—the largest of which carry 5,000 passengers—as a floating city. Each day people shower and flush toilets; crews launder tons of linens; staffs prepare 20,000 meals and dispose of the scraps; photo labs, dry cleaners, and beauty parlors use and toss tanks of toxic chemicals. At the same time, clean-up crews collect countless plastic containers, cardboard boxes, batteries, burned-out fluorescent and mercury vapor light bulbs, and medical wastes. We may assume that this mass of toxic trash is stored in holding bins and processed when the vessels return to port. But according to Oceana, an environmental protection group, we'd be wrong. Why? As the group stated in a February 1, 2003, article, "unlike cities . . . cruise ships are exempt from the . . . Clean Water Act." That means they are virtually free to dump these wastes and pollute at will. And pollute they do! In his book, Klein estimates that each day a large cruise ship produces 500,000 gallons of wastewater and 50,000 gallons of sewage. Ships may discharge gray water from showers, laundry, and dishwashing virtually anywhere. The Environmental Protection Agency discovered that some gray water actually had "higher levels of disease-causing bacteria than raw sewage." The reason? Cruise ships often combine chemical wastes and sewage with the gray water to circumvent regulations about dumping the most harmful products.

In May 2002, the Ocean Conservancy reported that because cruise ships use less water per flush, sewage on cruise ships is more concentrated than that from cities. An October 2003 report jointly published by Blue Water Network and Ocean Advocates confirmed that more than 98% of cruise ships discharge effluents that would be illegal on land. The Conservancy reveals that ballast water, used to stabilize the ship and control its buoyancy, poses another problem. Ships can suck up to thirty tanker trucks of ballast, including marine plants and animals, transport this biological soup thousands of miles, and discharge it, releasing non-native plants and animals to compete with and harm local species. Ballast water also carries diseases like cholera into clean areas.

Every day a cruise ship produces seven tons of garbage and solid waste, which workers often dump directly into the ocean. The damages from such practices are legion. First, according to the Smithsonian Institution's *Ocean Planet*, the polluted coastal water destroys shellfish beds and contaminates oysters, clams, and lobsters. Our next seafood platter may be palatable but poisonous. Second, Smithsonian says the sewage-polluted waters carry viral hepatitis, cholera, typhoid fever, and intestinal diseases. In one recent year, 2,400 United States beaches were temporarily closed because of bacteria. Unfortunately, some coastal states do not even monitor the water quality, and no federal laws require notifying the public of the pollution. Third, *Americas* of July/August 2003 explains that the raw sewage promotes massive growth of algae, which rob the water of oxygen and thus kill fish and other marine life. Recently such a huge "dead zone" has developed in the Gulf of Mexico. In addition, Oceana confirms that sewage has destroyed almost 90% of Caribbean coral reefs. Fourth, endangered species are succumbing to cruise ship pollution. For example, the *Anchorage Daily News* of July 22, 2001, reports that such pollutants are killing orcas, or killer whales, in Alaskan waters. In 2000, the orcas monitored were some of the most contaminated marine mammals ever measured. Some contained more than 500 times the level of contaminants considered safe.

William previews his speech.

William's analogy of a cruise ship as "a floating city" helps listeners comprehend the daily waste that such a ship produces.

William turns next to the harm—the effects—caused by the pollution he has documented.

Notice the use of a rhetorical question to provide a transition into William's next main idea.

How has such a devastating situation evolved? A number of factors have come together to create the disaster. First, laws governing the dumping of waste are inadequate. *Americas* of July/August 2003 reports that international laws are largely non-existent. U.S. laws are weak and applicable only to a narrow band of water along the U.S. coasts. For example, cruise ships may legally dump treated sewage 3 miles off the U.S. coast, but the definition of "treated" is so vague that ships often get away with dumping untreated sewage anywhere. Beyond 12 miles, ships can legally discharge raw sewage, which tides return to soil our shores. Second, the July 12, 2001, *Christian Science Monitor* reveals that most cruise lines register their fleets in foreign countries, exempting themselves from most U.S. laws and taxes. Such avoidance means that you and I, not the polluters, pay the bill for coastal clean-up.

Third, cruise ships openly violate the few laws and voluntary agreements that supposedly regulate them. One of the worst is Royal Caribbean Cruise Lines. Save Our Shores Foundation reports that this giant company's claim to be pro-environment is only a public relations ploy. In reality the line has been fined more than $30 million for illegally discharging oil, garbage, and sewage—and then falsifying its records as a cover-up. Royal Caribbean merely writes off these fines as business expenses and continues to pollute. And because so many regulations are non-binding agreements called Memoranda of Understanding, the October 2003 report *The Cruise Industry and Environmental History and Practice* tells us that the cruise lines feel free to violate them, claiming they are not breaking any laws but merely breaking their word. Rarely are violating ships caught. In fact, companies give financial bonuses to officers who routinely dump their wastes to save disposal and water treatment costs and so return from cruises under budget. Fourth, according to the General Accounting Office, the ships get away with illegal dumping because our Coast Guard, the agency responsible for monitoring compliance and conducting inspections, is so hopelessly over-extended that it can't do an adequate job. It uses less than 1 percent of its resources to monitor cruise ships. In addition, the Guard often schedules its inspections, allowing ships time to conceal illegal activities and falsify logs.

William uses negative visualization of the future as larger and larger cruise ships are launched.

Unfortunately, without extensive reform, the situation will get worse as cruise ships become bigger and more numerous. *The New York Times* of February 1, 2004, reports that the *Queen Mary 2* completed its maiden voyage on January 26. As long as the Empire State Building is high and twenty-three stories tall, the ship is the largest ocean liner yet built. But it won't hold that title for long. *CNN* of January 26, 2004, tells us that Royal Caribbean has ordered an even larger cruise ship scheduled for delivery in two years. *Americas* estimates that in the next 7 years the cruise business will double. Oceana reports that between 2001 and 2005 cruise lines expect to add 36 new ships, increasing the industry's capacity by 45%. What will our coastal waters be like then? Studies published by Bluewater Network and Ocean Advocates in October 2003 reveal that some ship-polluted Alaskan waters already have fecal bacteria levels 100,000 times the allowable standards.

Another rhetorical question serves as a transition to the satisfaction step of the presentation.

So what can we do to remedy this ever-growing threat? Obviously the government must replace the non-binding Memoranda of Understanding with much stricter regulations about cruise ship discharges, especially raw sewage. The *Congressional Record* of April 2, 2004, tells us that Representative Sam Farr of California has just introduced the "Clean Cruise Ship Act of 2004," which closes some of the loopholes in federal law that have allowed cruise lines to escape prosecution for some discharges of polluted water. If it can survive the expected powerful lobbying from the cruise industry, its impact could be significant. The bill requires cruise ships operating in U.S. waters to install the latest technology for treating emissions. Some devices, now available and reasonably priced, leave water cleaner than the natural ocean. Oceana estimates that companies could equip their ships with these devices for about $1.50 per passenger per day — about the price of a soft drink.

In addition, Congress must extend the Coast Guard's authority randomly to inspect the cruise ships and their logs. Of course, this extension means that the Guard must increase its budget and employ more inspectors. By levying stiffer fines for the violations, Congress can fund these additional services. You and I also have a part to play. As most of us will someday take a cruise, we must make sure we support responsible cruise lines, not those that repeatedly violate existing laws. In addition, we should support those few cruise lines actually registered in the United States who pay taxes to finance the monitoring and maintenance of coastal waters. According to a personal correspondence from Ross Klein on February 16, 2004, those are Cruise West, Glacier Bay, and American Safari. On board, we should watch for illegal dumping. We can videotape violations and even earn rewards for reporting violators. The *Juneau Empire* carried the story of an engineer who did just that. He reported a Holland American ship for dumping polluted bilge water in Alaska's Inside Passage and earned a half million dollar reward for his vigilance. As U. S. citizens, who comprise 82% of cruise passengers, we can pressure the cruise lines to clean up their act.

William includes himself and his listeners as potential cruise ship passengers who can and should take action. "This concerns you" is his underlying message.

Today we've exposed the dirty underside of the cruise ship industry, explored some reasons this nasty situation has developed, and finally examined several steps we must take to remedy this dangerous situation. For too long we've allowed the cruise ship industry to make their fortunes at the expense of our environment. It's time we told the cruise lines to shape up or ship out.

Finally, William summarizes his main points as he concludes his presentation.

PRINCIPLES **FOR A LIFETIME: Enhancing Your Skills**

Aware

Principle One: Be aware of your communication with yourself and others.

- Know whether your specific purpose is to change or reinforce an attitude, a belief, a value, or a behavior, and be realistic in assessing what you will need to do in your presentation to effect change.
- When you use cause-and-effect organization, you must analyze and then convince your listeners of the critical causal link.
- Relate personal experience to make you seem a more competent and trustworthy speaker.
- Have a brief summary of your qualifications and accomplishments ready for the person who will introduce you, to help enhance your initial credibility.
- To be a better informed consumer of persuasive messages, as well as a more ethical persuasive speaker, be aware of and avoid using common logical fallacies.

Verbal

Principle Two: Effectively use and interpret verbal messages.

- To create negative visualization, describe in detail how bleak or terrible the future will be if your solution is not implemented.
- To create positive visualization, describe in detail how wonderful the future will be if your solution is implemented.
- To select and narrow a topic for a persuasive presentation, pay attention to print and electronic media to help keep you current on important issues of the day.
- Word your central idea as a proposition to help you fine-tune your speaking objective and develop strategies for persuading your listeners.
- To make yourself seem more competent to your audience, cite evidence to support your ideas.
- Prepare a thoughtful conclusion to enhance your terminal credibility.
- Provide logical proof (evidence and reasoning) for your arguments and avoid logical fallacies to heighten your chances for success with your audience.
- Use emotion-arousing words to appeal to an audience's emotions.
- Use concrete illustrations and descriptions to appeal to an audience's emotions.

Nonverbal

Principle Three: Effectively use and interpret nonverbal messages.

- Maintain eye contact, use enthusiastic vocal inflection, and move and gesture purposefully to increase the likelihood that your audience will view you as dynamic.
- Dress appropriately to enhance your credibility.
- Maintain eye contact through and even after your closing sentence to enhance your terminal credibility.
- Use presentation aids to help evoke both positive and negative emotions as well as positive and negative visualization.

Listen and Respond

Principle Four: Listen and respond thoughtfully to others.

- Be prepared to answer questions after your presentation, regardless of whether there is a planned question-and-answer period.

Adapt

Principle Five: Appropriately adapt messages to others.

- Do everything possible to ensure that your audience's physiological and safety needs are met.
- To motivate an audience, appeal to their basic needs.
- If you are speaking to an apathetic audience or one that is not even aware that a problem exists, emphasize the problem portion of your problem-and-solution presentation.
- If your audience is aware of the problem you are discussing, emphasize the solution or solutions in your problem-and-solution presentation.
- Acknowledge and then refute the opposing points of view held by an unreceptive audience.
- In the need step of your motivated-sequence presentation, establish why your topic, problem, or issue should concern your listeners. Convince your audience that the problem affects them directly.
- In the action step of the motivated sequence, offer your audience members specific action they can take to solve the problem you have discussed.
- If you are speaking to a knowledgeable, receptive audience, do not spend a great deal of time on the need step of the motivated sequence; instead, emphasize the satisfaction and action steps.
- If you are speaking to a neutral audience, emphasize the attention, need, and visualization steps of the motivated sequence.

- Establish common ground with your audience.
- Consider the background and cultural expectations of your listeners as you develop your persuasive purpose.
- Make the most of your opportunity to speak to a receptive audience by identifying with them.
- If your audience is receptive, state your speaking objective overtly, tell your audience exactly what you want them to do, and ask audience members for an immediate show of support.
- Use emotional appeals with a receptive audience.
- Appeal to universal beliefs and concerns to persuade a neutral audience.
- Show a neutral audience how your topic affects both them and those they love.
- Be realistic about what you can accomplish with neutral and unreceptive audiences.
- Focus on areas of agreement with an unreceptive audience.
- If your audience is unreceptive, advance your strongest arguments first.

SUMMARY

Persuasion is the process of attempting to change or reinforce attitudes, beliefs, values, or behaviors. Several theories suggest how persuasion works—how listeners may be motivated to respond to a persuasive message. Cognitive dissonance is a sense of mental disorganization or imbalance that arises when new information conflicts with previously organized thought patterns. Cognitive dissonance may prompt a person to change attitudes, beliefs, values, or behavior. Maslow's classic hierarchy of needs is another approach that attempts to explain why people may be motivated to respond to persuasive appeals to various levels of need. Both fear appeals and positive motivational appeals can also motivate listeners to respond to your persuasive message.

Preparing and presenting a persuasive message require the same general approach as preparing any other kind of presentation. When you have a choice of persuasive topics, select a topic that is of interest to you and your listeners. Your specific purpose will target your audience's attitudes, beliefs, values, or behavior. Attitudes are learned predispositions to respond favorably or unfavorably toward something. A belief is one's sense of what is true or false. Values are enduring conceptions of right or wrong, good or bad. Of the three, attitudes are most susceptible to change; values are least likely to change. After clarifying your specific purpose, you can word your central idea as a proposition of fact, value, or policy.

Ways to organize your persuasive message include problem and solution, cause and effect, refutation, and the motivated sequence. The motivated sequence includes five steps: attention, need, satisfaction, visualization, and action.

A key to persuading others is to establish your credibility as a speaker. Credibility is an audience's perception of a speaker's competence, trustworthiness, and dynamism. Enhancing your initial credibility (what you do before you speak), your derived credibility (what you do during your presentation), and your terminal credibility (what you do after your presentation) will help you improve your overall credibility as a presentational speaker.

Reasoning, the process of drawing a conclusion from evidence, is integral to the persuasive process. The three primary types of reasoning are inductive, deductive, and causal. You can also reason by analogy. You can be an effective and ethical persuader by avoiding reasoning fallacies such as the causal fallacy, the bandwagon fallacy, the either-or fallacy, hasty generalization, personal attack, red herring, appeals to misplaced authority, and non sequiturs.

In addition to persuading others because of who you are (ethos) or how well you structure your logical arguments (logos), you can also move an audience to respond by using emotional appeals (pathos).

Finally, be prepared to adapt your persuasive messages to receptive, neutral, and unreceptive audiences. Throughout the persuasive speaking process, being aware of your messages and others' messages, effectively using verbal and nonverbal messages, listening and responding to your audience, and adapting to your listeners can enhance your skill as a persuasive speaker.

DISCUSSION AND REVIEW

1. Where might you turn if you needed ideas for a topic for a persuasive presentation?

2. Define attitudes, beliefs, and values. Why is it important that a persuasive speaker know which one he or she is targeting in a persuasive presentation?

3. What is a proposition of fact? Give one original example.

4. What is a proposition of value? Give one original example.

5. What is a proposition of policy? Give one original example.

6. List and explain four ways to organize a persuasive presentation.

7. When would you be most likely to organize a presentation by refutation?

8. List and explain the five steps of the motivated sequence.

9. What is credibility?

10. Define initial, derived, and terminal credibility, and explain how to enhance each one.

11. Define and provide an example of inductive reasoning.

12. How is reasoning by analogy different from using an analogy as supporting material?

13. Define and provide an example of deductive reasoning.

14. Define and provide an example of causal reasoning.

15. List and explain eight logical fallacies.

16. How can you appeal to your listeners' emotions in a persuasive presentation?

17. What is cognitive dissonance? How can you apply the theory in a persuasive presentation?

18. List and explain the five levels of Maslow's hierarchy of needs. How can you apply the theory in a persuasive presentation?

19. Provide specific suggestions for adapting to receptive audiences, neutral audiences, and unreceptive audiences.

PUTTING PRINCIPLES INTO PRACTICE

1. Watch a C-SPAN, CNN, or network news broadcast of a politician arguing for or against a particular proposition. Decide whether it is a proposition of fact, value, or policy. Identify the organizational pattern and the persuasive strategies the speaker uses.

2. Identify three nationally or internationally known speakers whom you consider to be credible. Analyze why these speakers are credible, according to the three components of credibility.

3. Identify the logical fallacy in each of the following arguments:

   a. We must raise taxes to finance the construction of new streets. Otherwise, we will have to rely on four-wheel-drive vehicles to get around.

   b. Breaking that mirror this morning was the reason I did so poorly on my history test.

   c. Everybody knows that you can't get a decent summer job around here.

   d. You should be concerned about your grade in that class because your new part-time job pays well.

   e. Jane grew up in a state that spends less money on education than any state in the United States; she could not possibly have any useful ideas about how to improve our children's test scores on standardized tests.

4. Develop a specific purpose statement and central idea for a persuasive message. Describe strategies you would use if you were to give this presentation to a receptive audience. Identify strategies you would use if you were to give this presentation to a neutral audience. Finally, suggest strategies you would use if you were to give this presentation to an unreceptive audience.

Chapter 4.5   *Practice Test*

MULTIPLE CHOICE. Choose the *best* answer to each of the following questions.

1. Peter is asking his mom if he can go to the concert this weekend. He tells her, "Everybody is going. I don't want to be the only one left out." Peter's logic suffers from the

    a. personal attack.

    b. causal fallacy.

    c. non sequitur.

    d. bandwagon fallacy.

2. The three types of propositions posed by persuasive speakers are propositions of

    a. opinion, fact, and policy.

    b. problem, cause, and effect.

    c. fact, value, and policy.

    d. attitude, belief, and value.

3. What error in reasoning is exemplified by the following: "All college classes are dull. I took four last semester and didn't enjoy any of them"?

    a. false cause

    b. hasty generalization

    c. invalid analogy

    d. circular thinking

4. Alex delivered a presentation at the Faculty Senate meeting supporting a change in the way honors graduates are selected. Alex's central idea is a proposition of

    a. fact.

    b. value.

    c. policy.

    d. attitude.

5. *The Rhetoric* is considered one of the first books written about persuasion. Its author was

    a. Cicero.

    b. Corax.

    c. Plato.

    d. Aristotle.

6. Persuasive speakers do all of the following *except*

    a. develop arguments using appropriate evidence.

    b. use force to achieve the presentation's goal.

    c. ask the audience to respond thoughtfully to the message.

    d. invite the audience to make a choice.

7. A speaker's credibility at the end of the speech is called

    a. derived credibility.

    b. initial credibility.

    c. demonstrated credibility.

    d. terminal credibility.

8. Mike gave a presentation to convince his audience that learning to play an instrument is more beneficial than learning to play a sport. Mike's central idea was a proposition of

    a. fact.

    b. value.

    c. policy.

    d. attitude.

9. What organizational pattern do the most effective fear appeals employ?

    a. cause and effect

    b. problem and solution

    c. if-then

    d. need-satisfaction

10. As long as the evidence in a presentation is credible,

    a. lower intensity fear appeals are more effective than higher intensity ones.

    b. higher intensity fear appeals are more effective than lower intensity ones.

    c. any amount of fear appeal will work.

    d. no amount of fear appeal will work.

11. A persuasive presentation that focuses on the audience's liking or disliking of something is attempting to change the audience's
    a. attitude.
    b. belief.
    c. value.
    d. dissonance.

12. All of the following are steps in Monroe's motivated sequence *except*
    a. need.
    b. motivation.
    c. attention.
    d. action.

13. When you create cognitive dissonance for an audience, you
    a. present them with information that is inconsistent with their current thinking.
    b. present them with information with which they disagree.
    c. act in an unexpected way.
    d. introduce an unknown idea.

14. Speaker credibility is associated with what component of persuasion?
    a. ethos
    b. pathos
    c. logos
    d. legos

15. Michelle tells her class that research indicates that 30 minutes of exercise is beneficial to everyone's health. She then concludes that everyone in her audience should spend 30 minutes a day working out in the campus gym. Michelle is using which kind of reasoning?
    a. inductive
    b. deductive
    c. intuitive
    d. counterintuitive

16. Marceau carefully prepares his presentation so that he does not reveal his persuasive purpose until late in the speech. He is assuming that his audience is

    a. receptive.
    b. neutral.
    c. unreceptive.
    d. naïve.

17. Rocio has prepared her presentation using mostly emotional appeals. She is assuming that her audience is
    a. receptive.
    b. neutral.
    c. unreceptive.
    d. naïve.

18. The President's exclamation "Either you are with us or you are with the terrorists" exemplifies which of the following logical fallacies?
    a. hasty generalization
    b. personal attack
    c. non sequitur
    d. either-or fallacy

19. According to Maslow's hierarchy, it would be inappropriate to persuade an audience to join a group on the basis of appeals to social needs if they
    a. were very hungry.
    b. had a negative self-image.
    c. had not reached their highest potential.
    d. were uncomfortable in social situations.

20. Arrange the following ideas according to Monroe's motivated sequence:
    I. The world's oil supplies will run out in our lifetime.
    II. Hybrid vehicles can buy humanity time to develop viable alternatives.
    III. Imagine going to fill up your car and paying $7.50 or even $10.00 per gallon for gas.
    IV. 345,200,000 gallons of oil are used in the U.S. every day.
    a. I, II, III, IV
    b. II, IV, III, I
    c. III, I, IV, II
    d. IV, II, I, III

TRUE/FALSE. Indicate whether the following statements are *true* or *false.*

1. T or F   A problem–solution format for a persuasive speech is especially useful when you are speaking to an unreceptive audience.

2. T or F   When using Monroe's motivated sequence, it is a good idea to *not* be too specific.

3. T or F   Creating cognitive dissonance in your audience's minds increases the likelihood that they will be persuaded by your speech.

4. T or F   The person who introduces the speaker plays an important role in establishing the speaker's initial credibility.

5. T or F   Reasoning by analogy is an example of deductive reasoning.

6. T or F   In order, the needs in Maslow's hierarchy are physiological, safety, social, self-esteem, and self-actualization.

7. T or F   Logical proof requires a major premise, a minor premise, and a conclusion.

8. T or F   Values are the hardest to change, followed by beliefs and then attitudes.

9. T or F   *Dynamism* refers to the characteristic of being a talented, charming, attractive speaker.

10. T or F   The false conclusion that A caused B because A preceded B is referred to as a hasty generalization.

FILL IN THE BLANK. Complete the following statements.

1. The experience of encountering information that runs counter to previously held beliefs is _____ _____.

2. Hasty generalization, personal attack, and red herring are examples of _____ _____.

3. A _____ relates to perceptions of what is true or false.

4. The stage of the motivated sequence at which you help the audience see themselves adopting your proposal is called _____.

5. The oversimplification of a problem to the point of offering only two choices is the _____ fallacy.

6. Aristotle's term for logical argument was _____.

7. The claim with which you want your audience to agree is your _____.

8. An argument with a major premise, minor premise, and conclusion is known as a _____.

9. The process of changing an audience's attitudes, beliefs, values, or behavior is _____.

10. If you argue that all students should be required to wear blazers because apple pie is your favorite dessert, then you are guilty of a _____ _____.

Technology and Presentational Communication

APPENDIX OBJECTIVES

1. Explain why speakers should exercise caution when using Internet sources of supporting material.

2. Describe the main concerns for speakers when they employ technological innovations in presentation aids.

3. Discuss how technology can help a speaker improve delivery.

At various points throughout the chapters on presentational communication in this text, we explored applications of technology to this context of communication. We won't repeat that information here, but we do want to offer a few reminders or cautions about the effects of technology on presentational speaking.

Source Material for Presentations

Times have changed. Instead of combing through dusty volumes in musty library stacks, most students who seek information simply type on a keyboard and click a mouse, and the information they seek appears on a computer screen. We also realize that, as college students, you're encouraged to employ your powers of critical thinking to assess the validity and usefulness of information before you use it in a speech or paper. But we have come to detect, through many semesters of teaching presentational speaking and conducting our own research, a sense among students that computers embody what can only be described as a "mystical" quality. Just as people decades ago believed that everything that appeared in print in the town newspaper just had to be true, many people believe that if it's on the computer screen, it counts as legitimate information. What we want to make sure you realize is that anyone with access to a computer and half a brain can learn to create a Web site. Just because something appears on a Web site doesn't mean it is necessarily reliable, legitimate, true, or useful.

Many Web sites are advocacy-based, meaning that they present only one side or a slanted view of an issue—the side they want to persuade you to agree with. Others are more even-handed, presenting multiple perspectives and allowing the reader to decide for herself or himself. It's acceptable to incorporate some of this kind of material into a presentation, but, at present, this information does not carry the same level of legitimacy that published research carries.

A related caution pertains to your ethical responsibility as a public speaker. You are expected to present the best information you can find—not the best information you can find the most quickly. Take time to hunt for the best information. Also realize that commonly used search engines, such as Yahoo!, Google, and Lycos, catalog only about 16% of the estimated 800 million Web pages that currently exist.[1] The research process is tedious and time-consuming, and computers have helped streamline it by a tremendous amount. However, the computer is but one tool to help you locate pertinent information. Other tools may take more time to use, but you may find that they provide more information of varying types than you could access via computer. You may also find yourself researching a topic that pre-dates the computerization of information. In a case like this, you don't want to discover that you've lost your library research skills because you constantly turn to a computer.

Technological Innovations and Presentation Aids

In Chapter 4.3 we provided information about a range of presentation aids, including computer-generated visual aids, that can be used to enhance a presentation. We also discussed some guidelines for using these aids, including this one: "Use technology thoughtfully." You want to avoid deciding to use technology to support a speech just because it will "wow" an audience. Keep in mind that there is nothing inherently dazzling about technology itself; it's all in how you *use* the technology.

In a presentational context, programs that generate images and text, such as Microsoft's PowerPoint™, may or may not help you get your message across to the audience.[2] We've seen presentations in which the technology outshone the speaker and overwhelmed the audience. And if your room isn't conducive to the technology, you may have to speak in the dark so that the presentation aids can be seen. This can also be a problem for speakers who rely on overhead projectors. A darkened room is not the best environment for a speaker, because you run the risk of losing some of your audience's attention. Also, some people (especially those who are quite nervous in speaking situations) let the darkness shield them and the presentation aids supplant their speech content. Remember that all presentation aids should *aid* the speaker; they should not *replace* the speaker.

Technology and Enhanced Speech Delivery

When we hear a recording of ourselves, most of us respond with "That's not my voice; I don't sound like that." The truth is, recording technology today is so sophisticated that it can capture sounds quite accurately—so indeed, you actually *do* sound like that. The way you hear your voice in your head is distorted, compared to the way others hear it when you speak. So if you want to know how you will sound when making a presentation, tape yourself and force yourself to listen to the playback, just as we advised in Chapter 4.3. This is one of the best ways to improve a speech—its content, organization, and delivery. But try not to be overly critical of yourself when you listen, as many of us tend to be. You want to note if you use too many filler sounds or words, such as "uh," "er," "okay," "you know," and "like" (our personal favorite). You want to attempt to slow down if you hear yourself rushing on the recording; you want to develop vocal variety so you don't speak in a monotone. But realize that you're developing a delivery style that is unique to you; don't try to change too much or you'll likely make yourself unduly nervous when you actually present the speech.

Aware

Verbal

If you're really daring, need an extra dose of reality, or are a narcissist, videotape yourself rehearsing or performing your speech. Of course, we're kidding when we say that, but we know that most people aren't thrilled with the thought of being videotaped. Most of us are thrilled even less with the thought of having to watch ourselves on tape. But, as we indicated in Chapter 4.3, a videotape of yourself is the absolute best form of pre- or post-speech feedback you can use as a tool to improve your speaking abilities. If you don't own a video camera, most colleges and universities have media centers that give students access to video equipment.

Nonverbal

When you watch the tape, imagine yourself as an audience member, sitting in the room listening to you speak. Are you bored by yourself as a speaker? Do you make yourself laugh? Are you understandable? Are you persuaded by you, if that's the goal? You might want to assess your presentation using the same criteria your instructor will use when you give the speech in class. As you watch, first note things you did well; then note those things you want to change. Try not to be overly harsh or distracted by such unchangeable things as your physical characteristics and appearance. Concentrate on the speech—how well it was organized; whether you cited your supporting materials adequately; whether you handled your note cards smoothly; whether you need to

Adapt

alter delivery elements like voice, eye contact, and movement; and whether the speech fit the specified time frame. It may be a humbling experience to watch your presentation on tape, but it will teach you a great deal.

PRINCIPLES FOR A LIFETIME: Enhancing Your Skills

Principle One: Be aware of your communication with yourself and others.

Aware

- Audiotaping or videotaping yourself making a presentation and then listening to or viewing the playback is an excellent way to become more aware of how you communicate as a speaker.

Principle Two: Effectively use and interpret verbal messages.

- Audiotaping or videotaping presentations and listening to or watching the playback is an excellent strategy to help speakers improve their use of language.

Verbal

Principle Three: Effectively use and interpret nonverbal messages.

Nonverbal

- Audiotaping or videotaping presentations and listening to or watching the playback is an excellent strategy to help speakers improve their nonverbal delivery.

Principle Five: Appropriately adapt messages to others.

Adapt

- When viewing a videotape of your presentation, imagine yourself as an audience member; then adapt the presentation to make the best impression possible on listeners.

SUMMARY

In this appendix we explored the effects of technology on presentational speaking. Speakers need to use caution when accessing source material for speeches from the Internet; some sources are more reliable than others. Computer searching should supplement, not replace, traditional library methods of research. Technology is improving our methods of generating and using presentation aids, but we warned about overusing or relying too heavily on technology. Aids simply help the speaker; they do not replace the speaker. Current technology can help speakers improve their delivery, especially through the use of audiotaped and videotaped speech rehearsals.

Sample Speeches for Discussion and Evaluation

Informative Speech

Taming Hostile Audiences:
Persuading Those Who Would Rather Jeer than Cheer

Larry Tracy[1]

Delivered to the Washington, D.C., Chapter of the National Speakers Association, Washington, D.C. January 8, 2005

Thank you, Sylvia, for that fine introduction. As professional speakers, we know how a poor introduction can be deflating. Sylvia, on the other hand, was somewhat inflating in her kind remarks.

I am frequently asked how I got into the field of presentations coaching after being a colonel in the U.S. Army. The first time that question was asked of me, my answer, I'm afraid, was a bit flippant. After reflection, however, I decided it was indeed quite accurate. I said that early in my career, I concluded (as did my superiors, I believe) that I could talk better than I could shoot. From that time on, I seemed to become the duty briefer no matter what my primary assignment. Ultimately, as Sylvia mentioned in her introduction, I was selected to head the Pentagon's top briefing team, responsible for daily intelligence presentations to the Chairman of the Joint Chiefs of Staff and the Secretary of Defense.

My experience with hostile and difficult audiences came later when the Department of State requested the Army to assign me to the Department for the specific task of speaking and debating controversial foreign policy issues throughout the U.S. and abroad. Initially, I found it flattering that State Department officials believed I was qualified to take on this task, but after the first few "confrontations," I realized these officials had decided it was better to place an Army colonel in jeopardy than a promising diplomat.

In all seriousness, however, that assignment was a wonderful life-changing experience. The almost 400 presentations, debates, and panels in which I participated caused me to enter the field of speech training as my post-Army career. I knew that few people in this field had the "real-world" experience I had gained and could now pass on to others.

Let me say something that may offend some of you. Although you are all professional speakers, I submit that you are not a true professional if you are only capable of speaking to groups that agree with you. The true professional speaker can deal with the jeers as well as the cheers. The true professional knows how to persuade the "nonpersuadable," not just preach to the choir.

There is no greater challenge in the field of speaking than the task of bringing around to your position audience members who are initially opposed to what you are advocating. Many people are inclined to take a fatalistic position at the prospect of dealing with such an audience. But that attitude is self-defeating. Bringing such an audience to your side by the lucidity of your reasoning, the coherence of your message, and the excellence of your presentation skills will indeed make you a complete speaker. As you have no doubt discovered, speakers in today's world must blend substantive mastery, focused structure, and stylistic elegance to a degree not required previously.

In today's contentious business and government climate, adversarial panels, debates, and presentations on controversial issues are more the rule rather than the exception. I want to divide today's presentation into two parts. In Part One, I'll emphasize the importance of mastering the fundamentals of the speaking art. In Part Two, I'll show how to apply these fundamentals to persuading audiences inclined to disagree with you.

Part One: The Fundamentals of the Speaking Art

I know that some of you are thinking "Hold on, we're professional speakers. We don't need any advice on "fundamentals." Just get to the good stuff—how to tame hostile audiences." Well, I disagree with those of you thinking that way. I have given over 3000 presentations, and I always review the fundamentals. Let me use a sports analogy to emphasize this point. By doing so, I am departing from the advice I teach in my workshops—"Men, go easy on the sports metaphors; you run the risk of alienating people in your audience who are not sports nuts." So please indulge me this one time, as the comparison is so apt.

Professional football players are superb athletes, who, in their games, employ complex formations, options, and plays. Yet, when they report to training camp, they initially practice only football fundamentals—blocking, tackling, running, passing, and catching. Only after honing these skills do these athletes move to their complex formations and plays.

Professional speakers should do no less. It is especially important when you are preparing to face a demanding audience. You may get by with a less-than-polished presentation when you are addressing people who agree with you and only wish to have their views reinforced. It is, however, sheer folly to speak to an audience opposed to you without a strict adherence to the fundamentals of the speaking art.

Now, just what am I referring to with the word *fundamentals*? I don't mean just the platform skills of body language, eye contact, gestures, and vocal inflection. They are indeed important tools for the speaker, but I mean something deeper. If your presentation does not take into consideration the objections, questions, and other obstacles to understanding, it is unlikely the audience will accept and act upon your message.

Don't think of a presentation as merely a series of words strung together, any more than a bridge is merely wires and steel haphazardly connected. Just as there are sound engineering principles in bridge construction that take into consideration soil composition, prevailing winds, stress and strain, etc., there are sound principles which must be followed in the construction of a presentation.

Your mission as a speaker, to either a supportive or nonsupportive audience, is to provide maximum information in minimum time in the clearest possible manner. Keep in mind that every presentation is actually four presentations: (1) the one you plan to deliver, (2) the one you actually deliver, (3) the one your audience hears you deliver, and (4) the one you wish you had delivered. I hope my presentation today will help you to deliver as you have planned and practiced, be on the same page as the audience, and have fewer of those "I wish I had said it this way" moments.

A motto of the National Speakers Association of a few years ago very elegantly described professional speakers as enjoying "The privilege of the platform." As a speaker, you have the rare opportunity to "write on the brains" of the people in your audience. Never undertake a presentation without that thought uppermost in your own mind.

To communicate effectively and persuasively with any audience, you need "actionable intelligence" on these people. Note that I do not use the term "audience analysis," which is a favorite phrase of most of my colleagues in the field of presentations training. That phrase reminds me of high school students dissecting a frog. When addressing an audience, you are dealing with living, breathing human beings with beliefs, attitudes, biases, prejudices, etc. Into that mix you will be adding new information. You must know their "what's in it for me" button, the pushing of which will cause them to listen to your message. You must know what problems these people have, so that your presentation can provide the information to solve these problems. This information must be delivered so it will be received by audience members. You must, in short, open the minds of these audience members.

So just how do you open the minds of an audience so your facts will be heard and accepted? You do so by going back to the teaching of history's greatest speech coach—Aristotle. He considered "Ethos," which we would call "source credibility," the most important part of a speaker's means of persuasion. He wrote in *The Rhetoric*, the seminal work on public speaking, that an audience which knew nothing of the subject being addressed would accept the position being advocated by the speaker if that person was considered to have "Ethos."

Moving that Aristotelian precept to our times, we base our view of whether a speaker has credibility on three elements:

1. Expertise
2. Believability
3. Likability

Your audience members want to know that you bring to the table information that will shorten their learning curve, that you have the credentials to speak on this issue, that you are telling the truth, not merely a glib speaker selling snake oil. Finally, they must like you. We all tend to accept information from people we like, and we reject it from people we do not like. Interpersonal skills are intimately connected to speaking skills.

Credibility is subjective. No one in this room, including me, can say "I have credibility to speak on my specialty." Your audience members will decide if you are credible. If they do so, you are in a position to bring them to your point of view. If they do not, you are wasting your time speaking to them.

With all that in mind, I want to show you a systematic way of following the fundamentals of speaking. It is what I call the S3P3 system, the heart of my executive workshops. It has worked for me, and it works for my clients who, for the most part are not nearly as experienced in speaking as you are. Therefore, I know it will work for you. Let me again ask you to open your mental PowerPoint, this time visualizing a pyramid supported by three pillars. The levels of the pyramid are, from base to apex, Planning, Practicing, and Presenting. The pillars are Substance, Structure, and Style.

Substance is the content of the presentation. Always remember that the purpose of a presentation is to convey information from speaker to audience. Style refers to how you look, how you sound, your choice of words—all those attributes we ascribe to a good public speaker. Substance without style is a dry and boring recitation of data. Style without substance is shallow and meaningless. Structure is the skeletal outline, or scaffolding, of the presentation. That's the word a young British Army lieutenant named Winston Churchill used in the title of a brilliant essay written in 1897, "The Scaffolding of Rhetoric." The future British Prime Minister emphasized that audience members needed a guide to show them where the speaker and they were going on this joint journey. A reading of Churchill's memorable World War Two speeches, [which were said to have] "marched the English language into battle," demonstrates that he followed the advice he developed in his youth.

Such organization is vital for an oral presentation. A written memo can have faulty structure, but can be reread. There is no instant replay of the oral presentation. Some examples of this structure are problem-solution, cause and effect, chronological. The presentation must have a beginning, a middle, and an end. It must also have transitions which send signals to the audience that new elements will be discussed.

Now, let's look at that pyramid, starting with that wide base. In Planning, you must develop a concrete objective, aimed at intersecting with the problems, needs, wants, and concerns of your audience. This is always important, but especially so when facing a demanding audience. Know specifically what you wish to have this audience do with the information you are providing. It is here where you draft your presentation, and this can best be done, in my opinion, by following my 3-1-2 system. While this system is counterintuitive, it virtually guarantees that you will have both focus and theme, vital for an oral presentation.

Take a stack of 3 × 5 cards. Mark one with a "3" and place on it the "bottom line" message you wish to impart to your audience. In front of these words, put "In summary," "In conclusion," or some other phrase signaling the end of your presentation. You now have your conclusion, as well as a mini-presentation, especially beneficial when making a business or sales presentation when time for the presentation is reduced at the last minute. Take another card, mark it with "1" and use it to tell the audience where you are taking them on this oratorical journey. Next, place the supporting points that flow from "1" to "3" on a series of cards marked "2A," "2B," "2C," etc.

Using the 3-1-2 system will enable you to present maximum relevant content within the limited amount of time your audience may have to listen to you. You'll have more focus, because you will know when you start drafting where you are going in the presentation. Most importantly, audience members will see a structure to your presentation, enabling them to follow and, in the best of cases, ultimately agree with your argument. Just remember: you draft 3-1-2, but when you have the allotted time, you deliver 1-2-3.

Now to Practicing, something many of us find rather odious. It is, however, vitally important, especially when preparing to face a difficult audience. Thorough practice will permit you to hone your presentation skills, anticipate questions, and it will certainly build your confidence.

I teach my clients a three-step practice process. First, practice by yourself, with a tape recorder and, if possible, a video camera. You are at your weakest at this stage and do not want anyone criticizing your performance. Listen for your "uh's" and "y'knows." The [fewer] of those abominations you utter, the less you will irritate your audience. Men, listen for a droning monotone. Ladies, listen for a high pitch. Next, ask a colleague to be your "audience." This should be a person who can offer constructive criticism and comments. The third stage is to convene a "Murder Board," a realistic simulation with colleagues role-playing your prospective audience. I'll cover this in more detail in just a few minutes when we focus on communicating with a demanding audience.

Finally, you reach that apex: Presenting. This is when you put voice to thought within a structure that facilitates audience comprehension and agreement with the position you are advocating, done with the style most appropriate to make your presentation memorable and successful. Eye contact, purposeful gestures, pleasant vocal inflection, skillful answering of questions, are all part of the presentation. If you have practiced well, you will present well.

For those of us who deliver similar presentations over and over, the challenge is to keep your material fresh. To do so, take a tip from the theatre. Actors who play the same role night after night refer to this as "creating the illusion of the first time." As speakers, you can add new material, and you can concentrate on getting yourself "pumped." Your obligation is to not be boring to members of your audience who are hearing your words for the first time.

Part Two: Persuading Hostile Audiences

Now let's see how we can apply these fundamentals to communicate with, and perhaps persuade, people who are adamantly opposed to our position.

We live in an increasingly high-tempo, fast-moving, information-laden, real-time age, and the pace is picking up. Audiences are knowledgeable, critical, impatient, and demanding. Public debates and panels on controversial issues are becoming common. Perhaps it has been the institutionalization of presidential and other political debates over the last several years that has led to this state of affairs. Perhaps there is a "Super Bowl" desire deep in our national psyche that craves the clash of ideas, issues, and rivals. A debate or confrontational panel means sharing the platform with a person or persons opposed to you, perhaps with an audience acting as cheerleader for these opponent(s). You will then know how the Christians in the Roman Coliseum felt as they looked at the hungry lions.

To be an effective presenter under such circumstances, a flexible "blueprint" must be developed for transferring information and perceptions from the speaker's mind to the minds of audience members. When facing a skeptical or hostile audience, you must keep in mind that the information you are presenting is probably at variance with the preconceived opinions and biases of audience members. Anticipating how audience members will react and what lines of attack any opponent(s) will follow is an absolute necessity. Knowing your vulnerabilities and developing responses/counterattacks will enable you to snatch victory from the jaws of defeat, if I may use an overdone cliché.

I'll illustrate how failure to develop an effective counterattack had profound consequences for one of our political leaders several years ago. To make this interesting, I'd like to make a wager with you that in a few minutes, as I recount this story, some of you will be able to repeat, almost verbatim, something you saw and heard on television about 16 years ago. Any takers?

I didn't think there would be. Let me tighten the focus. It's a cool October evening in 1988, and two Senators are in the vice-presidential debate. They are Lloyd Bentsen and Dan Quayle.

I'm starting to see some knowing nods. I told you you'd remember.

Quayle had been a controversial choice to be on the Republican ticket, due to his relative youth. To counter this perception, his campaign compared his age, and his time in the Congress, to that of the late President John F. Kennedy. In his memoirs, Quayle says that his "handlers," as he derisively referred to his debate prep team, feared Bentsen would turn the tables and make an unfavorable comparison of Quayle to Kennedy. They advised him to avoid any mention of Kennedy so Bentsen would not have an opportunity to skewer him. This was foolish advice, because in a debate one has no control over the questions. Quayle attempted to avoid the Kennedy comparison, but eventually, in response to a reporter's question, said he was the same age as Kennedy was in 1960, and had served the same number of years in the Congress as had the late president.

Now I see a lot of knowing smiles, and I would venture more than half of you know what happened next. Senator Bentsen said—and repeat after me—"Senator, I knew Jack Kennedy. Jack Kennedy was a friend of mine. Senator, you are no Jack Kennedy." What was Quayle's response? "That was uncalled for."

The remark by Bentsen, and Quayle's stunned reaction, was the most devastating and best-remembered exchange in the history of American political debates. Dan Quayle's image was permanently damaged, even though the Bush–Quayle ticket went on to win the November 1988 election.

The Bentsen–Quayle debate provides an excellent lesson for all presenters. You must seek to anticipate the most daunting objections and questions your audience will raise. Failure to do so could result in public humiliation, the fate suffered by then-Senator Quayle. Despite the fact that Quayle was, by all accounts, an effective Vice President, he never recovered from the Bentsen broadside. His every gaffe of the next four years was exaggerated by the media and TV comedians because it fit the image of the youthful, bumbling, politician established in the debate.

Could Quayle have neutralized Bentsen's broadside? Yes, with an intensive "Murder Board," which I've mentioned in passing and will discuss in a few minutes. Had Quayle and his advisers decided to act on their worst fears, rather than put their heads in the sand and hope for the best, think how effective this response to Bentsen would have been: "Senator, if you want to say who is not a John F. Kennedy, I would suggest you look at your running mate. The only thing Governor Dukakis and JFK have in common is the state of Massachusetts." Such a response would have taken little imagination to devise. A lemon could have been turned into lemonade by luring Bentsen into an "ambush," as a means of guaranteeing the hit on Dukakis. Quayle's risk-averse coaches, however, took the cautious approach, hoping to deny Bentsen the chance to launch the attack they feared. Quayle and the Republican Party were ill-served by such incompetence. If Quayle had delivered such a response, his supporters in the audience would have responded with robust applause, Bentsen's comment would not have captured the headlines, and Quayle would have been credited with a quick-thinking comeback. The exchange would probably have been forgotten, and Quayle, who did well in the rest of the debate, would have possibly been viewed as the winner, or at worst the debate would have been judged a draw. Instead, he was considered the clear loser.

Now let's move away from recent history and back to today. A presenter can connect with even a skeptical audience by showing that he or she shares certain views with members of the audience. You must develop rapport and seek to establish common ground with the audience. If you don't, there is no chance of success in bringing these people to your side. You simply must, at the outset, open the minds of audience members. Let me illustrate once again with a visual image. Imagine a car that is out of gas at point A. This is your prospective audience, which lacks the vital information you will be imparting. You wish to drive this car to point B—acceptance of your information. If the gas cap—the minds of audience members—is closed, any "gas" you pour will wind up on the ground. So how do you get that "gas cap" open? You can do so by getting audience members to like or respect you. You can establish personal contact, perhaps by phone, with key members of the audience well before the presentation. In so doing, you'll not only establish that needed "human connection," you'll also gain additional intelligence on why these people are opposed to you.

Arrive early so you can have conversations with people who are opposed to you. Learn more about their concerns, and why they are opposed to the position you are advocating. Perhaps you will learn who will be the troublemakers. You can speak with them in a nonconfrontational way. These people, in turn, may now see you more as a human being, not a remote corporate figure. During the actual presentation, mention the names of the people with whom you have conferred. Nothing is so sweet to the human ear as the sound of his or her name, especially if it is mentioned positively before others. These people that you mention will probably be less inclined to ask tough questions, as it could appear less than gracious after your kind remarks. Next, find that necessary common ground by emphasizing areas where you and the audience agree, even at a high level of abstraction. This at least puts you and the audience on the same page, even if it is a small page. After establishing that there are points of agreement, you can then move to the arguments supporting your position.

A technique I used in facing audiences initially opposed to the position I was advocating was to acknowledge that we in Washington had done a poor job of articulating our policy, and I could therefore understand why so many people in the audience were opposed to this policy. I would then say I hoped to fill in some of those gaps with my presentation. In this way, I was providing audience members with the opportunity to "save face," perhaps even [become] willing to change their mind as a result of the new information I was about to present. Remember that people don't want to admit they were wrong, and you cannot persuade people to change their mind; they must persuade themselves.

Now, let's look at three tactics for dealing with demanding audiences. First, The Murder Board: The term "Murder Board" comes from military briefings. It is a rigorous practice, a simulation of the actual presentation to be made. It consists of colleagues role-playing the actual audience, asking the type of questions this audience is likely to ask. As its rather macabre name implies, the Murder Board is intended to be more difficult and demanding than the actual presentation. In football terms, it is a full-pads scrimmage. This realistic practice session is the most effective shortcut to speaking excellence. It allows you to make your mistakes when they don't count. It allows you to be exposed to those tough questions, leading to focused research, which enables you to provide succinct, accurate answers in the actual presentation. In sum, the Murder Board increases the odds that you will shine. When faced with the audience inclined more to jeer than cheer, it is essential to have such rigorous preparation—unless you take some perverse joy in public humiliation.

Next, stay within your evidence: During the give-and-take of a presentation with a demanding audience, you may be tempted to go beyond the hard, factual evidence that is the underpinning of your argument. An analogy or metaphor may be stretched beyond its limits, or a conclusion stated that is simply not supported by the facts. This can destroy the credibility you have established up to that point and provide a lucrative target for those strongly opposed to you. Credibility lost is difficult to regain.

Finally, you simply must maintain your composure in the face of hostility: It is quite natural to let your emotions take over if a person in the audience starts to harangue you. Natural, but a recipe for disaster if you lose your temper. Audiences will adopt an "us against the speaker" attitude if you respond in kind to a heckler or a person making obnoxious remarks.

I'll illustrate with an example from my own speaking experience when I was called a liar by an audience member. I was on a panel at a major university, addressing U.S. Latin American policy. The three other members of the panel were professors from the university, all opposed to that policy. The audience was composed primarily of students, who, in the Q&A session, were aggressive but fair. Then a man in his 40s rose, asked a question to which I responded. This was then followed by two more, which were loud personal attacks against my honesty. I felt my Irish temper starting to boil. My instinct was to lash back. Fortunately, for reasons I still don't understand, I did not. Instead, I said, "Look, everybody in this auditorium wants to give me a hard time, and I just can't let you have all the fun." I broke eye contact, but he kept shouting.

At that point, another person shouted at the questioner "Will you sit down and shut up? We want to get at him too." That struck me as funny—perhaps I have a perverted sense of humor—and I laughed. The audience joined in, and even my adversaries on the panel laughed. We then had a fairly civil discussion of policy issues.

What would have happened if I had succumbed to the temptation of responding sharply to this man's accusations? The audience would have sided with him, I would have been booed, and the evening would have been quite unpleasant. The moral of this story? Keep your cool, no matter how provoked you may be. Your audience will respect you and may turn on the heckler who is taking up their time. I fortuitously learned a valuable lesson that day.

Let me make some final observations about our profession. Emotions do indeed play an important role with any audience, but it is still verifiable, factual data that persuades reasonable people to come to your side. Above all, remember that you cannot persuade an audience; audience members must persuade themselves. Never tell them that you are going to persuade, sell, or convince them. Do so and you are dead in the water. Allow audience members to "save face" by providing backing for your position with oral footnotes and with information they did not have prior to listening to you. Remember to maintain your composure, avoid personal attacks, and always keep in mind what you want your audience to do as a result of listening to your argument.

I think a fitting way to conclude may be with one of my favorite quotations about the true purpose of speaking to any group. It comes from the birthplace of speech training and the art of persuasion, ancient Greece. The people of Athens, although admiring the speaker with the stentorian voice, dramatic gesture, and clever turn of phrase, nevertheless realized the purpose of any presentation was to cause audience members to take the action the speaker wished them to take. So it was said, in comparing the greatest speaker of the day with one who had lived many years before: "When Demosthenes speaks, people say 'how well he speaks'. But when Pericles spoke, people said, 'Let us march.'"

Thank you, and good luck in all your speaking ventures, to friend and foe alike.

Persuasive Speech

Blinded by the Light

Erica Radcliffe[2]

On June 14, 2003, Bishop Thomas O'Brien was on his way home from celebrating mass. During his routine drive home, he heard a loud noise on the passenger side of his car and noticed his windshield had been damaged by what he thought was a rock. It wasn't until two days later that, according to *CNN.com* March 19, 2004, Bishop O'Brien was arrested by police, not for a cracked windshield, but rather for having struck and killed 43-year-old Jim Reed. In *The Washington Post* of February 10, 2004, Bishop O'Brien contends he never saw Reed in the roadway. The cause of his temporary blindness: the glare from streetlamps and headlights of oncoming traffic.

But this growing epidemic of excessive artificial nighttime lighting, better known as light pollution, isn't confined to this one tragic incident. According to an AAA publication of March 2003, nighttime glare from excessive lighting on roadways and from headlights is responsible for an average of 38,000 traffic accidents each year. But the effects of untamed illumination do more than put us at risk behind the wheel. Since *The New York Times* of August 30, 2003, reports that the United States wastes as much as 2 billion tax dollars every year in bad lighting, and because 99% of Americans live in areas tainted by light pollution, we must first look at the problems it creates, next investigate the causes, before finally figuring out some solutions that will help us flick the switch fueling light pollution.

Although often underestimated, excessive nighttime lighting can produce a plethora of safety, health, and environmental impacts. First, while bright light after dark may seem like a safety precaution, it can actually be a safety hazard. According to *The Santa Fe New Mexican* of July 27, 2003, too much lighting on sidewalks or in alleyways creates shadows, making unsuspecting passersby more susceptible to crime. Here we see a woman walking on what appears to be a well-lit sidewalk. However, in this photo she's gone, but she didn't go far; in fact, she only moved 4 feet to her left—now well hidden by the shadows created from the excessive lighting.

Light pollution also affects our safety on the road. According to *The Vail Daily* of September 25, 2003, after a nighttime fill-up, it takes our eyes 10 minutes to readjust from unnecessary lighting at gas stations once we're back on the road. And a study presented at the 2003 meeting of the National Transportation Research Board confirmed that only 5% of drivers recognized a pedestrian on a road with glare.

Light pollution not only affects our safety, but also has a direct impact on our health. *Discover Magazine* of July 2003 explains that light pollution can "trigger deadly hormonal imbalances." According to *ABC Science Online* of February 18, 2003, the increased and unnatural levels of light we are exposed to after dark is likely raising the risk of cancers. And an August 22, 2003, article by the Harvard Center for Cancer Prevention reports that nighttime light exposure may significantly increase the risk of breast and colon cancer. According to *Life Extension Magazine* of January 2004, light from sources as small as a night-light or television inhibits cancer-fighting melatonin production, compromising our immune systems, making us more susceptible to any number of diseases.

And if your eyesight is not as good as it used to be, recent studies have found that light pollution also affects our vision. *CNN.com*, updated daily and last accessed March 23, 2004, revealed that 55% of children who slept with a light on before the age of 2 were diagnosed with myopia, or nearsightedness, 30% more than those that slept in complete darkness, leading to increased risk of glaucoma, retinal detachment, and macular degeneration in old age. Finally, light pollution is leaving its mark on the environment. *The Norfolk Eastern Daily Press* of September 15, 2003, warns that every 100-watt bulb left on during the hours of darkness all year releases a quarter of a ton of carbon dioxide into the atmosphere, contributing significantly to global warming.

All of us are plagued by the three biggest causes of light pollution: industrialization, commercial competition, and our growing fear of the dark. Due to urban sprawl, the *Audubon Magazine* Web site accessed March 13, 2004, and updated monthly reveals that only 10% of us live in an area where we can see all the stars that should be visible under normal nighttime conditions. According to *The Providence Journal-Bulletin* of August 3, 2003, astronomers at Kitte Peak National Observatory have been complaining about the lights from Phoenix, an area that lies over 120 miles away.

Commercial competition is also responsible. The *Progressivegrocer.com*, updated daily and last accessed March 3, 2004, explains that many small businesses are now forced to expand their hours due to competition from larger chain stores. This rising need for 24-hour service only leads to more unnecessary excess lighting. Advertisements are also a problem. *American Demographic* of December 1, 2003, explains that outdoor advertising is a 6-billion-dollar industry on the rise; over the past 10 years, spending on outdoor ads has risen 97%. According to the February 10, 2004, *Pittsburgh Post-Gazette*, billboards "ruin drivers' night vision" as they use excessive lighting to get consumers' attention quickly on highways or busy city streets.

Finally, it's our own age-old fear of the dark. According to the previously cited *New York Times*, recent studies have found that contrary to popular belief, over-lighting does not reduce crime, but instead, as we saw earlier, merely alleviates our fear of crime, creating a dangerous false sense of security. So maybe it's time we conquered this fear, and we can start by looking at some solutions.

Although the problem seems glaring, it is one of the most easily curable forms of pollution, but must be addressed on a community, industry, and an individual level. The previously cited *Norfolk Eastern Daily Press* explains that the Norfolk city government now requires that white bulbs in street lamps be replaced with low-light-polluting orange bulbs. Road signs and billboards should be replaced with prismatic material, explains *The Pasadena Citizen* of September 16, 2003. This new, highly reflective material eliminates the need for overhead lighting on all road signs because it uses a car's headlights to light up the signs, illuminating them only when needed.

Businesses must also do their part. *The New Haven Register* of September 24, 2003, explains large light-emitting commercial buildings should surround their properties with fences and trees, reducing light pollution from the site. To eliminate unnecessary overnight light pollution, the previously cited *Vail Daily* explains that in that part of Colorado, business lights must be shut off 1 hour after closing. According to the May 17, 2003, *ABC News.com*, by going dark at night, some office buildings and school systems are saving as much as 1 million dollars every year.

But you can start fighting light pollution right now. The AAA Foundation for Traffic Safety offers tips to handle glare for safer driving at night. Please feel free to take one. And as soon as you get home, replace those 200-watt bulbs with 100s and turn out the lights when you leave a room. If you have a night-light, place it low on a wall facing away from you and keep it as dim as possible. If you tend to fall asleep with the TV on, many sets can now be programmed to shut off after a certain period of time. And according to the Home Depot Web site, last accessed March 23, 2004, you can purchase a Motion Sensor Security Light that only turns on when needed for as little as $12.97.

Today, we have seen the problems, looked at the causes, and finally, viewed some solutions to help us fight light pollution. Bishop Thomas O'Brien served Phoenix's 480,000 Catholics for 21 years. He now owns the title of the first-ever felony conviction for a U.S. Roman Catholic bishop. This is clearly one time Bishop O'Brien would have given anything not to be blinded by the light.

Notes

INTRODUCTION

1. For an excellent review of intrapersonal communication theory and research, see D. Voate, *Intrapersonal Communication: Different Voices, Different Minds* (Hillsdale, NJ: Lawrence Erlbaum, 1994).
2. D. Quinn, *My Ishmael* (New York: Bantam Books, 1996).
3. L. Barker, R. Edwards, C. Gaines, K. Gladney, and F. Holley, "An Investigation of Proportional Time Spent in Various Communication Activities of College Students," *Journal of Applied Communication Research 8* (1981): 101–109.

CHAPTER 4.1

1. J. Fitzgerald, "Metcalfe to MIT Geeks: Get to Writin'," *The Boston Herald* (April 28, 2005).
2. The sample presentation that is developed in this chapter is adapted from B. Johnson, "Coricidin: No Prescription Needed," *Winning Orations 2004* (Mankato, MN: Interstate Oratorical Association, 2004), 56–58.
3. S. B. Butterfield, "Instructional Interventions for Situational Anxiety and Avoidance," *Communication Education 37* (1988): 214–223.
4. Survey conducted by R. H. Bruskin and Associates, *Spectra* 9 (December, 1973): 4.
5. L. Fletcher, *How to Design & Deliver Speeches* (New York: Longman, 2001), 3.
6. K. Savitsky and T. Gilovich, "The Illusion of Transparency and the Alleviation of Speech Anxiety," *Journal of Experimental Social Psychology 39* (2003): 618–625.
7. K. Dwyer and D. Fus, "Perceptions of Communication Competence, Self-Efficacy, and Trait Communication Apprehension: Is There an Impact on Basic Course Success?" *Communication Research Reports 19* (2002): 29–37.
8. J. Ayres, "Speech Preparation Processes and Speech Apprehension," *Communication Education 45* (1996): 228–235.
9. P. Addison, E. Clay, S. Xie, C. Sawyer, and R. Behnke, "Worry as a Function of Public Speaking State Anxiety Type," *Communication Reports 16* (2003): 125–131.
10. J. Ayres and B. Huett, "An Examination of the Long-Term Effect of Performance Visualization," *Communication Research Reports 17* (2000): 229–236.
11. J. Ayres and B. Huett, "An Examination of the Impact of Performance Visualization," *Communication Research Reports 16* (1999): 29–39; Ayres and Huett, "An Examination of the Long-Term Effect of Performance Visualization."
12. L. Tracy, "Taming Hostile Audiences," *Vital Speeches of the Day 71.10* (March 1, 2005).
13. J. Humphrey, "Taking the Stage: How Women Can Achieve a Leadership Presence," *Vital Speeches of the Day* (May 1, 2001): 437.
14. Data provided by Center for Defense Information, "Chronology of Major Terrorist Attacks against U.S. Targets," *CDI Terrorism Project* (June 27, 2002) <http://www.cdi.org/terrorism/chronology-pr.html>; "September 11 Fatalities Make 2001 the Worst Year," *Airwise News* January 4, 2002 (June 27, 2002) <http://news.airwise.com/stories/2002/01/1010177858.html>.
15. W. Mossberg, "Product Review: Vertical Search Sites Promising," *Tucson Citizen*, April 6, 2005 (May 24, 2005) <www.tucsoncitizen.com/index.php?page=business&story_id=040605d1_vertical&toolbar=print_story>.
16. F. Fox, "Google or Yahoo?" *Bookmarks: Alkek Library (Texas State University–San Marcos) News 1* (2004), 2.
17. These criteria for evaluating Web resources are adapted from E. Kirk, "Practical Steps in Evaluating Internet Resources," May 7, 2001 (May 22, 2001)

<http://Milton.mse.jhu.edu:8001/research/education/practical.html>.

18. J. Heffernan et al., *Writing: A College Handbook*, 5e (New York: Norton, 2001), 53–54.

19. P. Gorski, "A Multicultural Model for Evaluating Educational Web Sites," December 1999 (May 22, 2001) <curry.edschool.Virginia.edu/go/multicultural/net/comps/model.html>; "Section 508," August 15, 2002 (May 26, 2005) <www.section.508.gov/index.cfm?FuseAction=Content&ID=11>.

20. "Section 508," August 15, 2002 (May 26, 2005) <www.section508.gov/index.cfm?FuseAction=Content&ID=11>.

21. M. Mirapaul, "Making Federal Web Sites Friendly to Disabled Users," *The New York Times* (June 11, 2001): B2.

22. U.S. Government Printing Office, "National Bibliography Program," *GPO Access*. May 9, 2005 (May 24, 2005) <www.access.gpo.gov/su_docs/fdlp/cip/index.html>.

23. B. Obama, speech delivered to the 2004 Democratic National Convention, July 2004. Available *America 2004: The Democratic National Convention*. (May 26, 2005) <www.dems2004.org/site/apps/nl/content3.asp?c=lu2LaPYG&b=131063&ct=158769>.

24. J. Potter, untitled speech. In *Winning Orations 2000* (Mankato, MN: Interstate Oratorical Association, 2000), 40.

25. M. Sanchez, "Diplomatic Immunity Unjustified." In *Winning Orations 1996* (Mankato, MN: Interstate Oratorical Association, 1996), 66.

26. M. Limon and D. Kazoleas, "A Comparison of Exemplar and Statistical Evidence in Reducing Counter-Arguments and Responses to a Message," *Communication Research Reports 21* (2004): 291–298.

27. S. Gomes, "Toxic Noise." In *Winning Orations 2000*, 28.

28. A. Hickman, "Race Against Time." In *Winning Orations 1997* (Mankato, MN: Interstate Oratorical Association, 1997), 102.

29. J. A. Dick, "The Dangers of Oral Polio Vaccination." In *Winning Orations 1997*, 89.

30. K. Clanton, "African American History." In *Winning Orations 2000*, 55.

31. R. Lamm, "How to Make an Environmentalist," *Vital Speeches of the Day 71.10* (March 1, 2005).

32. J. Celoria, "The Counterfeiting of Airline Safety: An Examination of the Dangers of Bogus Airline Parts." In *Winning Orations 1997*, 79.

33. N. Tremel, "The New Wasteland: Computers." In *Winning Orations 2000*, 37.

34. M. Curtin, "Importance of Language Education," *Vital Speeches of the Day 71.8* (February 1, 2005).

35. J. Pruitt, "College Credit Card Crisis." In *Winning Orations 1996*, 26.

36. Curtin, "Importance of Language Education."

37. See D. A. Lieberman, *Public Speaking in the Multicultural Environment* 2e (Boston: Allyn & Bacon, 1997).

38. J. T. Masterson and N. Watson, "The Effects of Culture on Preferred Speaking Style." Paper presented at the meeting of the Speech Communication Association, November, 1979.

39. L. Altman, "Wider Student Use Is Urged for New Meningitis Vaccine," *The New York Times* (May 27, 2005): A14.

40. The World's Easiest Quiz? Joke-of-the-Day.com (February 25, 1998) <http.www.joke-of-the-day.com> Copyright 1997/1998 JOKE-OF-THE-DAY.com/TWT. All rights reserved. Permission is granted to reprint or distribute Joke-of-the-Day's jokes as long as this full copyright notice is included, including the subscription information. To get a joke every day, e-mail us at Subscribe@joke-of-the-day.com.

41. W. W. Braden, *Abraham Lincoln, Public Speaker* (Baton Rouge: Louisiana State University Press, 1988), 90.

CHAPTER 4.2

1. L. Tracy, "Taming Hostile Audiences," *Vital Speeches of the Day 71.10* (March 1, 2005).

2. T. Martinet, "Ribbons: Function or Fashion." In *Winning Orations 2004* (Mankato, MN: Interstate Oratorical Association, 2004), 79.

3. D. A. Lieberman, *Public Speaking in the Multicultural Environment* 2e (Boston: Allyn & Bacon, 1997), 23.

4. Lieberman, *Public Speaking in the Multicultural Environment*.

5. A. Lee, untitled speech. In *Winning Orations 2004*, 19.

6. Y. Pavlovic, "Genetic Testing: Medical Miracle or Health Hazard?" In *Winning Orations 2000* (Mankato, MN: Interstate Oratorical Association, 2000), 111.

7. M. Erikson, "See Jane, See Jane's Dilemma." In *Winning Orations 1997* (Mankato, MN: Interstate Oratorical Association, 1997), 63.

8. R. A. Dankleff, "Rohypnol—The Date-Rape Drug of the Nineties." In *Winning Orations 1997*, 87.

9. S. Hamilton, "Cruise Ship Violence." In *Winning Orations 2000*, 95.

10. T. Longoria, "Let Go of Anger and Forgive" (Texas State University–San Marcos, 2005).

11. A. Greenspan, commencement address delivered to the Wharton School of the University of Pennsylvania, May 15, 2005 (May 24, 2005) <www.federalreserve.gov/boarddocs/speeches/2005/20050515/default.htm>.

12. E. Monaghan, "Mental Health Privacy." In *Winning Orations 2000*, 117.

13. C. Reed, "Decreasing Red Meat in Your Diet" (Texas State University–San Marcos, 2005).

14. A. Lincoln, "Gettysburg Address," delivered at Gettysburg, PA, November 19, 1863. Available Douglass Archives of American Public Address. August 19, 1998 (July 12, 1999). <http://douglass.speech.nwu.edu/linc_b33.htm>.

15. D. MacArthur, "Farewell to the Cadets," address delivered at West Point, May 12, 1962. Reprinted in *Contemporary American Speeches* 7e, edited by R. L. Johannesen, R. R. Allen, and W. A. Linkugel (Dubuque, IA: Kendall/Hunt, 1992), 393.

16. M. L. King Jr., "I Have a Dream," delivered in Washington, D.C., August 28, 1963. Reprinted in Johannesen et al., *Contemporary American Speeches*, 369.

17. T. Kirchhefer, "The Deprived." In *Winning Orations 2000*, 151.

18. K. Morris, "National Forests: For Ourselves and Our Posterity" (Texas State University–San Marcos, 2005).

19. The preparation outline on pages 62–65 and the delivery outline on pages 66–68 were adapted from a speech by B. Johnson, "Coricidin: No Prescription Needed," *Winning Orations, 2004*. (Mankato, MN: Interstate Oratorical Association, Larry Schnoor, Ex. Sec., 2004), 56–58.

CHAPTER 4.3

1. A. H. Monroe, "Measurement and Analysis of Audience Reaction to Student Speakers' Studies in Attitude Changes," *Bulletin of Purdue University Studies in Higher Education 22* (1937).

2. P. Heinbert, "Relationship of Content and Delivery to General Effectiveness," *Speech Monographs 30* (1963): 105–107.

3. A. Mehrabian, *Nonverbal Communication* (Hawthorne, NY: Aldine, 1972).

4. J. Detz, "Delivery Plus Content Equals Successful Presentation," *Communication World 15* (1998): 34.

5. Adapted from R. Ailes, *You Are the Message* (New York: Doubleday, 1989), 37–38.

6. P. Begala, "Flying Solo." PBS, *The Clinton Years: Anecdotes*. 2000 (July 14, 2002) <http://www.pbs.org/wgbh/pages/frontline/shows/clinton/anecdotes/#5>.

7. J. Wareham, "Doing It Off-the-Cuff," *Across the Board 35* (1998): 49–50.

8. Wareham, "Doing It Off-the-Cuff."

9. G. Orwell, "Politics and the English Language," reprinted in *About Language*, edited by W. H. Roberts and G. Turgeson (Boston: Houghton Mifflin, 1986), 282.

10. W. Safire, "Faithful, Even in Death," *The New York Times Magazine* (April 18, 1999): 72–74. Quotes from Vest's speech are from the text reprinted in this article.

11. J. F. Kennedy, inaugural address (January 20, 1961). In *Speeches in English*, edited by B. Aly and L. F. Aly (New York: Random House, 1968), 272.

12. J. Carter, address to the Democratic National Convention (July 2004). (August 1, 2004) <www.dems2004.org/site/pp.asp?c=1u12LAPYG&b=92959>.

13. G. W. Bush, Presidential victory speech, delivered at Austin, Texas, December 13, 2000 (December 14, 2000) <http://dailynews.yahoo.com/h/ap/20001214/el/recount_bush_text_1.html>.

14. E. Wiesel, "The Perils of Indifference," delivered at the White House, April 12, 1999 (July 1, 1999) <http://www.historyplace.com/speeches/wiesel.htm>.

15. H. R. Clinton, "Women's Rights Are Human Rights," delivered to the United Nations Fourth World Conference on Women, Plenary Session in Beijing, China, September 5, 1995 (July 1, 1999) <http://douglass.speech.nwu.edu/clin_a64.htm>.

16. J. F. Kennedy, "Address at Rice University on the Space Effort," delivered at Rice University, September 12, 1962 (July 1, 1999) <http://riceinfo.rice.edu/Fondren/Woodson/speech.html>.

17. S. A. Beebe, "Eye Contact: A Nonverbal Determinant of Speaker Credibility," *Speech Teacher 23* (1974): 21–25; S.A. Beebe, "Effects of Eye Contact, Posture and Vocal Inflection Upon Credibility and Comprehension," *Australian Scan Journal of Nonverbal Communication 7–8* (1979–80): 57–70; M. Cobin, "Response to Eye Contact," *Quarterly Journal of Speech 48* (1963): 415–419.

18. Beebe, "Eye Contact."

19. E. Adler, "Gestures May Give You a Hand with Speaking," *Austin American-Statesman* (November 25, 1998): E6.

20. J. C. McCroskey, V. P. Richmond, A. Sallinen, J. M. Fayer, and R. A. Barraclough, "A Cross-Cultural and Multi-Behavioral Analysis of the Relationship between Nonverbal Immediacy and Teacher Evaluation," *Communication Education 44* (1995): 281–290.

21. M. J. Beatty, "Some Effects of Posture on Speaker Credibility," library paper, Central Missouri State University, 1973.

22. R. Schmid, "Study: Posture Able to Communicate Fear," The Associated Press. November 16, 2004 (November 16, 2004) <news.yahoo.com>.

23. P. Ekman, W. V. Friesen, and S. S. Tomkins, "Facial Affect Scoring Technique: A First Validity Study," *Semiotica 3* (1971).

24. P. Ekman and W. Friesen. *Unmasking the Face* (Englewood Cliffs, NJ: Prentice-Hall, 1975).

25. "Bush's Smirk and Kerry's Smile Send the Wrong Message, Say Experts," The Associated Press. October 1, 2004 (October 1, 2004) <news.yahoo.com>.

26. Adapted from S. A. Beebe and S. J. Beebe, *Public Speaking: An Audience-Centered Approach* 5e (Boston: Allyn & Bacon, 2003), 292–293.

27. M. M. Gill, "Accents and Stereotypes: Their Effect on Perceptions of Teachers and Lecture Comprehension," *Journal of Applied Communication Research 22* (1994): 348–361.

28. Adapted from S. Linver, *Speak Easy: How to Talk Your Way to the Top* (New York: Summit Books, 1978), 204–205.

29. E. Bohn and D. Jabusch, "The Effect of Four Methods of Instruction on the Use of Visual Aids in Speeches," *Western Journal of Speech Communication 46* (1982): 253–265.

30. A. Wilson, "In Defense of Rhetoric," *The Toastmaster 70.2* (2004): 11.

31. U.S. Census Bureau, "Profile of General Demographic Characteristics: 2000," *American FactFinder.* December, 2004 (June 7, 2005) <factfinder.census.gov/>.

32. P. S. Sochaczewski, "How Can We Put Intimacy into Presentations?" *Consulting to Management 12* (2001): 37–38.

33. Detz, "Delivery Plus Content Equals Successful Presentation."

34. R. Raskin, "Have Your Calendar Call Mine," *Family PC* (June/July, 1999): 21–26.

35. UNAIDS, *AIDS Epidemic Update 2004,* December, 2004 (June 7, 2005) <www.unaids.org/wad2004/report_pdf.html>.

CHAPTER 4.4

1. J. R. Johnson and N. Szczupakiewicz, "The Public Speaking Course: Is It Preparing Students with Work-Related Public Speaking Skills?" *Communication Education 36* (1987): 131–137.

2. For an excellent discussion about teaching someone to perform a skill, especially a social skill, see M. Argyle, *The Psychology of Interpersonal Behavior* (London: Penguin, 1990).

3. For an excellent discussion of strategies for informing others see K. E. Rowan, "A New Pedagogy for Explanatory Public Speaking: Why Arrangement Should Not Substitute for Invention," *Communication Education 44* (1995): 236–250.

4. For an excellent discussion of factors affecting audience attention in public speaking, see D. Ehninger, B. E. Gronbeck, R. E. McKerrow, and A. H. Monroe, *Principles and Types of Speech Communication* (Glenview, IL: Scott, Foresman, 1986), 43.

5. This suggestion is based on an excellent review of the literature found in Rowan, "A New Pedagogy for Explanatory Public Speaking."

6. M. Groover, "Learning to Communicate: The Importance of Speech Education in Public Schools." In *Winning Orations 1984* (Mankato, MN: Interstate Oratorical Association, 1984), 7.

7. M. Klepper and R. Gunther, *I'd Rather Die than Give a Speech* (New York: Carol Publishing Group, 1995).

8. Our discussion of using humor is adapted from Klepper and Gunther, *I'd Rather Die than Give a Speech.*

9. Klepper and Gunther, *I'd Rather Die than Give a Speech.*

10. M. Knowles, *Self-Directed Learning* (Chicago: Follett Publishing, 1975).

11. A. Tisino, "The Power of Music" (Texas State University–San Marcos, 2005).

12. L. Hughes, *The First Book of Rhythms* (New York: Franklin Watts, 1954).

CHAPTER 4.5

1. S. McLaughlin, "The Dirty Truth about Your Kitchen: Using Common Sense to Prevent Food Poisoning." In *Winning Orations 1996* (Mankato, MN: Interstate Oratorical Association, 1996), 73.

2. McLaughlin, "The Dirty Truth about Your Kitchen," 75.

3. A. Maslow, "A Theory of Human Motivation." In *Motivation and Personality* (New York: Harper & Row, 1954), Chapter 5.

4. See I. L. Janis and S. Feshback, "Effects of Fear Arousing Communications," *Journal of Abnormal and Social Psychology 48* (1953): 78–92; F. A. Powell and G. R. Miller, "Social Approval and Disapproval Cues in Anxiety Arousing Situations," *Speech Monographs 34* (1967): 152–159; and K. L. Higbee, "Fifteen Years of Fear Arousal: Research on Threat Appeals, 1953–1968," *Psychological Bulletin 72* (1969): 426–444.

5. P. A. Mongeau, "Another Look at Fear-Arousing Persuasive Appeals." In *Persuasion: Advances through Meta-Analysis,* edited by M. Allen and R. W. Preiss (Cresskill, NJ: Hampton Press, 1998), 65.

6. Aristotle, *Rhetoric* (L. Cooper, trans.) (New York: Appleton-Century-Crofts, 1960).

7. A. Bogeajis, "The Danger of Child Safety Seats: Why Aren't They Safe?" In *Winning Orations 1996,* 10.

8. N. Barton, "The Death of Reading." In *Winning Orations 2004* (Mankato, MN: Interstate Oratorical Association, 2004), 33–35.

9. S. Groom, "Hope for Foster Care." In *Winning Orations 2004,* 60–62.

10. D. Ehninger, B. Gronbeck, R. McKerrow, and A. Monroe, *Principles and Types of Speech Communication* (Glenview, IL: Scott, Foresman, 1986), 15.

11. S. Nay, "Sex Offender Registries: A Call for Reform." In *Winning Orations 2004,* 87.

12. Nay, "Sex Offender Registries: A Call for Reform," 87.

13. Nay, "Sex Offender Registries: A Call for Reform," 88.

14. Nay, "Sex Offender Registries: A Call for Reform," 89.

15. Nay, "Sex Offender Registries: A Call for Reform," 89.
16. D. C. Bryant, "Rhetoric: Its Functions and Its Scope," *Quarterly Journal of Speech 39* (1953): 26.
17. B. Sosnowchick, "The Cries of American Ailments." In *Winning Orations 2000* (Mankato, MN: Interstate Oratorical Association, 2000), 114.
18. W. Stephens, "Cruisin' Out of Control," *Winning Orations, 2004* (Mankato, MN: Interstate Oratorical Association, Larry Schnoor, Ex. Sec., 2004), 103–105.

APPENDIX D

1. "Search Us," *Entertainment Weekly* (September 13, 1999): 17.
2. J. Downing and C. Garmon, "Teaching Students in the Basic Course How to Use Presentation Software," *Communication Education 50* (2001): 218–229; R. W. Bly, "The Case Against PowerPoint," *Successful Meetings 50* (2001): 51–52; T. A. Stewart, "Ban It Now! Friends Don't Let Friends Use PowerPoint," *Fortune 143* (2001): 210; T. Simons, "The Least We Can Do Is Allow PowerPoint to Die in Peace," *Presentations 16* (2002): 6; D. G. Levasseur, "Pedagogy Meets PowerPoint: A Research Review on the Effects of Computer-Generated Slides in the Classroom." Paper presented at the meeting of the National Communication Association, November, 2004; "Honk If You Hate PowerPoint," *PR Newswire.* November, 2004, <http://www.biz.yahoo.com/prnews>.

APPENDIX E

1. L. Tracy, "Taming Hostile Audiences," *Vital Speeches of the Day,* 71.10 (March 1, 2005). Tracy is author of The Shortcut to Persuasive Presentations (www.tracypresentation.com).
2. E. Radcliffe, "Blinded by the Light," *Winning Orations, 2004* (Mankato, MN: Interstate Oratorical Association, Larry Schnoor, Ex. Sec., 2004), 91–93.

Photo Credits

Answers to Practice Tests

CHAPTER 4.1

Multiple Choice

1. c	11. c
2. b	12. c
3. b	13. b
4. a	14. b
5. c	15. c
6. d	16. c
7. b	17. b
8. a	18. b
9. a	19. c
10. c	20. c

True/False

1. T
2. F
3. T
4. F
5. F
6. T
7. F
8. T
9. F
10. T

Fill in the Blank

1. hypothetical illustration
2. anxiety
3. systematic desensitization
4. presentational
5. general purpose
6. statistic
7. main ideas
8. central idea
9. specific purpose
10. description

CHAPTER 4.2

Multiple Choice

1. b	11. d
2. a	12. c
3. a	13. b
4. b	14. c
5. c	15. d
6. a	16. d
7. d	17. c
8. d	18. c
9. a	19. d
10. c	20. d

True/False

1. F
2. T
3. F
4. F
5. T
6. F
7. F
8. F
9. F
10. T

Fill in the Blank

1. complexity
2. problem-and-solution
3. delivery outline
4. cause-and-effect
5. soft
6. hard
7. spatial
8. transition
9. initial preview
10. chronological

CHAPTER 4.3

Multiple Choice

1. c	11. a
2. b	12. d
3. a	13. c
4. d	14. b
5. c	15. c
6. a	16. b
7. b	17. c
8. d	18. c
9. a	19. b
10. c	20. d

True/False

1. F
2. T
3. F
4. F
5. T
6. F
7. T
8. F
9. T
10. F

Fill in the Blank

1. extemporaneous
2. presentation aids
3. alliteration
4. figurative
5. personification
6. manuscript
7. impromptu
8. antithesis
9. memorization
10. inflection

CHAPTER 4.4

Multiple Choice

1. c	11. c
2. c	12. b
3. c	13. b
4. b	14. c
5. c	15. d
6. c	16. d
7. a	17. b
8. d	18. b
9. a	19. a
10. a	20. d

True/False

1. T
2. F
3. T
4. F
5. F
6. F
7. T
8. F
9. T
10. T

Fill in the Blank

1. analogy
2. procedure
3. inform
4. person
5. event
6. word picture
7. idea
8. motive
9. objects
10. redundancy

CHAPTER 4.5

Multiple Choice

1. d	11. a
2. c	12. b
3. b	13. a
4. c	14. a
5. d	15. b
6. b	16. c
7. d	17. a
8. b	18. d
9. c	19. a
10. b	20. d

True/False

1. F
2. F
3. T
4. T
5. F
6. T
7. F
8. T
9. F
10. F

Fill in the Blank

1. cognitive dissonance
2. logical fallacies
3. belief
4. visualization
5. either-or
6. logos
7. proposition
8. syllogism
9. persuasion
10. non sequitur

Key to the MyCommunicationLab Media Assets

The MyCommunicationLab assets are listed by type and title in the order in which they appear throughout each chapter.

CHAPTER 4.1

Explore	Speech Setting
Quick Review	An Overview of Presentational Speaking
Profile	PRCA-24
Quick Review	Understanding Speaker Anxiety
Profile	PRPSA
Explore	Overcoming Nervousness
Homework	Good Advice
Quick Review	Managing Speaker Anxiety
Explore	Topic
Explore	Audience Analysis
Homework	Different Audience, Different Approach
Visual Literacy	Visual Brainstorming
Explore	Visual Brainstorming
Quick Review	Selecting and Narrowing Your Topic
Watch	Demonstration: Internet Blogs
Watch	After Dinner Speech
Quick Review	Identifying Your Purpose
Watch	Introduction: Voting
Quick Review	Developing Your Central Idea
Quick Review	Generating Main Ideas
Explore	Researching Your Topic
Watch	Contemporary Education
Homework	Do Numbers Lie?
Quick Review	Gathering Supporting Material
Explore	Avoid Plagiarizing
Quick Review	Acknowledgment of Supporting Material

CHAPTER 4.2

Visual Literacy	Basic Organizational Patterns
Quick Review	Organizing Your Main Ideas
Explore	Organization
Explore	Testing for Relevance of Supporting Ideas
Homework	Organizational Challenge
Quick Review	Organizing Your Supporting Materials
Explore	Better Transitions
Watch	Transition: Getting to Know the Elderly
Quick Review	Organizing Your Presentation for the Ears of Others
Watch	Selecting a Speech Topic
Watch	Let Go of Anger and Forgive
Watch	Decreasing Red Meat in Your Diet
Explore	Compose
Homework	Well, That's about It
Watch	National Forests: For Ourselves and Our Posterity

Quick Review	Introducing and Concluding Your Presentation
Watch	Outlining: Of Our Immigration Story
Explore	Using the Microsoft Outlining Tool
Explore	Practicing with the Microsoft Outlining Tool
Explore	Creating a Speaking Outline
Quick Review	Outlining Your Presentation

CHAPTER 4.3

Explore	Methods of Delivery
Watch	Choosing a Speech Topic
Quick Review	Methods of Delivery
Explore	Language
Quick Review	Effective Verbal Delivery
Homework	Deep Breathing
Explore	Physical Delivery
Watch	Transition: Singing and Drumming in Africa
Watch	FDR Takes Office
Watch	Homicide Adaptation Theory (Bad Version)
Quick Review	Effective Nonverbal Delivery
Explore	Presentational Aids
Watch	Demonstration Speech: Baking a Cake
Watch	Writing Position Papers (Using PPT as Visual)
Watch	Starbucks
Explore	Speech Delivery
Quick Review	Effective Presentation Aids
Quick Review	Some Final Tips for Rehearsing and Delivering Your Presentation

CHAPTER 4.4

Watch	Informative: Hurricane Mitigation (No Visuals)

Explore	Informative Speeches
Watch	How to Use PowerPoint
Watch	Speech of Introduction
Watch	Truman's Decision to Drop the Bomb
Quick Review	Types of Informative Presentations
Quick Review	Strategies for Organizing Your Informative Presentations
Explore	Connecting Key Ideas
Quick Review	Strategies for Making Your Informative Presentation Clear
Explore	Presentational Aids
Explore	What's in It for Me?
Quick Review	Strategies for Making Your Informative Presentation Interesting
Explore	Scrambled Outline— Informative Speech
Quick Review	Strategies for Making Your Informative Presentation Memorable
Watch	The Power of Music

CHAPTER 4.5

Watch	Interstate Commerce Clause
Explore	Ethical Threats
Quick Review	Persuasion Defined
Explore	Persuasion
Explore	Maslow's Hierarchy of Needs
Quick Review	Motivating Your Audience
Quick Review	Selecting and Narrowing Your Persuasive Topic
Watch	Courting Responsibility
Explore	Proposition Me
Quick Review	Developing Your Central Idea as a Persuasive Proposition
Watch	Body Image Disturbance
Watch	Listen to Your Heart

Index